The 2nd U.S. Sharpshooters at Gettysburg

The 2nd U.S. Sharpshooters at Gettysburg

Like A Perfect Hornet's Nest

MARK W. ALLEN

McFarland & Company, Inc., Publishers
Jefferson, North Carolina

LIBRARY OF CONGRESS CATALOGING-IN-PUBLICATION DATA

Names: Allen, Mark W., 1963– author.
Title: The 2nd U.S. Sharpshooters at Gettysburg : like a perfect hornet's nest / Mark W. Allen.
Other titles: 2nd United States Sharpshooters at Gettysburg
Description: Jefferson, North Carolina : McFarland & Company, Inc., Publishers, 2024 | Includes bibliographical references and index.
Identifiers: LCCN 2024038755 | ISBN 9781476695952 (paperback : acid free paper) ∞
ISBN 9781476653907 (ebook)
Subjects: LCSH: Gettysburg, Battle of, Gettysburg, Pa., 1863. | United States. Army. Sharpshooters Regiment, 2nd (1861-1865) | United States. Army. Sharpshooters Regiment, 2nd (1861-1865)—Biography. | United States—History—Civil War, 1861-1865—Regimental histories. | United States—History—Civil War, 1861-1865—Campaigns.
Classification: LCC E492.7 .A45 2024 | DDC 973.7/6—dc23/eng/20240822
LC record available at https://lccn.loc.gov/2024038755

BRITISH LIBRARY CATALOGUING DATA ARE AVAILABLE

ISBN (print) 978-1-4766-9595-2
ISBN (ebook) 978-1-4766-5390-7

© 2024 Mark W. Allen. All rights reserved

No part of this book may be reproduced or transmitted in any form or by any means, electronic or mechanical, including photocopying or recording, or by any information storage and retrieval system, without permission in writing from the publisher.

Cover artwork: "Sharpshooters at the Slyder Farm" by Dale Gallon, used by permission www.gallon.com.

Printed in the United States of America

McFarland & Company, Inc., Publishers
  Box 611, Jefferson, North Carolina 28640
    www.mcfarlandpub.com

Table of Contents

Acknowledgments	vii
Preface	1
Introduction: 2nd Regiment, U.S. Sharpshooters	5
One—Setting the Stage: Initial Moves for an Upcoming Fight	19
Two—Pitzer Woods: A Reconnaissance Changes Everything	48
Three—Outguessing the Opponent: Positioning of Troops in the Early Afternoon	79
Four—Stepping Off and Rifles Blazing: The Attack and Defense of Slyder Farm	101
Five—Fall Back or Be Killed: The 2nd Regiment Retreats	116
Six—Among the Boulders: Defending Little Round Top	144
Seven—The Days After: Pickett's Charge, Picket Lines, and Conclusions	166
Appendix A: Abbreviated Order of Battle	179
Appendix B: Engaged Strengths on June 30, 1863, Muster Roll	184
Appendix C: Supplemental Figures	185
Appendix D: 2nd Sharpshooters Company Captains	189
Bibliography	197
Index	207

Acknowledgments

This work depended on help from many people. I am thankful to the following who have invested time and effort to help improve the book, and I greatly appreciate them. However, as helpful and instructive as they have been, any errors are mine alone.

Gettysburg licensed battlefield guide Gar Phillips gave his time over two visits on the southern end of the battlefield and the area around Slyder Farm. He reviewed an early draft of the manuscript and provided valuable insight, vastly improving the book. He was quick to answer questions and I appreciate his insight and willingness to help. Retired park ranger John Heiser of the Gettysburg National Military Park Library upon my two visits made me aware of many primary sources and patiently answered my many questions. After my visits, he was always quick to return my emails and offered a plethora of information when it came to the battlefield. Dr. David E. Allen, Dr. Thomas Goetz, Ryan Fairfield, Leslie Gilmore (USAF, retired), and Clarissa Field reviewed early drafts of the manuscript and offered valuable critiques that helped clarify the discussion.

Don Mounts with Global Military Research, LLC, obtained the regimental muster rolls and some of the photographs from the National Archives and Records Administration (NARA). He also examined pension files at NARA and searched in vain for company monthly returns. I highly recommend his services. Researcher Dave Johnson visited the Minnesota Historical Society on my behalf. Park ranger Matt Atkinson and cultural resources program manager Winona R. Peterson, both with Gettysburg National Military Park, helped with accessing information from Kathleen Georg Harrison's PowerPoint presentation given to the licensed battlefield guides on April 20, 2012. Nancy Hale took the time to look up various entries in the *Supplement to the Official Records of the Union and Confederate Armies* at her local library.

Dale Gallon gave permission to use his painting "Sharpshooters at the Slyder Farm" for the cover artwork. Brian T. White graciously shared many of his U.S. Sharpshooters images from his collection. Carla Carlson, assistant curator of historical manuscripts at the University of Southern Mississippi, provided the original and transcribed copy of the William Price Shreve Papers from their Special Collections. Sonya Eason, general chairman, Magazine Committee, with United Daughters of the Confederacy provided a copy of the article on Benjamin F. Carter of the Fourth Texas Infantry. Maureen Denfeld with *American Rifleman* magazine provided several articles from out-of-print back issues of that periodical.

The following individuals helped me with their respective collections: Paul Friday (New Hampshire Historical Society), Kate Phillips (Vermont Historical Society), Heather Moran (Maine State Archives), Mariessa Dobrick and Steve Picazio (Vermont State Archives), Rich Saylor and Aaron McWilliams (Pennsylvania State Archives), and Kris Rzepczynski and Jason Schultz (Archives of Michigan).

Last but not least, my wife Leilani assisted me while I tramped through the woods and along trails and patiently listened to me explain who was where and what they did and was my constant sounding board as I verbally worked out issues with troop locations and timing of events. She also reviewed the initial draft of the manuscript and made many helpful recommendations.

Preface

A detailed examination of the 2nd U.S. Sharpshooters' July 2, 1863, defense of the Union's left flank is a seldom-discussed topic in Gettysburg literature. Their actions normally get a page or two in most books, if there is any mention of them at all, as authors tend to focus on actions surrounding Devil's Den or Little Round Top. Most guidebooks do not mention the sharpshooters in detail, and battle maps of the area either fail to include the sharpshooters or have varying and usually incorrect deployment locations for the regiment. This story revolves around the 2nd Sharpshooters' defense of the Union's left flank from Slyder Farm to the Round Tops. This engagement is the definitive delaying action against their primary antagonists, the brigades led by brigadier generals Evander M. Law and Jerome B. Robertson, both under Major General John Bell Hood's division of Lieutenant General James Longstreet's corps.

The objective of this book is to tell the sharpshooters' important story and put their actions into context, knowing the events described did not happen in a vacuum. Union regiments engaged near Rose Woods, Houck's Ridge, Plum Run Valley, and the Round Tops affected the sharpshooters' actions that day, as did certain command decisions resulting from a reconnaissance into Pitzer Woods by the 1st U.S. Sharpshooters earlier that morning. I give only an overview of certain events that do not directly involve the sharpshooters, such as Confederate movements and many events involved with the advancement of Major General Daniel E. Sickles's line. Additionally, I discuss in general terms the sharpshooters' formation and recruitment. Charles Stevens has written on both topics, while Gerald Earley has written a history of the 2nd Sharpshooters. Roy M. Marcot has written books on the sharpshooters and on Colonel Hiram Berdan, commanding officer of the 1st and 2nd U.S. Sharpshooters. I recommend these resources for a deeper understanding of each topic.[1]

---

1. C.A. Stevens, *Berdan's United States Sharpshooters in the Army of the Potomac, 1861–1865* (St. Paul, MN, 1892); Gerald L. Earley, *The Second United States*

C.W. Tolles, Chief Quartermaster with the VI Army Corps during the Civil War, wrote, "The character of every battle is determined and controlled largely by the character of the ground on which it is fought."[2] Furthermore, understanding the terrain of a battlefield as it was at the time of the action is critical to the understanding of any battle.[3] Therefore, I used the Warren map as the base map for the figures.[4] Union brevet major General A.A. Humphreys, chief of engineers, ordered the survey, and Brevet Major General G.K. Warren, major of engineers and a West Point–trained engineer, conducted and supervised the work in 1868 and 1869. Civil engineer P.M. Blake revised the map in 1873.[5]

Former Gettysburg park ranger John Heiser said, "The Warren survey map is about the best to use for the earliest geographical database of the battlefield." The Warren maps accurately portray the woods, fields, fence lines, streams, and topography of the battlefield as precisely as possible using the tools available at the time. The Warren maps are the best primary source for locating the original breastworks, fence lines, wood lots, and other battle-era landscape features throughout the park.[6] I also used battlefield descriptions from participants or those familiar with the battlefield shortly after the battle, as the landscape would still have the same approximate configuration as it did during the war. Geomorphic agents and human activity would negligibly alter the landscape in the five years between the battle and the map's creation, and the major features would remain essentially the same for descriptive purposes.

Stated times of events varied, sometimes significantly, from person to person. I think Allen Guelzo sums this up best in his book, writing:

> America in the 1860s knew nothing about synchronized time. Clocks and watches were set by light and dark; there were no time zones, no standardized time-measurement schemes. Even meticulous timekeepers relied on

---

Sharpshooters in the Civil War: A History and Roster (Jefferson, NC, 2009); Roy M. Marcot, *Civil War Chief of Sharpshooters Hiram Berdan: Military Commander and Firearms Inventor* (Irvine, CA, 1989); Roy M. Marcot, *U.S. Sharpshooters: Berdan's Civil War Elite* (Mechanicsburg, PA, 2007), 7.

2. C.W. Tolles, "Army Movements," *The United States Service Magazine* 3 (New York, 1865), 541.

3. Glenn Foard, "English Battlefield 991–1685: A Review of Problems and Potentials," in *Fields of Conflict*, ed. Douglas Scott, Lawrence Babits, and Charles Haecker (Washington, D.C., 2009), 136.

4. G.K. Warren, *Battle Field of Gettysburg* [Washington, D.C., U.S. Army, Office of the Chief of Engineers 187–?] Map. Retrieved from the Library of Congress, https://www.loc.gov/item/99448794/ (accessed April 1, 2018).

5. *Ibid.*

6. John Heiser, former park ranger, Gettysburg National Military Park, personal communication, February 11, 2019.

the sound of church bells or public docks for uniformity. Of course, in the middle of the battle, few people were noticing bells, if they were being rung at all, and few were likely to be listening for the cheerful chiming of a courthouse clock. Soldiers set their personal watches by their own estimates, and in battle, those lacking watches were reduced to little more than a hazardous guess about the time. The participants themselves tried to establish some rough sense of the timing of the battle's events, and sometimes I have accepted their estimates or time notations, but always with the question in mind: Could this really have happened at that time?[7]

With that said, I have adjusted some of the stated times to a point where they fit within the flow of the action and have indicated these adjustments in the notes. Furthermore, *Gettysburg, July 2: The Ebb and Flow of Battle* by James A. Woods helped with timing issues, using maps with, in some cases, a minute-by-minute breakdown to describe the battle.[8]

Author Robert Bateman wrote that there are four levels of warfare: political, strategic, operational, and tactical. He defines the tactical level of war as the "level where men meet and fight from the individual level through the division. It is the realm of skirmishes, engagements, and battles. The tactical level of warfare is where one sees the face of battle." He further states, "This is fighting by privates and sergeants, lieutenants, captains, and colonels. This is the popular conception of war. This is war at the level of *Saving Private Ryan*."[9] This is the level I attempt to reach when describing the 2nd Sharpshooters at Gettysburg on July 2, 1863.

Before we begin, I leave you with this humbling statement from Oliver Norton of the 83rd Pennsylvania, present on Little Round Top the day of the battle. He wrote, "The correct story of Gettysburg has never been, will never be, written. None but the actors on the field can tell the story, and each one can tell of his own knowledge but an infinitesimal part. Many conscientious historians have attempted to weave a symmetrical whole from such disconnected threads as they can gather, but their accounts vary as their sources of information. Every man owes to the memory of those who died here, his best endeavor to tell truly the story of their deeds, that the historian of the future may have the material out of which to fashion a truer story of Gettysburg."[10] I have tried

---

7. Allen Guelzo, *Gettysburg: The Last Invasion* (New York, 2014), xxi.
8. James A. Woods, *Gettysburg, July 2: The Ebb and Flow of Battle* (Gillette, NJ, 2012).
9. Robert Bateman, "Understanding Military Strategy and the Four Levels of War," Esquire, 25 November 2015, http://https://www.esquire.com/news-politics/politics/news/a39985/four-levels-of-war/ (accessed May 10, 2018).
10. O.W. Norton, "Dedication of Monument 83D Regiment Infantry," in *Pennsylvania at Gettysburg: Ceremonies at the Dedication of the Monuments, Volume 1* (Harrisburg, PA, 1893), 432–433.

to weave a symmetrical whole from many disconnected threads, and I hope my effort honors the memory of the 2nd Regiment, U.S. Sharpshooters and their defense of the Union left flank at Gettysburg on July 2, 1863.

> O'er hills and through dark woods we roam,
> No Foe shall make us tremble;
> Our rifles crack, will drive them back,
> And every fear dissemble.[11]

---

11. S.G. Elder, *Berdan's Sharpshooters; Air Yankee Doodle* (New York), 1.

Introduction
2nd Regiment, U.S. Sharpshooters

> *A company of cool-headed, clear-eyed sharp-shooters is generally worth, in actual warfare, a brigade of ordinary troops.*[1]

In his official report after the Battle of Chancellorsville, Union colonel Samuel B. Hayman said, "The sharpshooters understand the true tactics of skirmishers, are possessed of enterprise and courage, and were maneuvered with great skill and address by Colonel Berdan, and I regard it as one of the best organizations of the volunteer service."[2] Colonel Hayman was referring to the combined actions of both the 1st and 2nd U.S. Sharpshooters on Saturday, May 2, 1863. Union colonel Hiram Berdan, commanding officer of both regiments, described their action in his official report on Chancellorsville, writing:

> I received general instructions from General Birney, which were to skirmish through the woods, keeping in the direction of a smoke which was rising from the woods on the southeast of our position. I deployed my First Regiment in the woods, using the Second Regiment as a reserve, and ordered them to advance and drive the rebels from the woods. My skirmishers soon engaged the enemy's skirmishers, consisting of a portion of the Twenty-Third Georgia, and drove them steadily from the woods, where they rallied at a large building, apparently used as a foundry. I then advanced my right and left, with flankers from the Second Regiment, and kept up so accurate and rapid a fire that the enemy dared not leave the cover of the building. I then ordered my men to cease firing, and called upon the rebels to surrender, upon which they came in, after throwing down their

---

1. *Harper's Weekly*, Saturday, July 4, 1863, 418.
2. *The War of the Rebellion: A Compilation of the Official Records of the Union and Confederate Armies*, 128 vols. (Washington, D.C., 1880–1901), series 1, vol. 25, part 1, 432. Hereafter cited as *OR*. All references are to series 1 unless otherwise noted.

arms and showing a white rag. The support of their skirmishers, with those who were able to escape, fell back along the road and rallied in a lane, covering in their retreat a wagon train, which was visible moving down the road. After sending the prisoners to the rear, I caused my left to gradually advance, keeping the attention of the enemy by desultory firing while I rapidly pushed forward my right in the woods until I had outflanked them and opened fire. They then attempted to come out of the railroad cut, in which they had taken shelter, and to retreat to the rear, but on meeting our fire they returned again to their cover, and very soon threw down their arms and surrendered. The whole number of prisoners taken was 365, including 19 officers, among whom was the major of the regiment. Our loss was trifling.[3]

Colonel Hiram Berdan, commanding officer, 1st and 2nd U.S. Sharpshooters. Library of Congress.

Two months later, on the afternoon of July 2, 1863, the 2nd Sharpshooters, acting as skirmishers on the extreme left of the Union line at Gettysburg, and with orders to observe and report Confederate activity in their front, would end up playing a critical, although frequently overlooked, role during the struggle for Little Round Top. Author Wiley Sword wrote, "In spite of the significance given to the 1st Sharpshooters Regiment's reconnaissance into Pitzer Woods earlier the same day, the greatest contribution at Gettysburg by either sharpshooter regiment was the 2nd Regiment's actions during the furious fighting with Lieutenant General James Longstreet's men in the Emmitsburg Road and Little Round Top sectors."[4]

Colonel Berdan, in the summer of 1861, proposed the idea of organizing sharpshooter regiments consisting of companies of men selected from multiple pro–Union states. The Federal government accepted Berdan's proposal and set forth the terms for candidate acceptance. Despite

---

3. *OR*, 25, pt. 1, 502.
4. Wiley Sword, *Sharpshooter: Hiram Berdan, His Famous Sharpshooters and Their Sharps Rifles* (Woonsocket, RI, 1988), 57.

the long-standing conviction that Hiram Berdan was the originator of the idea of a sharpshooter corps, there is some evidence that Lieutenant Colonel Caspar Trepp, a former Swiss officer with Crimean War service, may have first suggested the idea.[5] Captain Rudolph Aschmann, in command of Company A, 1st Sharpshooters during the Gettysburg battle, wrote this of Caspar Trepp:

Lieutenant Colonel Caspar Trepp, commanding officer, 1st U.S. Sharpshooters. Courtesy the Brian T. White Collection.

> It was a Swiss, my unforgettable friend and patron C. Trepp who became the founder and organizer of a system of sharpshooters. In July 1861 he called attention to the establishment of such a corps, and offered to organize one if men of influence could take care of the matter and effect the government's sanction. An American by the name of H. Berdan took an interest in this, went to Washington and soon obtained permission from the War Department to recruit in all loyalist states for a regiment of sharpshooters.[6]

Trepp lacked the needed political connections for such an idea and therefore collaborated with the well-known and eccentric inventor Hiram Berdan, who had the political aptitude to make the sharpshooters a reality. Berdan and Trepp envisioned the sharpshooters as a separate entity, not part of the regular infantry, and subsequently recruited the best marksmen from the northern states. Enticed with offers of extra pay along with an excuse from picket duty and the Sharps breech-loading rifle, enough qualified volunteers flocked to recruiters that Berdan created a second regiment and contemplated a third.[7] Interestingly, most if not all period accounts credit Berdan as the founder of the sharpshooters, and the

---

5. *Ibid.*, 10.
6. Heinz K. Meier, *Memoirs of a Swiss Officer in the American Civil War (Three Years in the Army of the Potomac or a Swiss Company of Sharpshooters in the North American War)*, trans. Hedwig D. Rappolt (Bern, Switzerland, 1972), 29.
7. Gary Yee, *Sharpshooters 1750–1900: The Men, Their Guns, Their Story* (Broadmoor, CA, 2009), 245.

newspapers in 1861, having no obvious reason to ignore Trepp, coined the name Berdan's Sharpshooters. These sharpshooters commenced active service in March 1862.[8]

Eventually, Berdan created two regiments, the 1st and 2nd U.S. Sharpshooters. The 1st Regiment reported to the Camp of Instruction in the fall of 1861. When complete, the regiment included one company each from New Hampshire (Company E), Vermont (Company F), and Wisconsin (Company G), three companies from Michigan (companies C, I, and K), and four companies from New York (companies A, B, D, and H). When the 2nd Regiment's organization was complete, it included one company each from Minnesota (Company A), Michigan (Company B), Pennsylvania (Company C), and Maine (Company D), and two companies each from Vermont (companies E and H) and New Hampshire (companies F and G). The purpose of these multistate regiments was to bring together the best northern marksmen possible and arm them with the most reliable rifles made. The men selected were also of a high grade in physical qualifications and intelligence. Berdan believed that with such men thoroughly equipped and so armed, sharpshooting and skirmishing would become invaluable to the Union cause.[9]

Captain Rudolph Aschmann, in command of Company A, 1st Sharpshooters regiment. Courtesy the Brian T. White Collection.

---

8. Earley, *The Second United States Sharpshooters*, 13; William F. Fox, *Regimental Losses in the American Civil War 1861–1865* (Albany, NY, 1889), 419.

9. Stevens, *Berdan's United States Sharpshooters*, 2–5; Fox, *Regimental Losses*, 419; Francis Peteler, "Narrative of the First Company of Sharpshooters," *Minnesota in the Civil and Indian Wars, 1861–1865*, 2nd ed. (St. Paul, MN, 1891), 507.

Sharpshooter eligibility required a recruit to make 10 consecutive shots whose aggregate distance from the center of the target would "string" less than 50 inches, an average of less than five inches for each shot. The distance to target and test for accuracy was 600 feet at a rest or 300 feet off hand. At these distances, many of the men could put all 10 shots inside the bullseye for each test.[10]

Charles Fairbanks of Bethel, Vermont, attended school during the winter and worked on the family farm during the summer. Hearing there was an officer in town getting recruits for "sharpshooters," Charles and a friend ran into town to try and enlist. Charles wrote, "When we reached the recruiting headquarters, some townsmen were there willing to enlist as sharpshooters if they could 'shoot well enough.' I stepped up to Major H.R. Stoughton, the recruiting officer, and told him that I wanted to enlist. The first step was to make a target. A soldier, in order to be competent to enter the sharpshooters, was required to shoot ten shots one hundred yards off hand at a ten-inch ring, and if each shot came inside the ring the man was accepted. Major Stoughton called me up to make the target. Making the first shot at the ten-inch ring brought a cheer from the crowd as I had nearly put the bullet in the center of the two-inch bullseye. The remaining nine shots were put inside the ring as well."[11] Charles Fairbanks joined Company E, 2nd Sharpshooters, and held the rank of private during the Gettysburg battle.

Wyman White, a machinist from Fitzwilliam, New Hampshire, described his enlistment test, writing, "A recruiting officer came to our town with his target rifle looking for recruits who could make the prescribed 'string' which was not more than forty-five inches in ten shots fired

Major Homer R. Stoughton, commanding officer, 2nd U.S. Sharpshooters. Library of Congress.

---

10. Fox, *Regimental Losses*, 419. "Offhand" means not resting the gun or your arms on anything to steady your aim, but only holding the gun against your shoulder and in your hands to shoot.

11. Janet Hayward Burnham, ed., *Notes of Army and Prison Life, 1862–1865* (Bethel, VT, 2004), 9–11.

off hand at two hundred yards distance. We set up our target. I commenced firing and when my string was completed, I had just twenty-three inches in the string, just half an inch more than half the limit."[12] Wyman White joined Company F, 2nd Sharpshooters and held the rank of private during the Gettysburg battle and attained the rank of first sergeant by the end of the war.[13]

Upon selection, the men attended the Camp of Instruction with the intent of drilling and disciplining the vast army of raw volunteers, molding the citizen into the soldier. The men spent time in camp learning company drill and battalion movements, guard and patrol duty, camp duties, and target practice and were soon able to execute the most difficult regimental drills.[14] More importantly, the sharpshooters learned basic infantry tactics and open-order skirmishing, which called for sending men forward of the line of battle, men whose duty was to engage and defeat the opponent's skirmishers and pick off their officers.[15] Private William B. Greene of Company G, 2nd Sharpshooters described skirmishing training in a letter home:

> I have been out about two miles from camp on a skirmish and Battalion drill for the first time. I was taken from my own company and put in to Co. B, a company that has been here two or three months. So after we had got out into the woods, the 2nd

Private Wyman S. White, Company F, 2nd U.S. Sharpshooters. Author's personal collection, scanned from carte de visite portrait photograph. This work is in the public domain and was published in the United States before 1927.

---

12. Russell C. White, ed., *The Civil War Diary of Wyman S. White, First Sergeant, Company F, 2nd United States Sharpshooters* (Baltimore, MD, 1993), 7–8.

13. Wyman White mustered into the Army on November 26, 1861, and was promoted to corporal on November 2, 1863; to sergeant on October 14, 1864; and to first sergeant on January 30, 1865. He transferred to the 5th New Hampshire Infantry on January 30, 1865. (John Foote Norton, *The History of Fitzwilliam, New Hampshire, From 1752 to 1887* [New York, 1888], 299.)

14. Stevens, *Berdan's United States Sharpshooters*, 5–6.

15. Yee, *Sharpshooters 1750–1900*, 266–267.

and 7th Company in the regiment were sent out as skirmishers to see if we could spy any rebels. Mind you we were on drill, not in the region of rebels. We went out a little way, deployed as skirmishers and went on at double quick time. We had not gone far before the order was given to halt just as if we had seen some enemy. When the order to halt is given when we are skirmishing we halt and run for the nearest tree and if there is none lay down flat on our bellies so to get out of the reach of the enemy's fire.[16]

As originally envisioned by many, including Colonel Hiram Berdan, as expert riflemen, sharpshooters would engage the enemy from beyond the range of the normal soldier. As skirmishers, they were to dominate the terrain before them and prevent harassment of their troops by enemy pickets or sharpshooters, enabling their infantry to maneuver into an advantageous position. However, early on, tactical doctrines for sharpshooters were yet to develop and there was no training for upper-echelon officers on the proper deployment of sharpshooters. Consequently, most sharpshooters fought as skirmishers.[17] The offensive use of sharpshooters was rare at the start of the war, but gradually, as some senior commanders began to understand the most effective use of their unique skills and the best methods to employ them, they played a more proactive part in preventing enemy advances.[18]

Both sharpshooter regiments were generally employed as skirmishers, trained to use "every wile and maneuver to conceal their own persons, while they watch every opportunity to pick off their antagonists. To run with a dodging, irregular, zigzag motion, so as to foil the eye of a marksman; to crawl like a reptile among vines and bushes; to hide behind trees, or rocks and stones, or in rifle-pits; to keep the eye stealthily but steadily fixed upon the foe; in short, to imitate in every possible manner the cunning of the savage or the beast of prey, these are the traits of the skirmisher. No trick is thought disgraceful; no stratagem to throw the enemy off his guard is thought unmilitary, if only successful; and, when he takes his murderous aim, the skirmisher is fully aware that, at the same moment, an unseen foe may be taking equally fatal aim at him."[19]

Consequently, they never suffered heavy losses as compared to standard infantry regiments. The sharpshooters were continually in demand as

---

16. William H. Hastings, *Letters from a Sharpshooter: The Civil War Letters of Private William B. Greene, Co. G, 2nd United States Sharpshooters (Berdan's), Army of the Potomac, 1861–1865* (Belleville, WI, 1993), 63.
17. Yee, *Sharpshooters 1750–1900*, 209–210, 212.
18. Martin Pegler, *Sharpshooting Rifles of the American Civil War* (New York, 2017), 44.
19. Arabella M. Willson, *Disaster, Struggle, Triumph: The Adventures of 1000 Boys in Blue* (Albany, NY, 1870), 180.

skirmishers due to their proficiency in skirmishing and having no equal in performing this task.[20]

Ultimately, the sharpshooters became expert skirmishers, operating in loose formations ahead of the army, relying on their initiative, field skills, courage, and marksmanship to inflict damage on the enemy out of proportion to their strength.[21] Operating in relatively small groups, sharpshooters and skirmishers possessed much greater flexibility than those in formation. They were also freer to follow their instincts of self-preservation. A skirmisher did not have to remain in the open when suddenly fired upon but could hide behind a tree or take whatever evasive steps were expedient.[22] Berdan's men knew how to use the terrain, adjust to any situation, and fight independently if necessary. They also knew they were an elite unit.[23]

Regimental historian Charles Stevens described their uniforms as "fine material, consisting of dark green coat and cap with black plume, light blue trowsers (afterward exchanged for green ones) and leather leggings, presenting a striking contrast to the regular blue of the infantry." Green uniforms were issued to Berdan's Sharpshooters to help them blend better with foliage. With their unique, black-buttoned green coats and kepis, calfskin knapsacks, and brown gaiters, the Berdan Sharpshooters considered themselves a cut above the regular regiments. With their rigorous training and advanced weaponry, the sharpshooters were the 1860s version of modern-day special forces.[24]

Soon after the Federal government mustered the 1st Sharpshooters into service, Colonel Berdan requisitioned Sharps breech-loading rifles. The Army initially issued the sharpshooters Colt revolving rifles, and Berdan's men took the Colts only when promised by an aide of Union army commander General George McClellan that they would receive their Sharps as soon as the Sharps Rifle Manufacturing Company made them. Private William B. Greene of Company G, while still at the Camp of Instruction, made three references to the Colt rifles and that the men were reluctant to take these rifles:

> January 27, 1862, Camp of Instruction. The story around camp is that the officers are going to try and have us take Colt's revolving rifles and I think if both regiments stick to it and not take them we shall be discharged.

---

20. Fox, *Regimental Losses*, 419.
21. Marcot, *U.S. Sharpshooters*, 7.
22. Brent Nosworthy, *The Bloody Crucible of Courage: Fighting Methods and Combat Experience of the Civil War* (New York, 2003), 248–249.
23. Jerry R. Desmond, *Turning the Tide at Gettysburg: How Maine Saved the Union* (Camden, ME, 2014), 56–57.
24. Stevens, *Berdan's United States Sharpshooters*, 5; Yee, *Sharpshooters 1750–1900*, 246, 285.

February 6, 1862, Camp of Instruction. We have received our rifles today. They are Colts revolving-five shooting ones. Some of the regiment refused to take them at first but concluded to at last.

February 7, 1862, Camp of Instruction. I answered mother's letter this morning and you probably know before this that we are armed against our will with Colts rifles. One of Gen. McLenon's [McClellan's] body guard was here today and the boy's told him just how the thing stood. He said the officers had no right to force us to take them but that it was Gen. McLenon's request for us to take them until Sharps could be made and he said that we should have Sharps rifles sure by four weeks, so you see we are going to have the guns we enlisted for and go for the same purpose as skirmishers.[25]

On May 8, 1862, Colonel Hiram Berdan wrote a letter to Hugh Harbison, treasurer of Colt's Firearm Manufacturing Company in Hartford, Connecticut. Berdan stated, "We are to-day exchanging our Colts revolving rifles for the Sharps rifles, and it occurs to me that to do this without explanation may be a cause of great injustice to your invaluable arm. The change is made in accordance with a promise made to the men when they were enlisted that they should have the Sharps rifles."[26] This was one of the few promises kept to the men, and they grudgingly took the Colts as interim weapons.[27] The manufacturer missed the four weeks mark, but by June 1862, both regiments exchanged their well-used Colts for Sharps rifles.

The open-sighted Sharps rifle was the best breech-loading gun manufactured at that time. This weapon combined accuracy with rapidity and was a perfectly safe and reliable weapon, just what a skirmish line needed for effective work.[28] And the men loved them. Captain Rudolph Aschmann, of 1st Regiment, Company A, wrote, "The Sharps rifles were all that we could have wished for. Besides being easy and quick to load in any position, they fired accurately even at great distances. They were easy to clean and keep in good working order, and more than any other gun in the army they had the look of a weapon worthy of a sharpshooter. They left nothing to be desired in the soundness of quality, and soon this rifle came to be so well-liked in the regiment that even the companies which were equipped with target rifles exchanged the latter for the new guns."[29]

The Sharps rifle was the result of a design formulated in 1848 by

---

25. Hastings, *Letters from a Sharpshooter*, 63, 71, 74.
26. Janet B. Hewett, Noah Andre Trudeau, and Bryce A. Suderow, eds., *Supplement to the Official Records of the Union and Confederate Armies*, 51 vols. (Wilmington, NC, 1994–97), Serial 93, vol. 1, part 3, 551.
27. Yee, *Sharpshooters 1750–1900*, 246.
28. Stevens, *Berdan's United States Sharpshooters*, 7, 163.
29. Meier, *Memoirs of a Swiss Officer*, 63.

Christian Sharps (1810–1874) and was a single-shot caplock breechloader. The Sharps rifles supplied to Berdan's sharpshooters differed from standard Army issue rifles in that they used factory-fitted double or set triggers, which provided the shooter with an extremely light trigger pull. The Sharps rifle was comparatively light, well-balanced, rugged in design, and simple in mechanical function. The rifle had a 30-inch-long round barrel that fired a combustible .52-caliber linen cartridge loaded with 67 grains of powder that propelled its 475-grain cylindro-conoidal bullet at a supersonic 1,400 feet per second. Although the manufacturer calibrated the ladder-pattern rear sight to 900 yards, the bullet was capable of considerably greater range. Besides accuracy and range, more than 1,000 yards in the hands of a skilled shooter, the major advantage that breechloaders had was the ability for the shooter to remain prone while reloading, instead of awkwardly manipulating a ramrod. A shooter could load and fire the breechloader at the rate of eight to 10 rounds per minute. This rapid ability to reload was a mixed blessing as sharpshooters often quickly ran out of ammunition, and they soon learned to carry a larger quantity of it. While 60 rounds were standard issue, on certain occasions, such as at Gettysburg, they carried many more in a second pouch. Nevertheless, these rifles proved to be an outstanding success with the men, even though historians sometimes overlook the devastating effect on enemy troops when these men were using the Sharps breech-loading rifles.[30]

On the afternoon of July 2, 1863, the men of Confederate major general John B. Hood's division experienced this devasting effect. Private Edwin Aldritt, Company A, 2nd Sharpshooters, wrote, "We sharpshooters were behind a stone wall and we made a quick work of the skirmishers. They brought up a regiment but had no chance. They had come across a clearing of about 200 yards and we shot them to pieces. Their loss was terrible, and they didn't get halfway before they broke and ran back for the woods. Our colonel told me to scout across the clearing to learn if they had retired or were bringing up reinforcements. I started and suddenly came across a wounded Confederate major. I gave him a swig out of my canteen and then he asked, 'What regiment is that behind the wall?' I told him we were the Second United States Sharpshooters. 'My God,' he said again, 'I never saw such shooting.'"[31]

Some first-person Confederate accounts state the sharpshooters' defensive line, stretching north to south across the fields of John Slyder's

---

30. Pegler, *Sharpshooting Rifles*, 23, 25, 35; Sword, *Sharpshooter: Hiram Berdan*, 57, 80, 82.

31. Daniel J. Hoisington, ed., "I Never Saw Such Shooting," in *Chanhassen: A Centennial History* (Chanhassen, MN, 1996), 48.

farm west of Big Round Top, was of no concern as advancing Confederate forces easily swept aside Union skirmishers, forcing them to retreat. For example, Colonel Robert M. Powell of the 5th Texas said, "On rushed the Texans, sweeping from their path cavalry ... crushing and destroying opposing forces at the foot of the mountain."[32] The understrength 2nd Sharpshooters, Powell's "forces at the foot of the mountain," impressively resisted the advancing Confederates. Interestingly, some Union soldiers made similar claims. For example, Edward Bennet with the 44th New York wrote, "The fact is two brigades of Major General Hood's Division met no obstacles on their way from the starting point to Round Top."[33] These statements are simply not accurate.

At Gettysburg, the Union's 2nd Sharpshooters engaged elements of two Confederate brigades containing five regiments from Brigadier General Evander M. Law's brigade and two regiments from Brigadier General Jerome B. Robertson's brigade. Combined, they had an engaged strength of approximately 2,750 men, whereas the understrength 2nd Sharpshooters' engaged strength, with only eight companies instead of the standard 10, was an estimated 169.[34] As detailed as these June 30 numbers are, they only give general guidelines for battlefield-engaged strengths, since they include units not present in the battle and do not account for stragglers or other losses for each unit between the time of the June 30 muster and the moment the unit reached the battlefield. Be that as it may, the estimated engaged strengths show a Confederate advantage of engaged combatants of approximately 15 to 1. Appendix B provides a breakdown of engaged strengths.[35]

What the 2nd Sharpshooters ended up performing was a delaying action across Slyder Farm and the western slope of Big Round Top. A delaying action is a battle fought by an outnumbered and outgunned force to try to slow down the advance of a superior force. The aim is to buy enough time for other friendly forces to either escape or arrive. This action also trades space for time by slowing down the enemy's momentum and inflicting maximum damage on the enemy without, in

---

32. Gregory A. Coco, ed., *Recollections of a Texas Colonel at Gettysburg* (Gettysburg, PA, 1990), 14.
33. Edward Bennet, "Fighting Them Over," *The National Tribune* (Washington, D.C., 1886), 3.
34. John W. Busey and David G. Martin, *Regimental Strengths and Losses at Gettysburg*, 4th ed. (Hightstown, NJ, 2005), 50, 131, 260–262. Initially, the 2nd Sharpshooters only engaged the Confederate skirmish line, not the combined engaged strength of 2,750. Later, on the slopes of Big Round Top, as the Confederate skirmish line passed to the south, the 2nd Sharpshooters engaged a much larger force of five Confederate regiments.
35. *Ibid.*, 6.

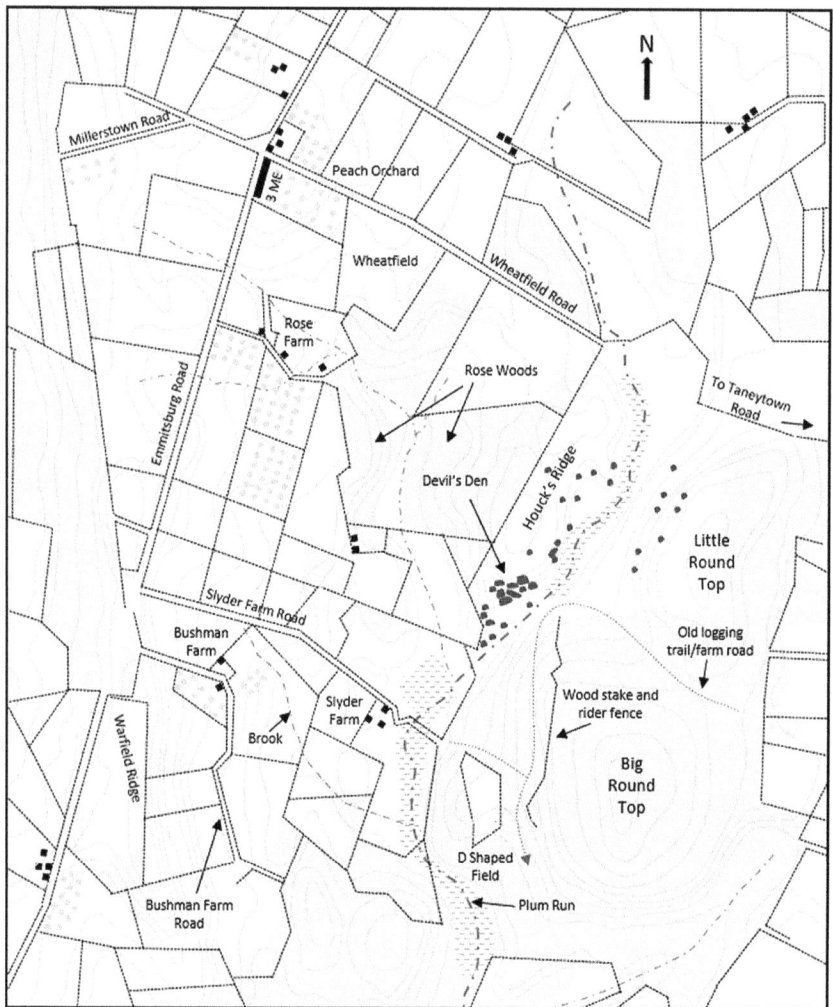

Major geographic and topographic features on the southern end of the battlefield. All maps are based on the Warren Map. North to top, the scale is 1:1000.

principle, becoming decisively engaged.[36] Delaying units use the terrain and obstacles to slow or hinder the enemy's advance, and a defending force can inflict heavy casualties against an advancing foe and minimize friendly casualties. Numerically inferior forces use restricted terrain to gain parity against a larger force. At Gettysburg, natural and

---

36. Military Factory, https://www.militaryfactory.com/dictionary/military-terms-alphabet-list.php?letter_group=D (accessed April 20, 2022).

manmade obstacles fragmented advancing Confederate units, depleting their strength, slowing momentum, and reducing their already limited manpower. Confederate colonel William C. Oates's decision to chase the 2nd Sharpshooters up Big Round Top consumed valuable time and further delayed the Confederates' mission of turning the Union's left flank and taking Little Round Top before the arrival of Union reinforcements.[37]

Eugene Nash of the 44th New York wrote that when General Longstreet visited Gettysburg in 1897, Longstreet stated that on July 2, 1863, he was "just three minutes late in occupying Little Round Top," and if he had occupied it first, "we would have had as much trouble getting rid of him as he did in trying to get rid of us." Nash continued, asking the questions, "Do great battles sometimes turn on small events? Do the happenings of three minutes of time change the fate of a battle?"[38] If one accepts that the 20th Maine "saved the day" at Little Round Top, should we accept, as author John J. Pullen suggests, that the 2nd Sharpshooters saved the minutes that made saving the day possible?[39] Posed another way, the essential question becomes: Did the 2nd Sharpshooters' delaying action slow the advancing Confederate battle line long enough for Union troops to occupy Little Round Top?

Berdan's Sharpshooters became the unique organization of the war, conceived under an innovative concept, to fight not as an infantry unit, but as skirmishers and snipers well in advance of the Union line of battle. Few regiments, if any, were more effective in their combat role, or more personally feared by the enemy, than the U.S. Sharpshooters.[40]

---

37. Phillip Thomas Tucker, *Storming Little Round Top: The 15th Alabama and Their Fight for the High Ground, July 2, 1863* (Cambridge, MA, 2002), 137. Oates was the commanding officer of the 15th Alabama Infantry Regiment.
38. Eugene A. Nash, "Dedication of Monument 44th Regiment Infantry," in *Final Report of the Battlefield of Gettysburg, Volume 1* (Albany, NY, 1902), 365.
39. John J. Pullen, ed., "Introduction," *Soldiers in Green: Civil War Diaries of James Mero Matthews, 2nd U.S. Sharpshooters* (Sandy Point, ME, 2002), iv.
40. Sword, *Sharpshooter: Hiram Berdan*, 8.

One

Setting the Stage

Initial Moves for an Upcoming Fight

(Around Midnight to about 10:00 a.m.)

A position is sometimes occupied as a matter of necessity, sometimes merely as a matter of tactical prudence.[1]

The study and the intimate knowledge of the terrain are the beginning and the end of tactics. Everything to do with the ground, its shape, its contours, its texture, even its color at different hours of the day, affects everything both opponents do and can do. The two adversaries have in common the battlefield terrain. Other things being nearly equal, the victory goes to the one who understands the terrain best and uses it to his advantage.[2] On July 2, 1863, the Union Army at Gettysburg, Pennsylvania, held one of the best examples of a defensive position occupied by either army during the war. The Union position was tactically strong with well-wooded hilltops. Meanwhile, Confederate troops advanced over a mostly open plain.[3] The ground opposite the Union left offered desirable positions from which to make the Confederate attack.

Equally important was the road network around and within the battlefield. An attacking force would find it desirable to seize the roads, while the defense would deem it equally important to hold them. These roads not only led through important military positions, but also formed lines of communication with distant strategic points: lines over which supply trains were moving, and routes on which troops were coming and going. Gettysburg was a junction of several major roads

---

1. Unknown, *Lectures on Land Warfare: A Tactical Manual for the Use of Infantry Officers* (London, 1922), 77.
2. Ralph Ingersoll, *The Battle Is the Pay-Off* (New York, 1943), 122.
3. Tolles, "Army Movements," 542–543.

found in that part of the country and many types of roads intersected the battlefield. These roads ranged from turnpikes, to farm roads, to logging trails, all of which could afford important tactical advantages for troop movement.

The primary roads traversing the immediate area are the Taneytown Road, east of the Round Tops, and Emmitsburg Road, west of the Slyder and Bushman farms. Two crossroads intersect Emmitsburg Road. The principal crossroad is Wheatfield Road, which extends at a right angle with Emmitsburg Road at the Peach Orchard and passes north of the Wheatfield and Houck's Ridge. Wheatfield Road eventually crosses Plum Run and continues to the east beyond Little Round Top. Wheatfield Road is named Millerstown Road west of Emmitsburg Road. A second crossroad is the Slyder farm road that extends eastward from Emmitsburg Road. The road traverses Slyder Farm, crosses Plum Run, and then starts up the western slope of Big Round Top, passing a cleared field bordered by a stone fence. Historians commonly refer to this field as the "D-shaped field" and it was possibly a livestock pen, as the ground is too rocky for farming.[4] At the time of the battle, the Slyder farm road merged with a logging or farm road that ran along the base of Big Round Top. The terrain and all these roads would be a factor in the battle on Thursday, July 2, 1863.

Three days earlier, on Monday, June 29, the 2nd Sharpshooters, on their way to Gettysburg, marched through the town of Taneytown, Maryland. The citizens of Taneytown, displaying good intentions and Union pride, flocked to the road to see the Union troops as they marched through their town. Passing through town, the sharpshooters bivouacked near the village at dark, continuing their march toward Emmitsburg, Maryland, the next day. The regiment arrived at Emmitsburg on Tuesday, June 30, sometime between 5:00 p.m. and dark; however, there was a very different feeling there than the day before at Taneytown. Only a few of the people in Emmitsburg were moving about, and even the priests who were out remained silent as they went about their tasks. The First Division, III Army Corps, to which the 2nd Sharpshooters belonged, camped near Emmitsburg for the night as the men, trying to stay dry, hastily pitched their tents in the rain. Maybe it was because secessionists had burned part of the town. Maybe it was

---

4. William F. Fox, "New York at Gettysburg," *Final Report of the Battlefield of Gettysburg, Volume 1* (Albany, NY, 1902), 37, 42–43; William R. Balch, *The Battle of Gettysburg: An Historical Account* (Philadelphia, PA, 1885), 36; J. Warren Gilbert, *The Blue and Gray: A History of the Conflicts During Lee's Invasion and Battle of Gettysburg* (Harrisburg, PA, 1922), 58; Henry J. Hunt, "The Second Day at Gettysburg," in *Battles and Leaders of the Civil War: Volume 3, The Tide Shifts* (Secaucus, NJ, 2010), 283.

the coming darkness combined with the approaching rain. Or was it that the people the sharpshooters talked to seemed to feel that a great battle was close at hand? Either way, Emmitsburg felt different to some of the men.[5]

On Wednesday, July 1, the division broke camp and marched through town looking for a proper place to camp, which they soon found on the other side of Emmitsburg. The weather was still rainy, but most men were hopeful that a day or two of rest was coming. However, as soon as the men set up camp and consumed noon rations, orders came to pack up, and by 5:00 p.m. the division was again on the move. Private Wyman White wrote, "By the hasty way we were prompted, it looked as though we were to counter some move of the enemy."[6] With rain in the morning, it became hot and humid in the afternoon as the division, headed toward the town of Gettysburg, forced-marched 11 miles over rough and muddy roads.[7] For most of the afternoon, the sharpshooters could hear cannon fire in the distance to the north, ceasing at about 7:00 p.m. They would also sporadically meet citizens going in the opposite direction, fleeing from their homes. The sharpshooters arrived on the battlefield at 8:30 p.m. and camped for the night southeast of Little Round Top. The men slept soundly on their arms that night; however, Wyman White wrote that "all felt that the great battle was to come the next day ... that the enemy would renew the battle at early morn."[8]

Earlier that evening, around 7:00 p.m., as the sharpshooters were making their way to the Gettysburg area, Major General Daniel E. Sickles arrived on the battlefield. Soon, he and his officers were engaged in readjusting the lines, forming new ones, and ensuring that their men had enough ammunition in anticipation for the battle that was soon to come.[9] As troops began arriving in the Gettysburg area, one of the first things Sickles did was establish a picket line along Emmitsburg Road. The 63rd Pennsylvania and the 4th Maine were the first two regiments to move into position, followed shortly by the 99th Pennsylvania.

Major John A. Danks, commanding the 63rd Pennsylvania, wrote, "On Wednesday, July 1, the Sixty-third, with the rest of the brigade, moved from camp in the field near Emmitsburg, Md., to a point near Gettysburg, Pa. From this point the regiment was ordered on picket, and

---

5. Pullen, *Soldiers in Green*, 159; White, *Civil War Diary*, 161. Sergeant James Matthews, Company D, references a report that part of Emmitsburg had been burned by a "secesh," which was an informal term for a supporter, soldier, or sympathizer of the Confederacy during the Civil War.
6. White, *Civil War Diary*, 161; Pullen, *Soldiers in Green*, 160.
7. Peteler, "Narrative of the First Company," 508; White, *Civil War Diary*, 162.
8. Burnham, *Notes of Army and Prison Life*, 49; White, *Civil War Diary*, 162–163.
9. *OR*, 27, pt. 1, 115.

posted on line with the Emmitsburg pike." Furthermore, Captain Robert A. Nesbitt of Company A wrote, "On the evening of July 1st, the regiment moved out along the Emmitsburg Road, our left opposite the Peach Orchard, and facing where the enemy was posted in the woods. The extreme left, where Company B was stationed, and just on the left of the orchard the members of the Sixty-third Regiment tore down the rail fences and built a rifle pit, facing the enemy across an oats field. Here we remained all night, pickets in the road."[10]

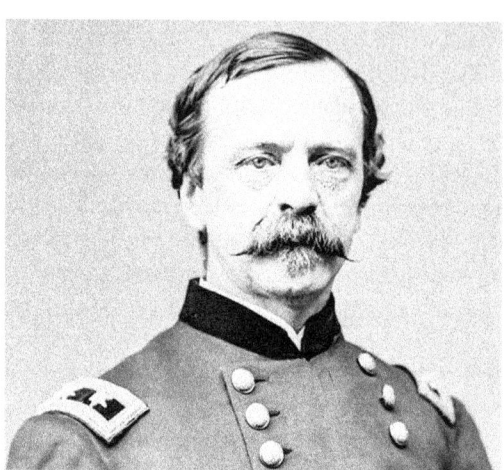

Major General Daniel E. Sickles, commanding officer, III Army Corps. Library of Congress.

The 99th Pennsylvania also arrived in Gettysburg by way of the Emmitsburg Road. At about 7:40 p.m., just shortly after sunset on July 1, the regiment bivouacked for the night in the Peach Orchard just east of Emmitsburg Road. At about 3:45 a.m. on July 2, Major John W. Moore was to place his regiment in the line of battle on the right of the brigade, which formed the extreme left of the Union line. The first streakings of the morning light broke from the horizon as the men of the 99th Pennsylvania took up their position to the left of the Peach Orchard.[11]

The 4th Maine arrived on the field with Sickles's corps about 7:00 p.m. on July 1, having moved up from Taneytown by way of Emmitsburg. Colonel Elijah Walker, commanding the 4th Maine, was trying to get a little sleep when, at about 8:30 p.m., he heard one of his captains calling for him. Walker answered, "I am here, captain. Is it our turn to establish

---

10. *OR*, 27, pt. 1, 498; Gilbert Adams Hays, *Under the Red Patch: Story of the Sixty Third Regiment Pennsylvania Volunteers 1861–1864* (Pittsburgh, PA, 1908), 194.

11. *OR*, 27, pt. 1, 513; Albert Magnin, "Dedication of Monument, 99th Regiment Infantry," in *Pennsylvania at Gettysburg, Ceremonies as the Dedication of the Monuments, Volume 2*, ed. John P. Nicholson (Harrisburg, PA, 1893), 531. With sunrise occurring at about 4:45 a.m. on July 2, the "first streakings of the morning light" would appear around an hour earlier, at 3:45 a.m. Although it depends largely on where you are on Earth, the sky starts to lighten up around an hour before sunrise (Astronomy Scope, *Dawn vs. Sunrise*).

a picket line?" The captain responded, "Yes, it is the order of General Sickles that your regiment establish a picket line, the right to connect with the I Corps pickets and the left with those of the II Corps." Lieutenant Charles F. Sawyer, who took over command of the regiment after Walker was wounded later in the day, wrote in his report that they were to connect "on the left with the 99th Pennsylvania Volunteers." Walker's picket line was to extend along a portion of the front of the left wing, as the Union line existed at that hour. Walker reluctantly obeyed, moved to the front about half a mile, and established a line by a rail fence, some 30 or 40 rods (165–220 yards) west of the Emmitsburg Road, linking up with the I Corps pickets, as directed, but failed to find any troops on his left except for a few cavalry scouts. The reason Walker did not connect on his left with the 99th Pennsylvania is that, as described above, Major Moore did not deploy the 99th Pennsylvania until just before dawn the next morning. More importantly, Walker noted, verifying the statement of Major Danks, that Confederate pickets were in the woods in front of the 4th Maine. Walker wrote, "During the night the enemy were massing in the woods in front of us. The enemy's pickets, at this time, occupied the woods directly in our front, 30 and 50 rods [165 and 275 yards] from our line, in which woods the enemy were assembling throughout the night."[12]

By the time General Sickles arrived on the battlefield, Major General Winfield S. Hancock, commanding the II Corps, had already placed troops on the left of the line.

Colonel Elijah Walker, commanding officer, 4th Maine Infantry. Maine State Archives Collection.

At 3:00 p.m. I arrived at Gettysburg and assumed the command. The Third Corps had not yet arrived from Emmitsburg. Orders were at

---

12. Charles Hamlin, C.T. Stevens, S.W. Thaxter, G.W. Verrill, and C.E. Nash, "Fourth Maine Regiment," *Maine at Gettysburg* (Portland, ME, 1898), 159; Elijah Walker, "Regimental Dedication of Monument," *Maine at Gettysburg* (Portland, ME, 1898), 179–180; *OR*, 27, pt. 1, 509; David L. Ladd and Audrey J. Ladd, eds., *The Batchelder Papers: Gettysburg in Their Own Words, Volume 2* (Dayton, OH, 1994), 1093–1094.

once given to establish a line of battle on Cemetery Hill, with skirmishers occupying that part of the town immediately in our front. Brig. Gen. John W. Geary's division, of the Twelfth Corps, arriving on the ground subsequently, and not being able to communicate with Maj. Gen Henry W. Slocum, I ordered the division to the high ground to the right of and near Round Top Mountain, commanding the Gettysburg and Emmitsburg Road, as well as the Gettysburg and Taneytown Road to our rear.[13]

Lieutenant Charles F. Sawyer commanding the 4th Maine after the wounding of Colonel Walker in the late afternoon of July 2. Maine State Archives Collection.

Brigadier General John W. Geary reported to Hancock, who informed Geary that the right could maintain itself, and the immediate need for a division on the left was imperative. At Hancock's direction, Geary moved his Second Division to the extreme left of the line of battle, as reports indicated the enemy was attempting to flank the Union line, and cavalry was already skirmishing in front of that position. Geary completed this movement by 5:00 p.m., and noted the importance of the Round Tops, writing, "These hills I regarded as of the utmost importance since their possession by the enemy would give him an opportunity of enfilading our entire left wing and center with a fire which could not fail to dislodge us from our position."[14] This movement extended the Union line at that time from about half a mile west of the Baltimore Turnpike to the Round Tops, which Geary occupied with two regiments of his First Brigade.

Big Round Top is the most conspicuous elevation in the vicinity of Gettysburg. Brigadier General Evander Law said of Big Round Top, "It rose like a huge sentinel guarding the Federal left flank, while the spurs and ridges trending off to the north of it afforded unrivaled positions for the use of artillery. The thick woods which in great part covered the sides of Round Top and the adjacent hills concealed from view the rugged

---

13. *OR*, 27, pt. 1, 368.
14. *Ibid.*, 825.

nature of the ground, which increased fourfold the difficulties of the attack." Directly north of Big Round Top, separated by a slight depression, is Little Round Top, which is an irregular rocky rise of ground with sloping sides. During the battle, considerable tree growth existed on the hill except on the top and western face where the local population had previously stripped timber, leaving nothing but an immense mass of boulders. The western slopes of the Round Tops descend to the low, marshy ground of Plum Run Valley.[15]

Brigadier General John W. Geary, commanding the Second Division, XII Army Corps. Library of Congress.

Brigadier General Geary ordered Colonel Charles Candy, as sunset approached, commanding Geary's First Brigade, to move forward two regiments to the left and "occupy a high range of hills overlooking the surrounding country and watch for any attempted advance of the enemy on the left of the army."[16] Colonel John H. Patrick, commanding the 5th Ohio, commenced operations and proceeded to the extreme left of his line, to occupy a "hill covered with trees," referring to Big Round Top. Colonel Candy placed the 147th Pennsylvania under Colonel Patrick's command, to extend and increase the front of his position. Patrick wrote, "We deployed as skirmishers in our front across an open valley to a light strip of woods, and in front of that timber facing an open field, for the purpose of guarding against a flank movement of the enemy."[17]

---

15. Terrain descriptions compiled from Evander M. Law, "Round Top and the Confederate Right at Gettysburg," *The Century Magazine* 33, no. 2 (December 1886), 299; Gilbert, *The Blue and Gray*, 58–59; Thomas Rafferty, "Gettysburg," *Personal Recollections of the War of the Rebellion, An Address Delivered at a Meeting of the Commandery, State of New York, Loyal Legion*, Nov. 7, 1883, ed. James Grant Wilson and Titus Munson Coan (New York, 1891), 6–7; A.T. Cowell, *Tactics at Gettysburg as Described by Participants in the Battle* (Gettysburg, PA, 1910), 40; Eugene A. Nash, *A History of the Forty-Fourth Regiment New York Volunteer Infantry in the Civil War, 1861–1865* (Chicago, 1911), 143–144; Fox, "New York at Gettysburg," 36; A.M. Judson, *History of the Eighty-Third Regiment Pennsylvania Volunteers* (Erie, PA, 1865), 66.
16. *OR*, 27, pt. 1, 825.
17. Ibid., 839.

In position at the northern base of Little Round Top, Colonel Patrick ordered the 147th Pennsylvania out on picket duty for the night. The men advanced several hundred yards in the direction of Emmitsburg Road, taking an advanced position on rough, rocky ground, and occupied a stone fence as protection. The 147th Pennsylvania crossed the Plum Run Valley and deployed near the northern end of Houck's Ridge. The ridge commands the long approaches and open fields to the west and south, with the ridge's summit about 80 feet above the Plum Run Valley floor. Rose Woods lies to the west and extends nearly to the Peach Orchard. The mostly wooded ridge trends in a northwesterly direction, with Devil's Den on the south and Wheatfield Road to the north. Here the 147th Pennsylvania, except for the reserve on Little Round Top, stood alert against approaches by the enemy.[18]

Colonel Charles Candy, commanding the First Brigade, Second Division, XII Army Corps. Library of Congress.

As already noted, Captain Robert Nesbitt of the 63rd Pennsylvania and Colonel Elijah Walker both wrote that Confederate troops were massing in the woods in their front and probably moving into position for an attack. Both Nesbitt and Walker were correct in their assumptions. On July 2, Colonel R. Lindsay Walker commanded the artillery reserve of Major General William D. Pender's division, Lieutenant General Ambrose P. Hill's Third Army Corps. Walker moved the battalions of Major William J. Pegram, Major David G. Mcintosh, Major John Lane, and a part of Lieutenant Colonel John J. Garnett's battalion, under Major Charles Richardson, into position on the right of the Fairfield turnpike, about one mile in advance of the position of the previous

---

18. Joseph A. Moore, "Dedication of Monument, 147th Regiment Infantry," in *Pennsylvania at Gettysburg, Ceremonies as the Dedication of the Monuments, Volume 2*, ed. John P. Nicholson (Harrisburg, PA, 1893), 702–703. Terrain descriptions compiled from Fox, "New York at Gettysburg," 37; Jennings C. Wise, *The Long Arm of Lee or the History of the Artillery of the Army of Northern Virginia, Volume II* (Lynchburg, VA, 1915), 640. Note: At the time of the battle, names such as Devil's Den, Round Top, Culp's Hill, Cemetery Ridge, and so on were unknown to the soldiers in either army.

day.[19] The report filed by Captain Ervin B. Brunson for Pegram's battery stated that the battalion "bivouacked the night 1st near the position we occupied during the day. At an early hour in the morning, we took position a mile to the right of the pike, in advance of the position we occupied the day before, and opposite the Yankee center, about 1,400 yards from the crest upon which his artillery was massed."[20] Sunrise on July 2, 1863, was at about 4:45 a.m., and Brunson's comment about taking position "at an early hour of the morning" is clearly about a time before dawn and/or sunrise.

Colonel John H. Patrick, commanding the 5th Ohio Infantry of Colonel Candy's First Brigade. Library of Congress.

On the evening of July 1, Colonel William L.J. Lowrance with the 34th North Carolina found Brigadier General A.M. Scales's brigade on the extreme left of the division, numbering in all about 500 men, without any field officers, except Lieutenant Colonel G.T. Gordon and himself. Lowrance observed few line officers, and many companies were without a single officer to lead them or to inquire after them. Lowrance wrote in his report, "In this depressed, dilapidated, and almost unorganized condition, I took command of the brigade, and remained at the point where I found it until after nightfall."[21] The reason Lowrance took command of the brigade is that Brigadier General Alfred M. Scales, who commanded the Fourth Brigade of Pender's division, received wounds from Union artillery earlier in the day. General Scales wrote,

> I immediately ordered my brigade to advance. We passed over them, up the ascent, crossed the ridge, and commenced the descent just opposite the theological seminary. Here the brigade encountered a most terrific fire of grape and shell on our flank, and grape and musketry in our front. Every discharge made sad havoc in our line, but still we pressed on at a double-quick until we reached the bottom, a distance of about 75 yards

---

19. *OR*, 27, pt. 2, 610.
20. *Ibid.*, 678.
21. *Ibid.*, 671.

from the ridge we had just crossed, and about the same distance from the college, in our front. Here I received a painful wound from a piece of shell, and was disabled. Our line had been broken up, and now only a squad here and there marked the place where regiments had rested.[22]

Lowrance next states that he "was ordered to the extreme right of the line; and, having arrived at this place designated, I sent out a strong picket to the front and right, so as to guard against any surprise, and then ordered the few who were still in ranks to stack arms for the night. It was then 1 o'clock."[23] Lowrance never states in his official report who is ordering the movements of his brigade, but more than likely orders originated from Major General William Pender.

Lowrance continues, "At early dawn on the morning of the 2d, I was ordered to a position on the right of and on line with the artillery, which left me still on the extreme right of the line, and was ordered to hold the position at all hazards."[24] The artillery mentioned is Pegram's battalion, which had relocated a few hours earlier. The time reference of "early dawn" indicates that this movement happened after Pegram's move and probably concluded sometime between 3:45 a.m. and 4:00 a.m. Lowrance immediately realized several things upon reaching his assigned position. First, the location was an important point on the immediate right of Pegram's artillery and Lowrance's brigade was its only guard with no support. Second, he considered it hazardous in the extreme, taking into consideration his brigade's weakness as to numbers and the importance of the position. As a result, Lowrance threw out a strong line of skirmishers, extending fully one-half mile to the right, inclining to the rear. The skirmish line was under the command of Lieutenant A.J. Brown of the 38th North Carolina, who "most gallantly held the line against several strong skirmish lines thrown against him until 1 p.m., at which time the brigade was relieved by Maj. Gen. Richard H. Anderson's Division, and then I was ordered to move by the left flank and join my division, which I did."[25] The time was now close to 4:45 a.m. and sunrise was not far off.

About an hour earlier, Union major general George G. Meade decided to reinforce his right as he believed it was closer to the Confederate lines. Around 4:00 a.m. on July 2, Meade ordered Brigadier General John W. Geary to abandon his position near the Round Tops and to occupy the eastern slopes of Culp's Hill to the right of Brigadier General James S. Wadsworth. Geary's division camped near the Round Tops the

22. Ibid., 670.
23. Ibid., 671.
24. Ibid.
25. Ibid.

ONE—*Setting the Stage* 29

night of July 1, with the 5th Ohio and 147th Pennsylvania guarding the left of the line. At 5:00 a.m., Geary's division departed its position, leaving vacant all the portion of the line he occupied, from Major General Daniel E. Sickles's left to Little Round Top.[26] As Geary's men departed, the 5:00 a.m. reveille awakened the men of the 1st and 2nd Sharpshooters. As the sharpshooters awakened from their sleep, they would eventually fall into line, about-face to the west, and deploy as skirmishers facing the town of Emmitsburg.[27] Little did either regiment know what the day held in store for them.

Shortly after dawn, when there was enough light to see, the 63rd Pennsylvania moved forward from the Peach Orchard into position upon the skirmish line. The regiment rested behind Joseph Sherfy's house, at a fence that was parallel to Emmitsburg Road. At about 5:00 a.m., the enemy made their appearance in front of the Union skirmish line and opened fire. Firing continued during the day, and at three different times the enemy deployed and advanced a strong skirmish line as if they intended full columns to follow, but in every instance, the Union skirmishers drove them back after a severe skirmish.[28]

Colonel Elijah Walker with the 4th Maine reported similar events. Walker wrote that all was quiet, until daylight, at which time a desultory skirmish fire began between the opposing picket lines, which continued until between 9:00 and 10:00 a.m. Several times the enemy picket line advanced into the opening but the men were

Major General George G. Meade, commanding the Army of the Potomac. Library of Congress.

26. *OR*, 27, pt. 1, 825; Fox, "New York at Gettysburg," 36; The Comte De Paris, *History of the Civil War in America, Volume 3* (Philadelphia, PA, 1888), 590.
27. White, *Civil War Diary*, 163; Pullen, *Soldiers in Green*, 160.
28. Samuel P. Bates, *History of Pennsylvania Volunteers, 1861–5, Volume II* (Harrisburg, PA, 1869), 495; *OR*, 27, pt. 1, 498; R. Howard Miller, "Historical Sketch, Dedication of Monument, 63D Regiment Infantry," *Pennsylvania at Gettysburg, Ceremonies as the Dedication of the Monuments, Volume 1*, ed. John P. Nicholson (Harrisburg, PA, 1893), 360.

glad to take cover in the woods.[29] Walker knew the enemy was in force on his front and had fears of an attack. After the war, Walker would write that early that morning he reported a large force in the woods in front of him and asked for support near at hand. But his superiors disregarded the report, all claiming that there was no force in the woods and that the main force had fallen back. Walker claims he "was twice ordered to advance and drive the enemy's pickets out of the woods. These orders I did not attempt to execute." Lieutenant Charles F. Sawyer, also of the 4th Maine, corroborates this, writing in his official report, "On the morning of the 2d, some picket firing took place, which was not responded to."[30] From 10:00 a.m. and for the next hour, there was relative quiet on this part of the picket line, when at about 11:00 a.m. the 1st Massachusetts relieved the 4th Maine, who then rejoined the brigade.[31]

At 5:00 a.m., as pickets west of Emmitsburg Road fired at one another and as reveille roused the men of the 1st and 2nd Sharpshooters, Brigadier General Geary prepared to move his division. It seems that General Geary, upon receiving his orders earlier that morning stating the III Corps would relieve him, waited for some time for them to arrive at his location. He eventually sent a staff officer to Sickles with instructions to explain the position and its importance and to say that if Sickles could not send any troops to relieve him, would Sickles send one of his staff to see the ground, and to place troops there on their arrival. General Sickles replied that he would attend to it in due time; however, no officer or troops came, and after waiting until his patience was exhausted, Geary withdrew and joined his corps.[32]

In obedience to Major General Slocum's orders, Geary moved his division to the right and assumed a position with the rest of the Second Division on the left of the First Division, XII Corps, and to the right of the I Corps.[33] As Geary's Division moved to the right of the Union line, Brigadier General J.H. Hobart Ward ordered Major John Moore with his regiment, the 99th Pennsylvania, to report to Major General David B. Birney. Moore received Ward's order sometime before 6:00 a.m., as Moore had put his regiment in line of battle about 3:45 a.m., writing in his report that his regiment was "lying in this position for two to three hours" before receiving Ward's order to report to Birney. Moore

---

29. Elijah Walker, "Regimental Dedication of Monument," 180; *Maine at Gettysburg* (Portland, ME, 1898), 159.
30. Ladd and Ladd, *The Batchelder Papers*, 1093–1094; Elijah Walker, "Regimental Dedication of Monument," 98, 180; *OR*, 27, pt. 1, 509.
31. *Maine at Gettysburg*, 159; *OR*, 27, pt. 1, 509, 547.
32. George G. Meade, "Letter from George G. Meade to G.G. Benedict, March 16, 1870," in *The Life and Letters of George Gordon Meade, Volume II* (New York, 1913), 353.
33. *OR*, 27, pt. 1, 839, 825, 846, 836.

returned his regiment to the brigade and took a position somewhat to the right of Little Round Top. Moore wrote, "This position I held for over an hour," remaining there until about 7:00 a.m., when General Ward advanced the balance of the brigade.[34]

At 10:00 p.m. the previous day, General Meade broke up his headquarters, which until then had been at Taneytown, and proceeded to the field in Gettysburg, arriving there at 1:00 a.m. on July 2. As soon as it was light, he proceeded to inspect the position occupied and made arrangements for posting the several corps as they should reach the ground.[35] Meade, after having settled upon the positions for the respective corps to occupy, sent Brigadier General Henry Hunt, Meade's chief of artillery, to examine the lines for a second time and to make sure that the artillery was everywhere properly posted. Hunt indicated this examination happened "at or near daylight."[36]

As previously noted, General Meade ordered Geary to abandon his position,

Brigadier General J.H. Hobart Ward, commanding the Second Brigade, First Division, III Army Corps. Library of Congress.

Major General David B. Birney, commanding the First Division, III Army Corps. Library of Congress.

---

34. *OR*, 27, pt. 1, 513; Magnin, "Dedication of Monument, 99th Regiment Infantry," 532; C.H. Fasnacht, *Historical Sketch, Dedication of 99th Pennsylvania Monument, Gettysburg, PA, July 2, 1886* (Lancaster, PA, 1886), 9.
35. *OR*, 27, pt.1, 115.
36. George Meade, *The Life and Letters of George Gordon Meade, Volume II* (New York, 1913), 63; *OR*, 27, pt. 1, 232.

which Geary did about 5:00 a.m. that morning. Meade then directed Sickles to take the ground Geary had left, but Sickles did not receive his orders until almost an hour later, at 6:00 a.m.[37] Meade wrote, "The position of General Sickles, commanding the Third Corps, was indicated to him in two specific ways—to relieve the division of General Geary, by occupying the line upon which he had been posted the night before by General Hancock; and to connect his right with the left of the Second Corps, prolonging his line on the ridge up to, and on to, Little Round Top, and, if practicable, to occupy it."[38] Sickles acknowledged that at a "very early hour on Thursday morning I received a notification that General Meade's headquarters had been established at Gettysburg, and I was directed by him to relieve a division of the 12th corps, (General Geary's division, I think,) which was massed a little to my left, and which had taken position there during the night."[39]

Brigadier General Henry J. Hunt, Chief of Artillery, Army of the Potomac. Library of Congress.

It was now sometime after 6:00 a.m. and the III Corps had yet to occupy Geary's old position on the left of the Union line. Recall that Geary's position extended as far as Big Round Top and the commanding aspect of this hill indicated it was an important point to hold on the Federal left. However, with Geary having departed at an early hour, Sickles, entirely preoccupied with his own troops, claimed he was unaware of the position Geary held and the extent of his line, claiming Geary left no one behind to supply Sickles with the necessary information.[40]

Major General David B. Birney, commanding the Third Division of III Corps, wrote in his official report that he relieved Geary's division at 7:00 a.m. under orders from Major General Sickles. Birney "formed a line,

---

37. David Craft, *History of the One Hundred Forty-First Regiment, Pennsylvania Volunteers, 1862–1865* (Towanda, PA, 1885), 118.
38. George Meade, *The Life and Letters, Volume II*, 63–64.
39. United States, *Report of the Joint Committee on the Conduct of the War* (Washington, D.C., 1865), 297.
40. The Comte De Paris, *History of the Civil War*, 590.

resting its left on the Sugar Loaf Mountain and the right thrown in a direct line toward the cemetery, connecting on the right with the Second Division of this corps. My picket line was in the Emmitsburg road, with sharpshooters some 300 yards in advance." Birney would later claim that "I took position with my left at and on Round Top about 9 o'clock in the morning and threw out skirmishers along the Emmitsburg road to cover the left."[41] This two-hour difference between Birney's *Official Report* (7:00 a.m.) and his testimony to the Joint Committee on the Conduct of the War (9:00 a.m.) is likely Sickles via Birney, moving part of his skirmish line from the Emmitsburg Road to Little Round Top, to satisfy Meade's requirement to occupy Geary's position. I explain this in detail shortly.

Brigadier General Hobart Ward, by direction of Birney, ordered his direct reports into position, putting the Second Brigade about one mile east of the Emmitsburg Road.[42] By 7:00 a.m., General Ward was advancing several units forward to the skirmish line, including the 3rd Maine, both Sharpshooters regiments, and skirmishers from the 99th Pennsylvania, whom Ward pulled off the skirmish line only an hour earlier. Ward ordered Colonel Moses B. Lakeman, commanding the 3rd Maine, to form his regiment in line of battle parallel to and facing Emmitsburg Road, on the right of the brigade, during the early morning. This position was on the line that General Sickles was establishing with the III Corps before he advanced his line to the Peach Orchard later in the afternoon.[43] Birney then ordered Major John Moore to send out a detachment of men from the 99th Pennsylvania in support of the 3rd Maine, which was engaged in skirmishing with the enemy on Emmitsburg Road.[44] While the 99th Pennsylvania was lying in the rear of the Wheatfield, a detail of men under the command of Second Lieutenant Sylvester Bonnafon moved in the direction of the Sherfy house. Advancing in an oblique line through the Peach Orchard, the detail deployed as skirmishers and crossed the Emmitsburg Road, entering the field beyond. In this advanced position, they discovered a rebel skirmish line advancing in an oblique direction toward the left of their line. The two skirmish lines exchanged shots and the Union skirmishers fell back to where the III Corps was then in the line of battle. A short time later, Colonel Hiram Berdan's 1st Sharpshooters would encounter the same line of rebel skirmishers.[45]

41. *OR*, 27, pt. 1, 482; United States, *Report of the Joint Committee*, 366.
42. *OR*, 27, pt. 1, 493.
43. *OR*, 27, pt. 1, 507; *Maine at Gettysburg*, 127–128.
44. *OR*, 27, pt. 1, 513.
45. Fasnacht, *Historical Sketch*, 8–9; Albert Magnin, "Dedication of Monument, 99th Regiment Infantry," 532.

On the morning of July 2, Colonel Berdan received instructions from Birney to assume command of the 1st and 2nd Sharpshooters and to report directly to division headquarters. In accordance with instructions he received, Berdan "posted the 2nd Regiment, Major Homer R. Stoughton commanding, on our left, to act as flankers, and the 1st Regiment on our front."

Colonel Moses B. Lakeman, commanding the 3rd Maine Infantry. Maine State Archives Collection.

Lieutenant Colonel Caspar Trepp, in command of the 1st Regiment, indicated the time was early morning, most likely starting their move into position around 7:00 a.m. in conjunction with other regiments of the brigade. Their instructions were to protect the left flank of the III Corps.[46]

It is a common misperception that Major Stoughton initially moved his regiment to the area between Little Round Top and Houck's Ridge, southeast of the Peach Orchard. However, evidence shows that Berdan's order to Major Stoughton to act as flankers was in reference to the left of the 1st Sharpshooters along Emmitsburg Road. For example, there is the statement by William P. Shreve, aide-de-camp to Colonel Berdan. Shreve enlisted in the 9th Regiment, New York State Militia, on June 4, 1861, and on October 4, 1861, attained the rank of quartermaster sergeant, Company H, 2nd Regiment, U.S. Sharpshooters. Shreve remained in this capacity until his promotion in the winter of 1862 to aide-de-camp, a position he held during the Battle of Gettysburg.[47] Shreve wrote, "Colonel Berdan was stationed at the Peach Orchard ... I remember of being there but once during the day. Major Stoughton of the second regiment was there."[48]

There is also commentary from several men in the 2nd

---

46. *OR*, 27, pt. 1, 514–515, 516.
47. Shreve (William Price) Papers, The University of Southern Mississippi—McCain Library and Archives, https://lib.usm.edu/spcol/collections/manuscripts/finding_aids/m029.html (accessed May 4, 2022).
48. William P. Shreve, *William Price Shreve Papers*, M29, Historical Manuscripts, Special Collections, The University of Southern Mississippi Libraries.

One—Setting the Stage 35

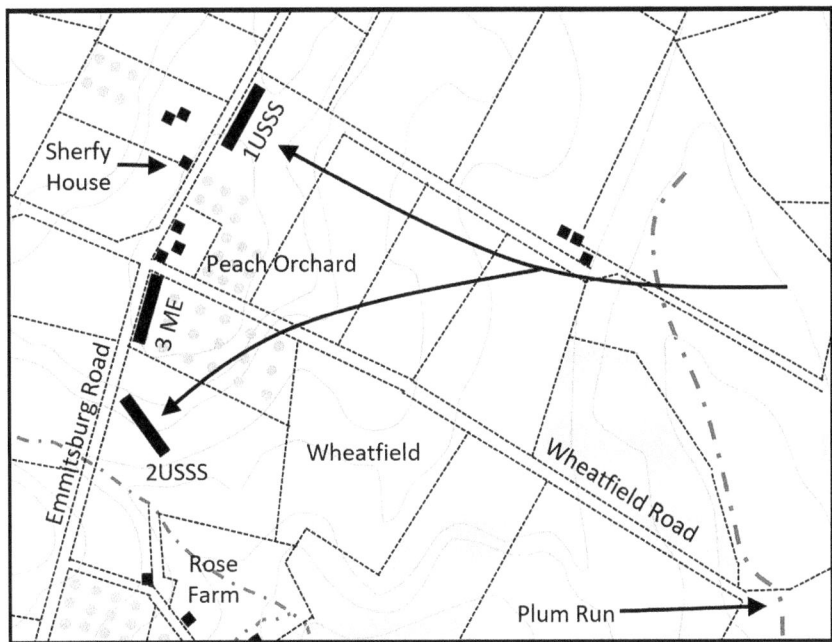

The approximate location of Colonel Berdan's two regiments at about 7:00 a.m. on July 2, 1863. Arrows indicate movement directions around 7:30 a.m. after receiving orders from Colonel Berdan to move to their respective new locations. Additionally, Lieutenant Hannibal Johnson of the 3rd Maine stated his regiment was in the Peach Orchard during the morning of July 2, 1863 (Johnson, *Sword of Honor*, 10).

Sharpshooters that verifies their initial position. Private Charles Fairbanks of Company E wrote, "Sickles placed our regiment in front of the line of battle … near the peach orchard on the Emmitsburg Road." Private Wyman White of Company F indicated that "when we fell in that morning, we faced about and deployed as skirmishers facing back towards Emmitsburg, the right of our line extending across the Emmitsburg Pike." Sergeant James Matthews of Company D confirms their initial direction of march that morning, stating, "Were awakened about 5 o'clock and marched a short distance back in the direction we came yesterday. The enemy swung their right into the road which we came on last night."[49]

Additionally, the official reports of Trepp and Stoughton indicate Berdan placed both regiments into position as previously described,

---

49. Burnham, *Notes of Army and Prison Life*, 49; White, *Civil War Diary*, 163; Pullen, *Soldiers in Green*, 160.

but then changed their orders a short time after getting into position. Stoughton wrote that on the morning of July 2, Berdan placed the 2nd Sharpshooters in line on the extreme left of the III Corps, and he remained there for nearly one hour. At this time, around 8:00 a.m., Berdan issued new orders. Trepp wrote that "dispositions were changed" and that he was to send 100 men on a reconnaissance in front of the right of the III Corps. Likewise, Berdan instructed Stoughton to place his regiment in a position to cover a ravine near Sugar Loaf Hill (Little Round Top).[50]

First Lieutenant William P. Shreve, aide-de-camp to Colonel Berdan. Courtesy the Brian T. White Collection.

By 7:00 a.m., Berdan had both sharpshooter regiments positioned along Emmitsburg Road, near the Peach Orchard. Trepp deployed six 1st Regiment companies, A, B, C, G, H, and K, as a skirmish line, from the Peach Orchard northward, extending the line about a half mile, parallel with the Emmitsburg Road. Aide-de-camp William Price Shreve noted that Berdan deployed the balance of the two regiments not positioned on the skirmish line to the Peach Orchard, including 1st Regiment companies D, E, F, and I, which Trepp kept in reserve, Colonel Berdan himself, plus the 2nd Regiment further to the left, acting as flankers.[51]

When General George Meade arrived in Gettysburg, he selected the Lydia Leister farm on the western side of the Taneytown Road, directly behind Cemetery Ridge, for his permanent headquarters. Around 7:00 a.m., Meade was on horseback in a field on the east side of Taneytown Road, somewhat south of the Leister house. At this time Brigadier General John Gibbon rode up, just in advance of his II Corps. Meade instructed Gibbon to place the corps in position on Cemetery

---

50. *OR*, 27, pt. 1, 516, 518.
51. Stevens, *Berdan's United States Sharpshooters*, 302; Shreve, *William Price Shreve Papers*.

Ridge extending the line toward the Round Tops, and that the III Corps would connect with his left.[52] Gibbon acknowledged the orders and moved off to place his II Corps in the position indicated by Meade.

The Confederate pickets under the command of Lieutenant A.J. Brown had engaged the Union skirmishers for over an hour. Brown's men made several attempts to advance, but the Union skirmish line's accurate shooting turned them back, retreating to the cover of the woods. While this was going on, Confederate Brigadier General Cadmus M. Wilcox's Brigade, consisting of five Alabama regiments, was moving to the Confederate right, and deploying into the woods, unbeknownst to the men of the Union skirmish line. The day before, during the afternoon of July 1, Wilcox marched his brigade along the Chambersburg and Gettysburg turnpike, and upon reaching Gettysburg, Wilcox halted the brigade and remained to the rear of Major General Richard H. Anderson's Division. At 7:00 a.m. on July 2, Wilcox's brigade rejoined the division and advanced, bearing to the right, to take a position in the line of battle. Major General Anderson accompanied Wilcox to the right, indicating the position Wilcox was to occupy. Wilcox wrote, "The right of my line, as thus directed, was thrown forward, resting against a heavy and thick woods, and ran thence back obliquely to the rear across an open field, terminating at a stone fence 100 yards from the right of Perry's Brigade, the ground occupied by the left of my line being lower than the right, and ascending slightly in the latter direction. In front of my line in the open fields were several farm-houses, with barns, orchards, and the usual enclosures. The enemy's pickets were seen about these and some 600 or 700 yards distant." Wilcox, not knowing whether the enemy occupied Spangler Woods against which the right of his line was to rest, ordered the 10th Alabama, under the command of Colonel William H. Forney, to occupy the woods, and the 11th Alabama, under the command of Colonel John C.C. Sanders, to form in line in the open field on Forney's left.[53]

According to an 1886 letter from George Meade, Jr., to Henry Hunt, sometime between 8:00 a.m. and 9:00 a.m., General Meade instructed his aide, Captain George Meade, Jr., to find General Sickles and indicate to him where the general's headquarters was, to inquire of him if his troops were yet in position, and to ask him what he had to report.[54] Moreover, in his letter, George Meade, Jr., stated that his account of the

---

52. George Meade, *The Life and Letters, Volume II*, 63; Hunt, "The Second Day at Gettysburg," 294.
53. *OR*, 27, pt. 2, 616–17.
54. George Meade, *The Life and Letters, Volume II*, 66.

timing was *"as near as I am able to judge"* (emphasis added).⁵⁵ As we will soon see, this instruction probably happened much earlier in the morning, probably closer to 7:00 a.m., and likely happened after Meade received a status report from an officer on Sickles's staff. As mentioned in this book's preface, stated times of events varied, sometimes significantly, from person to person. This is likely one of them. In the following, we see the III Corps going into position by 7:00 a.m.

Brigadier General Cadmus M. Wilcox, commanding Wilcox's brigade of Anderson's division, Third Corps. Library of Congress.

Captain Meade rode at once down Taneytown Road, reaching the temporary headquarters of the III Corps in a small patch of woods on the west side of the road. Only Captain George E. Randolph, General Sickles's chief of artillery, seemed to be about. Captain Meade expressed to this officer his wish to see General Sickles, who was reportedly sleeping in his tent after a hard march and being up most of the night. Meade delivered to Randolph the message given to him by General Meade, and Randolph said that he would see General Sickles at once, went into the tent, and after a few minutes' absence, returned. He then informed Captain Meade that the III Corps was not yet in position, and that General Sickles was in some doubt as to where he should go.⁵⁶

Captain Meade reported back to General Meade with Sickles's reply. The general, in his sharp, decisive way, told Captain Meade to ride back as rapidly as possible to General Sickles, and to say to the general that his instructions were to go into position on the left of the Second Corps; that his right was to connect with the left of the Second Corps; and that he was to prolong with his line the line of that corps, occupying the position that General Geary had held the night before. By the time Captain Meade had again reached General Sickles's headquarters, Meade found "the tents about to be struck, the general just mounted,

---

55. George Meade, *Letter to Henry J. Hunt, July 22, 1886*, http://www.gdg.org/Research/Hunt/hajuly22_1886.html (accessed May 10, 2022).
56. George Meade, *The Life and Letters, Volume II*, 66.

while several of his staff officers, also mounted, were gathered around Sickles. Captain Meade delivered his message to the general in person, whereupon he replied that his troops were then moving, and would be in position shortly, adding something as to General Geary's not having had any position, but being massed in the vicinity. Sickles then rode off in the direction of the front."[57]

The whole III Corps then present at Gettysburg was going into position by 7:00 a.m., as seen in the official reports by Birney, Ward, and Berdan. This movement was more than likely in response to General Meade's original orders to Sickles at 6:00 a.m. However, Sickles, claiming not to know where Geary's position was, did not have Birney or Ward deploy any troops to Little Round Top. Captain Meade's visit likely prompted Sickles into action to correct this oversight by readjusting his lines. We see this in Sickles's reply to Captain Meade that "his troops were then moving," as Birney would soon move the 2nd Sharpshooters from the extreme left of his skirmish line back to the Little Round Top area, effectively putting troops in Geary's vacated position as Meade ordered.

At about 7:30 a.m., Berdan received orders to adjust the positions of his sharpshooters. First, Berdan ordered Major Stoughton to place his regiment in a position to cover a ravine near "Sugar Loaf hill." The 2nd Sharpshooters marched back down Wheatfield Road in the direction of Little Round Top.[58] In Plum Run Valley, Major Stoughton posted his regiment to cover the ravine between Little Round Top and Houck's Ridge. He placed Company H on the western slope of Little Round Top, with vedettes overlooking the ravine. Sergeant James Matthews of Company D said the men of Company H were high up on Little Round Top with a commanding view of Emmitsburg Road. Company D was in the ravine near the woods, to watch the enemy's movements in that direction. Companies A, E, G, and C (left to right, facing west) formed a line perpendicular to Wheatfield Road. Stoughton held companies B and F in reserve, placing the two companies onto the ridge running from near "Devil's Den" to the woods to the right. This arrangement put the left of the Union line at the foot of Little Round Top.[59] Stoughton is specific when listing the company order. The order listed, A-E-G-C and B-F, left

---

57. Ibid., 67.
58. *OR*, 27, pt. 1, 518. As a reminder, Sugar Loaf Hill is Little Round Top.
59. *OR*, 27, pt. 1, 518; G.G. Benedict, *Vermont in the Civil War: A History of the Part Taken by the Vermont Soldiers and Sailors in the War for the Union, 1861–1865, Volume 2* (Burlington, VT, 1888), 765–766; Marya (Abbott) Kellogg and Robert Kellogg, eds., *The Curtis Abbott Papers: Letters and Memoirs from a Civil War Veteran's Long Life* (Scottsdale, AZ, 2015), 215; Pullen, *Soldiers in Green*, 160; White, *Civil War Diary*, 163; *Maine at Gettysburg*, 349.

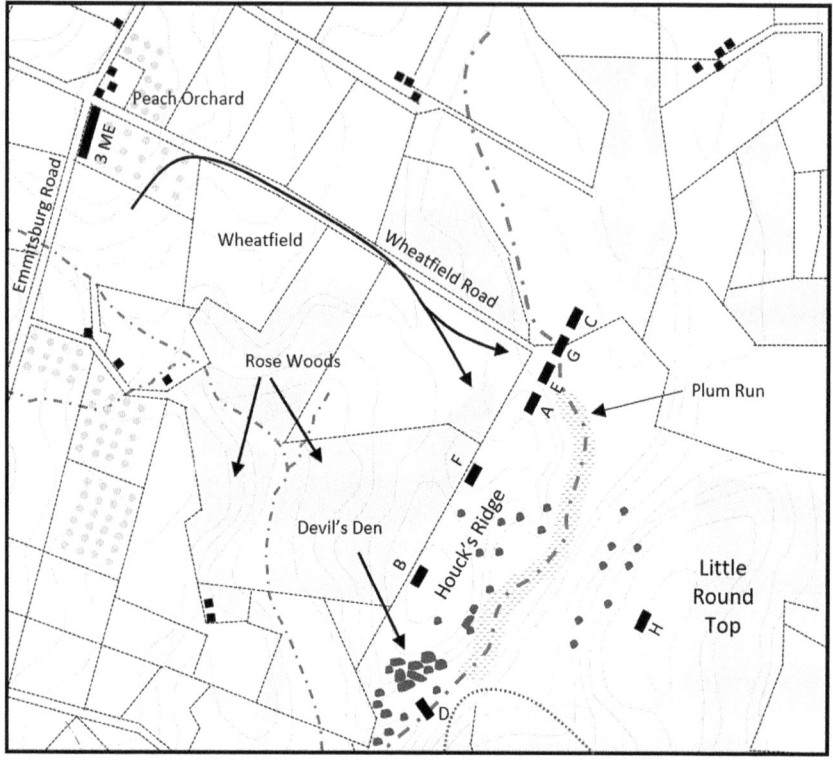

Placement of the 2nd Sharpshooters to cover Plum Run Valley between Houck's Ridge and Little Round Top. The 2nd Sharpshooters were in position around 8:00 a.m.

to right, facing west is important to help know the arrangement of the companies in the Slyder Farm area later in the day.

With Stoughton's regiment in place sometime between 8:00 a.m. and 8:30 a.m., Sickles had finally occupied the position General Meade designated, but as Sickles had only deployed one of his two divisions, he could not reach beyond the base of Little Round Top and did not set foot upon the hill itself. General Meade believed the decisive struggle would take place on his right and was not inclined to weaken either his right wing or his center for the benefit of the left. Astonishingly, Meade appeared to underestimate the importance of the defensive dispositions on the Union left.[60]

After giving Stoughton his orders to cover the ravine, Berdan next had Trepp send forward a detachment of 100 sharpshooters

---

60. The Comte De Paris, *History of the Civil War*, 591–592.

to reconnoiter the front and right of the III Corps line and discover, if possible, what the enemy was doing. Berdan claimed to go out with the detail and post them on the crest of the hill beyond Emmitsburg Road,[61] but chances are Berdan passed the task to Trepp, who in his official report wrote, "I received an order to send 100 men on a reconnaissance in front of the right of the Third Army Corps. This detachment I conducted in person and deployed them. The command was given to Capt. John Wilson, a very efficient officer, and I returned to the regiment."[62] Trepp, in front with the detachment, deployed 1st Sharpshooters companies B, G, and K in a skirmish line on either side of the Peter Rogers house.[63] Companies B and G, under the immediate command of Captain Frank E. Marble, were together in an open field behind a fence, 200 yards in advance of Emmitsburg Road. Company K was farther to the right, and Company C was on their left "at the brick house," which was the Joseph Sherfy farmhouse, as all the Peter Rogers buildings were wooden structures. Companies A and H were between Companies B and C, situated along Emmitsburg Road. The skirmish line was in position by 8:00 a.m. and all six companies soon became engaged, with the firing not letting up until the middle of the afternoon when the action became general on this part of the line.[64]

Captain Rudolf Aschmann, of Company A, stated that the skirmish line was "to discover and observe the enemy's position. His position was soon found out." Aide-de-camp Shreve wrote, "We accordingly advanced a line extending both sides of the Peter Rogers house but mostly to the right." The ground descended beyond the Rogers house and was perfectly open and cleared for perhaps a quarter of a mile, when it began to ascend again. The sharpshooters advanced until they drew fire from the Confederate skirmishers. At that point, the sharpshooters lay down and continued to exchange shots with the enemy. Aschmann continued, "Hardly had we pushed ahead a very short stretch when we were received by heavy infantry fire which prevented any further advance and did severe harm to several companies at the center. We retreated a short distance, leaving the dead and wounded on the field, and took up position along the main highway leading to Emmitsburg. This road lay about 100 steps in front of our artillery which now started directing, right over our heads, a very heavy fire at the enemy. However, the enemy's cannoneers did not stay idle either, and soon an artillery duel of gigantic proportions made the earth tremble. We ourselves

---

61. *OR*, 27, pt. 1, 515.
62. *OR*, 27, pt. 1, 516.
63. Stevens, *Berdan's United States Sharpshooters*, 302.
64. *Ibid.*

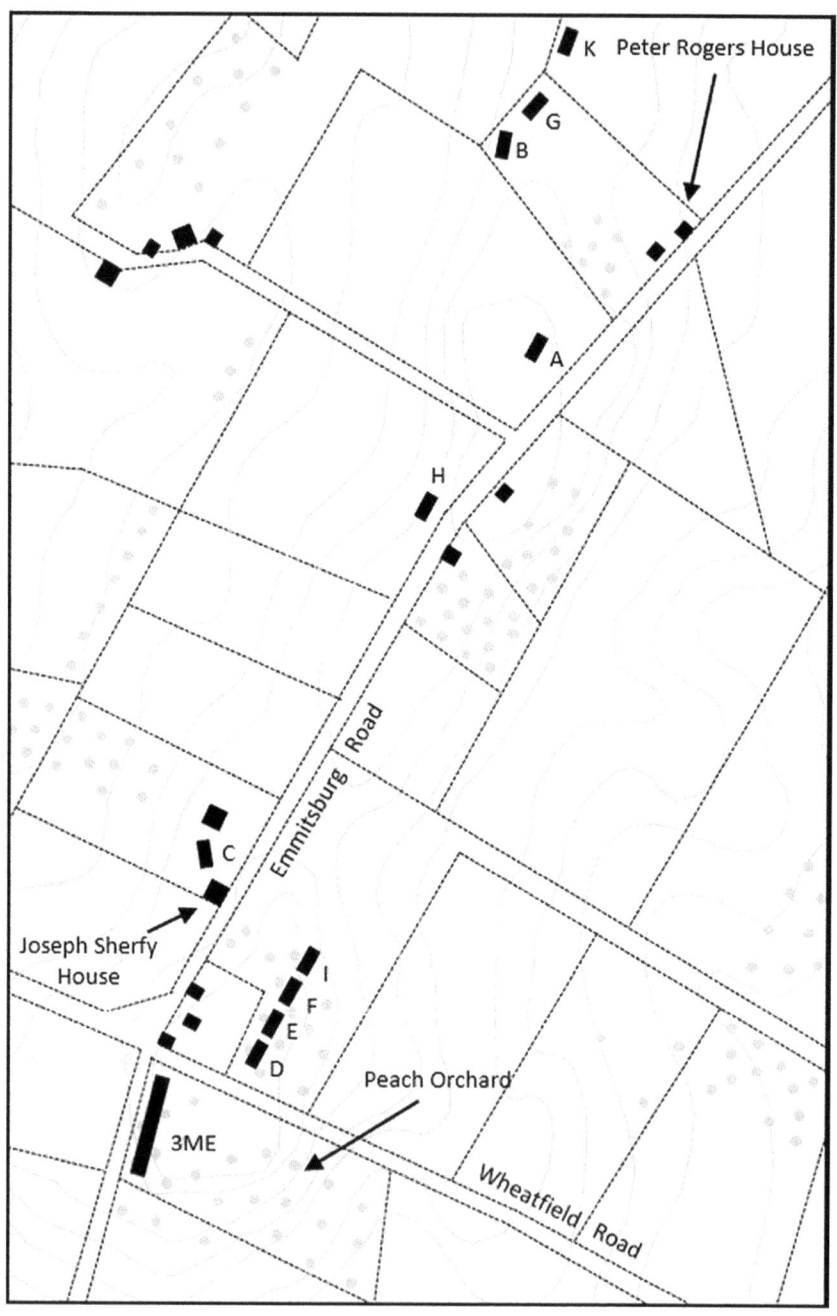

Approximate locations of the 1st Sharpshooters on the skirmish line along Emmitsburg Road.

kept up a brisk fire at the enemy marksmen who tried to advance several times but were repulsed at each attempt. The Confederate artillery did some excellent shooting and caused great devastation among our infantry and artillery."[65]

Additional support from the Union left came from Colonel Thomas C. Devin, commanding Brigadier General John Buford's Second Cavalry Brigade. Devin was reconnoitering the rear of the enemy's right when he noticed, "Our sharpshooters became engaged with a division of the enemy advancing to feel our lines in front of my position. I immediately dismounted and deployed two squadrons in support of Berdan's Sharpshooters (who were engaged in my front) and formed the brigade into line on the left of the [Colonel William Gamble's] First Brigade, with one section of Tidball's [Calef's] battery in position." As the III Corps was coming into position, Buford ordered Devin's Second Brigade to march to Taneytown, and then on to Westminster.[66]

The Confederate artillery was that of Pegram's Battalion, positioned on the high ground west of Emmitsburg Road and the Union skirmish line. The Union responded with guns from Lieutenant John H. Calef's Battery A, Second U.S. Artillery (often referred to as Tidball's battery in the *Official Reports*) and Captain A. Judson Clark's Battery B, First New Jersey Light Artillery. Lieutenant Calef, positioned south of Emmitsburg Road and right of the Peach Orchard on the morning of the 2nd, wrote, "The attack commenced directly in front of where my battery was parked. Dispositions were made to receive the

Colonel Thomas C. Devin, commanding the Second Brigade, First Division, Cavalry Corps. Library of Congress.

---

65. Heinz K. Meier, *Memoirs of a Swiss Officer*, 117; Shreve, *William Price Shreve Papers*; Frederick Phisterer, *New York in the War of the Rebellion, 1861–1865* (Albany, NY, 1912), 4316. Rudolph Aschmann mustered in as a private, Company A, 1st Sharpshooters, on August 27, 1861. The Army promoted him through the ranks until attaining the rank of captain, Company A, on July 1, 1863.

66. *OR*, 27, pt. 1, 939; Hillman A. Hall, W.B. Besley, and Gilbert G. Wood, *History of the Sixth New York Cavalry, Second Ira Harris Guard, Second Brigade, First Division, Cavalry Corps, Army of the Potomac 1861–1865* (Worchester, MA, 1908), 142.

enemy, who were driving our skirmishers rapidly. For want of men, I could serve but five guns." At approximately 9:00 a.m., Colonel John Pulford moved his 5th Michigan regiment to the front to support Calef's battery. He wrote that he "went out to the front and formed a line of battle to the right of Tidball's battery, remained in this position about an hour when the battery was ordered off and I received an order from Maj. General Birney to rejoin my brigade." At about 9:30 a.m. Captain Clark moved his battery to the front and left and placed in line on the rise of ground midway between General Sickles's headquarters at the Trostle farm and the Peach Orchard. Clark wrote that he "remained in his position until 2:00 p.m. At this time, the enemy's infantry was discovered passing in column across the Emmitsburg road to our left and front, and distant about 1,400 yards, and, by direction of General Sickles, I placed my battery in position, and opened fire upon their position." Calef noted that his battery had hardly gotten into position when an order came from Brigadier General John Buford for Calef, with his battery, to follow the First Brigade of Buford's Division and march with it to Taneytown for supplies and forage.[67]

On the morning of July 2, General Robert E. Lee, commanding the Confederate Army, was on horseback, examining in person the Federal right. He feared the Union forces were maneuvering him out of position, intent on forcing his army back across the Potomac without any opportunity to fight. Not fully appreciating the strength of the Union position and misled by the hope that a large fraction of the Union Army was out of reach, Lee determined to strike, and only hesitated to determine the best point to attack. He rode to the left and conferred with generals Richard S. Ewell and Jubal A. Early. Both Ewell and Early discouraged Lee from attacking in their

Lieutenant John H. Calef, commanding Battery A, Second U.S. Artillery. National Archives.

---

67. *OR*, 27, pt. 1, 525, 585, 1032; Ladd and Ladd, *The Batchelder Papers: Volume 1*, 46.

front, instead urging that Lieutenant General James Longstreet attack the right. The reason Ewell and Early discouraged Lee from attacking in their front was that the Union Army's center and right occupied excellent defensive positions on Cemetery Hill and Culp's Hill. Lee returned from the meeting with Ewell and Early around 9:00 a.m., deciding to entrust the main attack to Longstreet; however, Lee had not yet given Longstreet formal orders to proceed. The two men rode to the Confederate right and devoted the rest of the morning to reconnoitering the ground upon which the First Corps would advance.[68]

General Robert E. Lee, commanding the Army of Northern Virginia. Library of Congress.

Lieutenant General James Longstreet, commanding the First Corps, Army of Northern Virginia. Library of Congress.

Major General John B. Hood's Division had arrived at Gettysburg shortly after daybreak and commenced filing into an open field with troops stacking arms and resting as they awaited orders. A short distance beyond this open field, Hood joined generals Lee, Longstreet, and A.P. Hill in observing the Union Army's position. Lee was anxious for Longstreet to attack that morning, but Longstreet believed it was

---

68. Oliver W. Norton, *The Attack and Defense of Little Round Top, Gettysburg, July 2, 1863* (New York, 1913), 253; E.P. Alexander, *Military Memoirs of a Confederate: A Critical Narrative* (New York, 1907), 391; The Comte De Paris, *History of the Civil War*, 596–597.

better to wait for the arrival of General George Pickett's Division.[69] Lee had carefully examined Union positions before deciding to attack the Union left. Lee wanted Longstreet to extend his line along Emmitsburg Road by placing General Lafayette McLaws's and John Bell Hood's divisions opposite the Union left. Longstreet's line would form at right angles to this road and attack, sweeping down the Union line from their left.[70] Longstreet's orders were very vague, as Lee did not give his instructions in the precise and peremptory form. Consequently, Longstreet, not seeing any advantage in pressing the attack, lost precious time, through either design or mental sluggishness. Meanwhile, Lee, relying upon Longstreet's promptness, proceeded to examine the Union right, which Ewell was still preparing to attack.[71]

Major General John B. Hood, commanding Hood's Division, First Corps, Army of Northern Virginia. Library of Congress.

Both armies were experiencing problems moving their respective troops into their desired positions. On the Confederate side, Lee wanted to attack, but Longstreet pushed back, wanting to wait for more troops to arrive. For the Union, it was Sickles getting his line established later than Meade expected. For the 2nd Sharpshooters, still on watch in the Plum Run Valley, two events would cause them to be heavily involved in the upcoming afternoon's conflict. The first event, which was about to happen, involved Brigadier General John Buford's cavalry division posted on the left flank of the Union line. Unbeknownst to General Sickles, General Meade authorized Major General Alfred Pleasonton to send Buford's division to Westminster, Maryland, 30 miles away, leaving

---

69. J.B. Hood, *Advance and Retreat: Personal Experiences in the United States and Confederate States Armies* (New Orleans, LA, 1880), 56–57.
70. Norton, *The Attack and Defense*, 253; Alexander, *Military Memoirs*, 391; The Comte De Paris, *History of the Civil War*, 596–597.
71. The Comte De Paris, *History of the Civil War*, 597.

the extreme left flank of the Union's line unprotected. The second event arose from Colonel Berdan's failure to discover what force the enemy had in the woods west of the Union skirmish line. Berdan said, "It was impossible with this force to proceed far enough to discover what was being done by the enemy in the rear of this woods." First Lieutenant Charles A. Stevens of Company G wrote, "As our scattered force was too small to hazard the attempt to skirmish the front, on that part of the field, exposed to the destructive fire of evidently overwhelming numbers, Col. Berdan reported his inability to discover what force the enemy had ahead of us; stating to both Birney and Sickles his belief that they were concentrating behind the woods for a demonstration on our extreme left to attack our corps on the flank, and suggested a reconnaissance."[72]

Brigadier General John Buford, commanding First Division, Cavalry Corps. Library of Congress.

Major General Alfred Pleasonton, commanding Cavalry Corps, Army of the Potomac. Library of Congress.

---

72. Stevens, *Berdan's United States Sharpshooters*, 302; *OR*, 27, pt. 1, 515.

Two

Pitzer Woods

A Reconnaissance Changes Everything

(10:00 a.m. to 2:00 p.m.)

Seek, and ye shall find ...[1]

Brigadier General John Buford's cavalry moved off the field at about 10:00 a.m., followed by Colonel Thomas C. Devin's Sixth New York Cavalry and Lieutenant John H. Calef's battery. Both had been supporting the 1st Sharpshooters. Buford wrote, "July 2, the division became engaged with the enemy's sharpshooters on our left and held its own until relieved by General Sickles' corps, after which it moved to Taneytown, and bivouacked for the night. The next day, July 3, it moved to Westminster, to guard the trains of the army at that point." Earlier that morning, Major General Daniel Butterfield, General Meade's chief of staff, ordered Major General Alfred Pleasonton, Commanding Officer Cavalry Corps, to have General Buford collect all the trains in the vicinity of Taneytown and take them down to Westminster. According to Pleasonton, Buford's First Division held a position on the Union left at Gettysburg until relieved by the III Corps. Interestingly, Butterfield, in his orders to Pleasonton, makes no reference to the III Corps relieving Buford.[2]

General Meade incorrectly believed that Brigadier General David M. Gregg, commanding the Second Cavalry Division, had relieved Buford. At 10:40 a.m., Pleasonton sent Gregg a dispatch, stating, "You will hold your force well in hand in your present position, with pickets and scouts well out. The enemy are in heavy force on the road from Heidlersburg to Gettysburg and toward Berlin. You will see that our flank and rear are

---

1. Matthew 7:7 (King James version).
2. Fox, "New York at Gettysburg," 36; *OR*, 27, pt. 1, 914, 927–928; *OR*, 27, pt. 3, 1086.

not turned without giving timely information. I understand your position to be 3 miles from Gettysburg, on the Hanover Road."[3] When Meade discovered this situation, he told Pleasonton that Sickles's flank should not be left unprotected.[4] At 12:50 p.m., Butterfield sent to Pleasonton a dispatch stating, "The major-general commanding directs me to say that he has not authorized the entire withdrawal of Buford's force from the direction of Emmitsburg, and did not so understand when he gave the permission to Buford to go to Westminster; that the patrols and pickets upon the Emmitsburg Road must be kept on as long as our troops are in position."[5] Almost an hour later, at 1:45 p.m., with no cavalry in position on the left flank, Pleasonton sent a dispatch to Gregg, stating "You will detail a regiment from your command to picket on the left of our line, lately occupied by General Buford, who has been withdrawn. You will then move your command to the north of Gettysburg, toward the Heidlersburg Road, to ascertain if the enemy is in that position in force. You will make these dispositions as soon as practicable and report the same."[6] Gregg's Cavalry Division never arrived on the Union left, and Sickles went into battle with only infantry protecting his left flank.[7] With Buford's departure, Major Stoughton and his regiment would remain on the extreme left of the Union line and the 2nd Sharpshooters would eventually move forward in the afternoon, becoming the pickets that Gregg's calvary was supposed to be. This was the first event that affected the 2nd Sharpshooters; the second event happened because of decisions made from an upcoming reconnaissance, which was now just a couple of hours away.

Major General Daniel A. Butterfield, General Meade's chief of staff. Library of Congress.

At the earliest dawn on July 2, Major Henry E. Tremain was up and in the saddle. Tremain, who mustered into the U.S. Volunteers as

---

3. *OR*, 27, pt. 3, 490.
4. Fox, "New York at Gettysburg," 36.
5. *OR*, 27, pt. 3, 490.
6. *Ibid.*
7. Fox, "New York at Gettysburg," 36.

a major and aide-de-camp in April 1863, served on the staff of General Daniel Sickles at Gettysburg. Sickles's III Corps had gone into bivouac the night before on the left of the II Corps. Tremain's first duty concerned inspecting the lines and posting pickets, assigning Brigadier General Andrew A. Humphreys's pickets the right front, and Major General David B. Birney's pickets the left front and flank. As Tremain performed his inspection, he noticed that neither the batteries nor the infantry was occupying any special posts selected for defense or offense, as that awaited the light, which had now come. Each division commander at once set about arranging a confirmed line of pickets. Birney's division was missing two brigades; however, Brigadier General Charles K. Graham, commanding the First Brigade of Sickles's First Division, III Army Corps, was in the process of bringing to the field the detached brigades left the day before at Emmitsburg.[8]

The day before, on July 1, Sickles sent an update to General Meade at 9:30 p.m. indicating he had left his First and Third brigades and two batteries at Emmitsburg, to protect the approaches through Emmitsburg toward his left and rear. Furthermore, Sickles asked that if his corps was to remain in position at Gettysburg, he hoped Meade would relieve his brigades and batteries in Emmitsburg and have them join Sickles in Gettysburg.[9] Not knowing Meade's intentions, around 11:00 p.m. Sickles ordered General Graham to "proceed at once to Emmitsburg, Md., and assume command of all the troops of this corps now there. The position is of the utmost importance, as it covers the left and rear of this army, and must be held at all hazards." However, as Graham approached Emmitsburg, one of

Major Henry E. Tremain, aide-de-camp to General Daniel Sickles, Army III Corps. Library of Congress.

---

8. Henry E. Tremain, *Two Days of War: A Gettysburg Narrative and Other Excursions* (New York, 1905), 36–39.
9. *OR*, 27, pt. 3, 468.

Meade's aides met Graham with orders for him to assemble the troops and march to Gettysburg without delay. Graham left Emmitsburg between 4:00 and 5:00 a.m., and the remaining III Corps brigades would begin arriving in Gettysburg around 9:00 a.m.[10]

As Major Tremain examined the Union lines, he noted, "The mists of the morning had risen, and in the clear light of day it was easy to discern the advantages of defense afforded or denied by the surrounding country. The enemy's pickets, too, were discovered to be stronger and nearer to us than had been supposed; and at times they evinced no little activity, so that at some points our little party were kindly cautioned against undue exposure."[11] Tremain reported his inspection to General Sickles, expressing concern about that "crossroad running west towards Fairfield, that intersected the Emmitsburg highway near Humphreys' left picket." Sickles ordered Tremain to have Birney picket the Millerstown Road as far toward the enemy as practicable and to keep Sickles fully informed. As

Brigadier General Andrew A. Humphreys, commanding Second Division, III Army Corps. Library of Congress.

Brigadier General Charles K. Graham, commanding First Brigade, First Division, III Army Corps. Library of Congress.

---

10. *OR*, 27, pt. 3, 464; James A. Hessler, *Sickles at Gettysburg* (New York, 2010), 96, 110.
11. Tremain, *Two Days of War*, 40.

previously mentioned, pickets were already in position west of Emmitsburg Road, near Tremain's "crossroad."

It was about this time, probably around 7:00 a.m., that an aide, sent to explore the ground on the left and rear of the III Corps, reported that he could discover no troops there, or evidence of them having been there. General Birney, who had yet to move any troops to Little Round Top to occupy General Geary's former position, confirmed that fact. That order and/or movement was still at least 30 minutes away. Sickles had Tremain go to General Meade's headquarters and report the location of the III Corps picket lines, the fact that General Graham was to bring from Emmitsburg the balance of the corps, and the absence of any adjoining troops at Sickles's left and rear. Tremain then returned to III Corps headquarters, but his report likely prompted General Meade to send Captain Meade to Sickles for an update, as described in the preceding chapter.[12]

The III Corps troops, except for their pickets, were yet unposted. Tremain wrote, "They were in large part reclining where they had spent the night; and their location proved to be on low ground, easily commanded by the land in front."[13] Tremain was referring to the Peach Orchard, and Sickles's troops, in their current position, would be at the mercy of anyone that possessed that elevated ground. Sickles, easily recognizing this problem when "the morning mists had arisen," mounted his horse, and he and Tremain rode to General Meade's headquarters. The interview there between the two generals was brief. General Sickles asked Meade to go over the ground on the left and examine it. Meade said his engagements did not permit him to do that. Sickles then asked Meade to send General Warren with him, or have Warren go by himself. Meade said General Warren's engagements were such as to make it inconvenient for him to go. Finally, Sickles asked him to send General Hunt, which Meade granted. General Meade told Hunt that Sickles, then with him, wished Hunt to examine a new line, as Sickles thought that assigned to him was not a good one, especially since he could not use his artillery there. Sickles and Tremain, joined by Brigadier General Henry Hunt, left Meade's headquarters and quickly rode away. With Major Tremain being familiar with the land, Sickles had Tremain conduct the party in and around the picket lines.[14]

Hunt accompanied Sickles directly to the Peach Orchard, where he pointed out the ridges as his proposed line. The ridges commanded all

---

12. *Ibid.*, 42.
13. *Ibid.*, 42–43.
14. *Ibid.*, 43; United States, *Report of the Joint Committee*, 298.

the ground behind, as well as in front of them, and together constituted a favorable position for *the enemy* to hold, which was one good reason for Sickles taking possession of it. However, at Hunt's insistence, Sickles ordered a reconnaissance to ascertain whether the enemy occupied the woods across Emmitsburg Road. Hunt did not await the result of the reconnaissance but returned to III Corps headquarters by way of Round Top, to examine that part of the proposed line. As Hunt was leaving, Sickles asked whether he should move his corps forward. Hunt answered, "Not on my authority; I will report to General Meade for his instructions." Hunt had not reached the Wheatfield when a sharp rattle of musketry showed that the enemy held the woods in front of the Peach Orchard.[15]

When Sickles and Tremain returned to III Corps headquarters, the subject of posting the main line became a practical and imminent one. Moreover, a lively skirmish fire opened on Brigadier General Humphreys's pickets, and Tremain surmised it "betokened some activity on the part of the enemy, although indeed, it might well be without import." However, Sickles sent Tremain in that direction for a report. Some of the men at one picket post took Tremain under the shelter of an old farm building, through the apertures of which he could, in concealment, glean an excellent outlook upon the opposing picket line. It was too thick a line to be without significance to Tremain's mind and he did not like it. Major Tremain reported on his return that the enemy was doing something behind their skirmish line—but what, he did not know.[16]

---

15. Hunt, "The Second Day," 301–302; *OR*, 27, pt. 1, 130–131. It is fair to assume that the Hunt–Sickles reconnaissance happened at or just after 11:00 a.m. since Hunt claims, in his testimony in the *Report of the Joint Committee on the Conduct of War*, that he returned to Meade's headquarters about 11:00 a.m. after inspecting the lines. However, this is the only place Hunt mentions a time. Tying the Hunt–Sickles reconnaissance with other events suggests that Hunt and Sickles made their examination of the Peach Orchard somewhat earlier, around 8:30 to 9:00 a.m. Hunt performed three examinations of the lines that day. The first was with Meade early in the morning while it was still dark. The second was at or near daylight. Along with his general inspection, Hunt, in his official report, said, "At or near daylight, Major-General Slocum reported to the commanding general that there was a gap between the left of his line and the right of the First Corps, which he feared would be taken advantage of by the enemy, as he apprehended an immediate attack. The general commanding then gave me directions to make the necessary arrangements to meet the emergency" (*OR*, 27, pt. 1, 232). With sunrise at about 4:45 a.m., it is improbable that the second inspection, even with addressing the issue reported by General Slocum, would take six hours (5:00 a.m. to 11:00 a.m.). Three to four hours seems reasonable, putting Hunt back at Meade's headquarters between 8:30 and 9:00 a.m. The third examination was with Sickles, which Hunt does not mention in his official report. Granted, Tremain's account played a big part in this conclusion, but his narrative tied with other events (i.e., positioning of III Corps troops, his initial report to Meade, Graham's arrival after the Peach Orchard visit, Hunt's insistence on Berdan's reconnaissance, etc.) suggests a pre–9:00 a.m. visit to the Peach Orchard.
16. Tremain, *Two Days of War*, 44–45.

Meanwhile, word had come that General Graham's column was well along on its march. Tremain wrote, "There was a natural apprehension that the skirmish fire mentioned might indicate a movement of the enemy towards us by the cross-road or Cashtown Road at our left front." Therefore, Sickles ordered General Birney to reconnoiter that road with great caution. This he at once proceeded to do.[17] In due time, General Graham's column arrived after a most expeditious march; Tremain commented that "there was no little satisfaction among our headquarters party that the entire corps was assembled and quite ready for any task to which it might be assigned."[18] The time was now about 9:00 a.m.

At this point, we know that Sickles, at Hunt's insistence, planned to order a reconnaissance into the enemy-held woods across Emmitsburg Road. At about 9:00 a.m., Birney ordered his aide-de-camp Captain J.C. Briscoe to take some of Berdan's sharpshooters and reconnoiter the woods on the west side of Emmitsburg Road, but the question is, which reconnaissance is Birney referring to? It seems Birney may have given Berdan three separate orders for a reconnaissance that morning.

The orders for the first reconnaissance came at 7:30 a.m., when Birney had Berdan send forward a detachment of 100 sharpshooters to discover, if possible, what the enemy was doing. This task Berdan delegated to Lieutenant Colonel Caspar Trepp, who moved three companies from the 1st Sharpshooters northward to the Rogers house and deployed them, returning to the regiment located in the Peach Orchard.[19]

Major Tremain wrote, "There was a natural apprehension that the skirmish fire mentioned might indicate a movement of the enemy towards us by the cross-road or Cashtown Road at our left front."[20] Sometime before 9:00 a.m., Sickles ordered Birney to reconnoiter Millerstown Road, using a few companies of Berdan's sharpshooters with proper supports. Birney gave this task to Captain Briscoe. Briscoe wrote, "About ten A.M., the major-general commanding directed me to take out one hundred and fifty sharpshooters under Colonel Berdan and feel the enemy, who were supposed to be in the woods west of and parallel to the Emmitsburg Road."[21] The time was likely closer to 9:00 a.m., as Briscoe's reported times in his report all seem an hour off when compared to other events.

When Briscoe arrived at the Rogers house, Berdan reported his

---

17. *Ibid.*, 45.
18. *Ibid.*
19. *OR*, 27, pt. 1, 515–516.
20. Tremain, *Two Days of War*, 45.
21. J.C. Briscoe, "Capt. J.C. Briscoe's Report of Gettysburg," in *Life of David Bell Birney, Major-General United States Volunteers* (Philadelphia, PA, 1867), 400.

sharpshooters drove in the enemy's pickets twice but stated the enemy was "in force with infantry and artillery."[22] At this point, Colonel Berdan decided it was impossible with the 100-man detachment to proceed far enough to discover what the enemy was doing in the rear of the woods in his front. Berdan was on his way to report this fact to Major General Birney.[23] However, it is likely that Briscoe then informed Berdan of Birney's updated orders, which included supporting infantry that, in this case, was the 4th Maine under Colonel Elijah Walker. These updated orders were the second orders asking for a reconnaissance.

Colonel Walker, in two separate postwar documents, indicated that about 9:00 a.m., Colonel Berdan came to him stating that General Birney ordered Berdan to join with the 4th Maine and drive the enemy pickets out of the woods. Walker said to Berdan that the division could not do it and that they had better not make the attempt. Walker soon convinced Berdan, with both men agreeing, that an attack on the rebels' flank was the only practicable move that they could make. Berdan left, saying he would report the results of his observations, and would state to General Birney his and Walker's views regarding the enemy. A while later, Walker noted that "the 3rd Maine and the Sharpshooters were sent into the woods, on the enemy's flank, to see what was in our front."[24] This third reconnaissance would be the actual and familiar reconnaissance into Pitzer Woods, and the one Berdan and his 1st Sharpshooters are known for at Gettysburg. Probably around 10:00 a.m., Berdan reported to Birney, discussed the conversation Berdan had with Walker, and probably addressed the advantages and disadvantages of a direct versus flank maneuver. Birney, with input from Berdan and possibly Briscoe, developed a new plan for the reconnaissance.

A little before 11:00 a.m., Birney noted, the firing between his and enemy skirmishers became very sharp and seemed to increase. Believing the enemy's constant fire indicated a movement toward Birney's left, he asked permission from General Sickles to send "a regiment and a battalion of sharpshooters to make a reconnaissance and feel the enemy's right." Meade granted permission to send 100 of Berdan's Sharpshooters, with the 3rd Maine as a support, and see whether they could discover what the enemy was up to in Pitzer Woods.[25]

At 11:00 a.m., Birney issued orders for the reconnaissance. Berdan was to send out another detachment of 100 sharpshooters "farther to

---

22. Ibid.
23. *OR*, 27, pt. 1, 515.
24. Ladd and Ladd, *The Batchelder Papers, Vol. II*, 1093–1094; Walker, "Regimental Dedication of Monument," 180.
25. *OR*, 27, pt. 1, 482; United States, *Report of the Joint Committee*, 366.

the left of our lines, and to take the Third Maine Volunteers as support, with directions to feel the enemy, and to discover their movements, if possible."[26] Birney again sent Captain J.C. Briscoe with the reconnaissance, under the command of Colonel Berdan, likely in an advisor or observation role, since Briscoe would later claim he watched "this affair from the roof of a blacksmith's shop on the Millerstown Road."[27] Birney ordered General Hobart Ward to move Colonel Moses B. Lakeman's 3rd Maine, a small regiment with about 200 men, into position as support for a body of sharpshooters under command of Colonel Berdan. Once Ward relayed the order to Lakeman, Captain Briscoe had Lakeman and his regiment report to Berdan. Finally, Berdan notified Lieutenant Colonel Caspar Trepp to ready 100 men for a reconnaissance.[28] With six of his companies on the skirmish line to the north, Trepp readied companies D, E, F, and I, who were still in reserve at the Peach Orchard.

At this time, Sickles had both of his flanks on good defensible terrain; however, his center was on low ground and the potential of the enemy occupying the Peach Orchard troubled him. Sickles feared that this low ground would prohibit his artillery dispositions. Worse yet, if the enemy gained the higher Emmitsburg Road ridge that included the Peach Orchard, their guns would dominate his line. When Sickles looked west from the center of his initial position, these advantages must have been very evident to him.[29]

The repercussion of the upcoming foray across Emmitsburg Road and into Pitzer Woods would eventually give Sickles the reason he needed to advance and lengthen his line, forcing the 2nd Sharpshooters farther to the left and forward, acting as a hybrid picket/skirmish line. In the meantime, Berdan, Briscoe, Trepp, and Lakeman were preparing to advance down Emmitsburg Road. The time was approximately 11:10 a.m.

An hour earlier, about 10:15 a.m., an impatient General Robert E. Lee directed Lieutenant General Longstreet to attack without Brigadier General Evander M. Law's brigade, who had yet to arrive at Gettysburg. Longstreet was to move opposite the Union left with his available troops and deploy along the Emmitsburg Road. Longstreet, fearing his force too weak for an attack, petitioned Lee to wait until Law's Brigade arrived. Lee yielded to Longstreet's request and his move would wait for

---

26. *OR*, 27, pt. 1, 515; Benedict, *Vermont in the Civil War*, 743.
27. *OR*, 27, pt. 1, 482; Briscoe, "Capt. J.C. Briscoe's Report," 400.
28. *OR*, 27, pt. 1, 507, 516.
29. Matt Spruill, *Decisions at Gettysburg: The Nineteen Critical Decisions That Defined the Campaign* (Knoxville, TN, 2011), 62; Hessler, *Sickles at Gettysburg*, 104, 116.

Law's arrival. Around 11:00 a.m., Law finally reached Gettysburg, joining General Hood's division west of town.³⁰

Brigadier General Evander M. Law, commanding Law's Brigade, Hood's Division, First Corps, Army of Northern Virginia. Library of Congress.

General Lee intended to make the principal attack on the Union's left, which would also improve the effectiveness of his artillery. Shortly after 11:00 a.m., Lee instructed Longstreet to place McLaws's and Hood's divisions to the right of General A.P. Hill, partially enveloping the Union left. Once in place, Longstreet was to turn the Union left flank with his right division and attack the Peach Orchard with his left division. General Hill was to first threaten the Union center and prevent reinforcements from moving to either wing, while at the same time his right-most division was to support Longstreet's attack. General Ewell was to make a simultaneous demonstration upon the Union right and make a real attack should opportunity offer.³¹

With orders in hand, Longstreet and his commanders made their preparations to depart, and the Confederate line began to extend beyond the Union's left flank. As Longstreet proceeded southward, he was to avoid exposing this movement from the view of the Federal signal station on Little Round Top. However, engineers guiding Longstreet's Corps took a road that would have disclosed the move, and additional delays resulted from seeking a more concealed route.³² The amount of time lost up to this point haunted Longstreet. His two divisions, with McLaws preceding Hood, marched along a winding road through

---

30. James Longstreet, *From Manassas to Appomattox: The Memoirs of the Civil War in America* (Philadelphia, PA, 1896), 358; The Comte De Paris, *History of the Civil War*, 600–601; Law, "Round Top," 297. Law says 12 M (or noon), but Law's timing throughout his article is about one hour ahead, so his 12 M is actually 11:00 a.m.

31. *OR*, 27, pt. 2, 318–319; Cowell, *Tactics at Gettysburg*, 39–40; The Comte De Paris, *History of the Civil War*, 597–598.

32. Longstreet, *From Manassas to Appomattox*, 366–367; Alexander, *Military Memoirs*, 391.

woods that led to Emmitsburg Road, enabling Longstreet's Corps to extend beyond the Union left.[33] The movement was time-consuming, with frequent halts and deflections from the direct course to conceal their movements from the Union signal station.[34]

General Lee remained primarily a spectator of the struggle after instructing his general staff in their separate roles in the upcoming action. He received few messages and issued scarcely any orders, as the complex nature of his battle plan was too difficult for him to properly guide and control once the troops begin maneuvering into position.[35] Lee's apparent spectator role will be an interesting development later in the afternoon when General Hood and General Law present another option to Longstreet in attacking the Union left.

Brigadier General Cadmus M. Wilcox had deployed the 8th, 9th, and 10th Alabama, the right of his line, into Spangler Woods sometime around 8:00 a.m. Private Bailey McClelen of the 10th Alabama wrote that "Wilcox's brigade was up and before sunrise was in line of march passing regiments, brigades, and it looked like Lee's whole army—their guns were all stacked. It soon became apparent to our minds that Wilcox's brigade had been selected to reconnoiter for the army and open the battle for the South." Once Wilcox indicated where his regiments were to go, Colonel Hilary A. Herbert of the 8th Alabama noted, "The brigade was moving by the right flank below the crest of a ridge that was to our left between us and the enemy—this to avoid being seen as we were taking our position in the intended line of battle." With the brigade behind the ridge, Lieutenant George Clark, with the 11th Alabama, wrote, "the brigade ... on reaching the proper point fronted and began to move forward in line to the position assigned us for the battle." With the brigade in line, Colonel Herbert stated that the "10th Alabama was in front, the 11th next, and the 8th next." Private McClelen continued, "After passing our troops who had bivouacked that night in our front, we came to a wood which was clear of any undergrowth. Here we halted for the purpose of putting out skirmishers in our front, however, we deployed into line of battle on our first halt and before sending skirmishers in advance." He further stated that the 10th Alabama advanced but a short distance after their skirmishers went forward, when orders came to lie down and wait for further developments.[36]

---

33. The Comte De Paris, *History of the Civil War*, 607.
34. Law, "Round Top," 297.
35. The Comte De Paris, *History of the Civil War*, 600.
36. Norman E. Rourke, ed., *I Saw the Elephant: The Civil War Experiences of Bailey George McClelen, Company D, 10th Alabama Infantry Regiment* (Shippensburg, PA, 1995), 41; Maurice S. Fortin, ed., "Colonel Hilary A. Herbert's 'History of the Eighth

As Longstreet was beginning to move his corps to the Confederate right, Wilcox had his three right regiments deployed along the southern edge of Spangler Woods, ready to push forward and sweep Pitzer Woods in their front. The 10th Alabama, Colonel William H. Forney commanding, and 11th Alabama, Colonel John C.C. Sanders commanding, with the 8th Alabama, Lieutenant Colonel Hilary A. Herbert commanding, in reserve just behind the 11th, were still lying down awaiting orders. So were the skirmishers who had advanced just a short distance a while earlier.

Near the Peach Orchard, Berdan and Trepp had readied four 1st Sharpshooters companies for the reconnaissance and started the advance beyond the Union lines. The 3rd Maine moved out to Emmitsburg Road, beyond the picket line of Birney's Division, and joined the sharpshooters.[37] This was the proverbial calm before the storm, as everything was about to change. Berdan moved down Emmitsburg Road some distance beyond the Union's extreme left but did not indicate how far he went down the road.[38] Captain Briscoe, Birney's aide-de-camp, wrote, "Advancing from the Peach Orchard, out the Millerstown Road, we entered the woods." Birney stated the same thing, likely getting his information from Briscoe. Birney wrote, "They advanced from the Peach Orchard out the Millerstown Road and entered the woods."[39]

Both are incorrect as other accounts indicate they went south on the Emmitsburg Road about one-half mile before turning west, marching about three-quarters of a mile before entering the woods. For example, Sergeant Hannibal A. Johnson, with the 3rd Maine, said that the regiment was in the Peach Orchard when Berdan ordered the reconnaissance. Johnson wrote, "We advanced, and for half a mile outside our lines pierced the enemy's territory, when a dense wood obstructed our front."[40] Another account states that "the Third Maine, preceded by the Sharpshooters, advanced to, and moved southward along the Emmitsburg Road for some distance, then left it and advanced toward a dense wood on the west side. In approaching this wood, the command

---

Alabama Volunteer Regiment, C.S.A.,'" *Alabama Historical Quarterly* 39, no. 1–4 (Montgomery, AL, 1977), 114; George Clark, "Wilcox's Alabama Brigade at Gettysburg," *Confederate Veteran* 17, no. 5 (May 1909), 229.

    37. *OR*, 27, pt. 1 515–517; Benedict, *Vermont in the Civil War*, 743; Briscoe, "Capt. J.C. Briscoe's Report of Gettysburg," 400; Stevens, *Berdan's United States Sharpshooters*, 313–314. Trepp stated he followed the aide-de-camp (Briscoe) and makes no mention of Colonel Berdan until Berdan issued the command to fall back, firing.

    38. *OR*, 27, pt. 1, 515.

    39. Briscoe, "Capt. J.C. Briscoe's Report," 400; *OR*, 27, pt. 1, 482.

    40. Hannibal A. Johnson, *The Sword of Honor: A Story of the Civil War* (Worcester, MA, 1906), 10.

was forced to move three-quarters of a mile through an open field."[41] Finally, Trepp wrote, "We entered the woods, advancing as skirmishers, we met the enemy's skirmishers very soon after crossing the road."[42] Using these distances, the departure point from Emmitsburg Road was about halfway between the Peach Orchard and the George Rose farm. Based on these accounts, the road Trepp stated he crossed was Millerstown Road.

Both officers and men believed these woods were concealing the enemy, and marching almost a mile over an open field was a trying time for the men. Sergeant Lewis J. Allen with Company F, 1st Sharpshooters, wrote, "I felt as we descended to the woods that the enemy could easily note our sparse force and arrange to capture or destroy us at his leisure."[43] Lieutenant Colonel Trepp was also upset with the route taken, so much so that he wrote the following in his official report: "Following the aide-de-camp, I conducted this second detachment directly to and followed the road in plain view of the enemy. This detachment might have been marched from the original position to a point where the engagement took place perfectly concealed from view of the enemy and without loss of time. As we marched, the enemy must have seen every man from the time we reached the road until we entered the woods on the Fairfield Road, giving the enemy time enough to counter-maneuver." However, they were unmolested as they made this movement and entered the woods without incident.[44] It was now about 11:30 a.m. Berdan's reconnaissance was just entering the woods south of Millerstown Road.

At this time, Wilcox ordered the 10th and 11th Alabama to advance, with his skirmishers moving forward out in front of the two regiments. The 11th

Sergeant Hannibal A. Johnson, 3rd Maine Infantry. Maine State Archives Collection.

---

41. *Maine at Gettysburg*, 128.
42. *OR*, 27, pt. 1, 517.
43. L.J. Allen, "Berdan Sharpshooters," *The National Tribune* (Washington, D.C., 1886), 3.
44. *OR*, 27, pt. 1, 516–517; *Maine at Gettysburg*, 128. Fairfield Road is the same road as Millerstown Road.

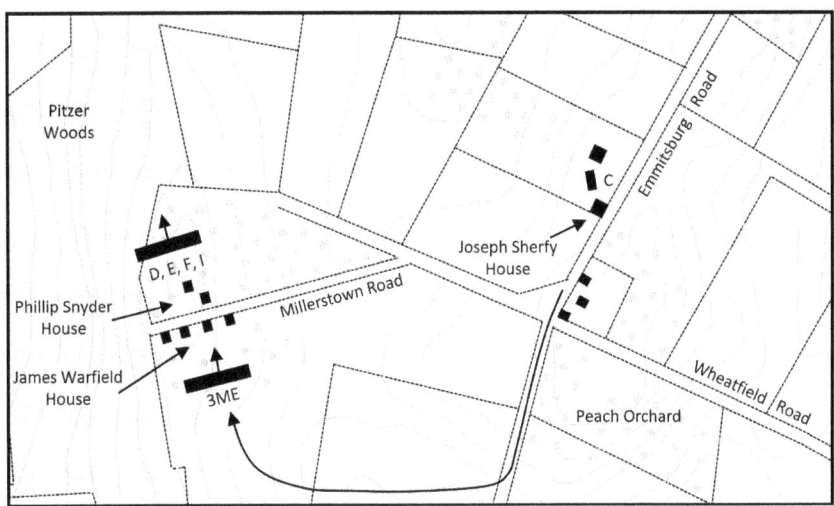

The approximate path of Berdan's reconnaissance from the Peach Orchard into Pitzer Woods, with the 3rd Maine as support. The position shown is just before contact with Confederate pickets.

Alabama was to take a position in line behind a fence, and the 10th Alabama was to keep on a line with the 11th, to protect the regiment from any enemy fire that might originate from the woods. The remaining regiments Wilcox held in the rear pending discovery of the enemy in the woods. Lieutenant George Clark wrote that the 11th Alabama occupied the left of the line, and after moving forward a short distance entered a valley and an open wheat field. The 11th, being in the

Sergeant Lewis J. Allen, Company F, 1st U.S. Sharpshooters Regiment. Vermont Historical Society.

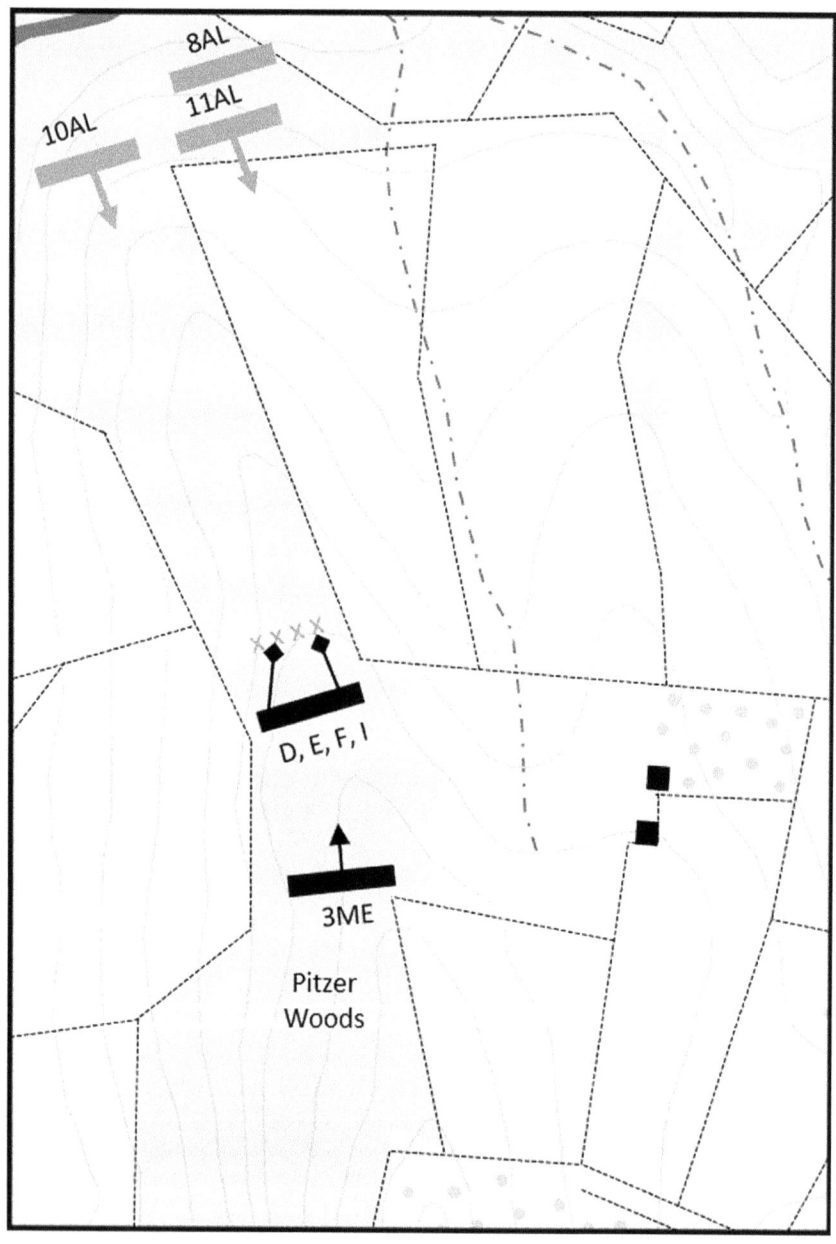

Encounter in Pitzer Woods. Berdan's men rout and pursue Confederate pickets, and the 3rd Maine is advancing close behind.

open field, advanced more easily than the 10th, who were advancing through wooded terrain.⁴⁵ However, moving in the open fields created a problem for the advancing line. At 11:45 a.m., First Lieutenant Aaron B. Jerome, a Union signal officer on Little Round Top, sent Major General Butterfield a dispatch that enemy skirmishers were advancing from the west, approximately one mile from Jerome's location.⁴⁶ Jerome had spotted Wilcox's skirmish line advancing to the south from Spangler Woods.

Also watching events unfold were Corporal Curtis Abbott and the men of Company H from Stoughton's 2nd Regiment. Stoughton had placed Company H high on Little Round Top earlier in the morning. Abbott wrote that they were "under the signal flags that waved on Little Round Top, full of the rest and nimbleness which comes from easy marches and regular sleep and is necessary to skirmishers even more than two lines of battle. We were witnessing from this distance our brothers of the same arm, and the occasional smoke puffs of their rifles as they disappeared in the recesses of the wood, where they were reconnoitering the enemy's right."⁴⁷

A few minutes earlier, around 11:35 a.m., Berdan's reconnaissance party advanced rapidly into the woods, moving forward in a northerly direction parallel to Emmitsburg Road.⁴⁸ Upon reaching Millerstown Road, Berdan used the road to quickly deploy the sharpshooters in a line running nearly east and west. Trepp arranged his four companies, "D and E on the left, F and I on the right, Third Maine

Corporal Curtis Abbott, Company H, 2nd U.S. Sharpshooters Regiment. Vermont Historical Society.

---

45. *OR*, 27, pt. 2, 617; Clark, "Wilcox's Alabama Brigade," 229.
46. *OR*, 27, pt. 3, 487.
47. Kellogg and Kellogg, *The Curtis Abbott Papers*, 256.
48. Stevens, *Berdan's United States Sharpshooters*, 304; Charles J. Buchanan, "Oration by Lieut. Charles J. Buchanan," *New York at Gettysburg: Final Report of the Battlefield of Gettysburg, Volume 3* (Albany, NY, 1902), 1068; *OR*, 27, pt. 1, 515.

as reserve."⁴⁹ Corporal Charles Buchanan of Company D stated that the sharpshooters "deployed rapidly near those frame buildings skirting these woods and the road leading by yonder schoolhouse." Buchanan is referring to the Snyder and Warfield farmhouses and the Millerstown Road, which leads to a schoolhouse, shown on the Warren map, a mile or so to the west.⁵⁰ Sergeant Lewis Allen of Company F said the sharpshooters entered the woods and "dropped off in skirmish groups and deploying 'left in front' moved at right angles to our line of march across the enemy's front." They then obliqued cautiously into the grove, taking a northwesterly direction.⁵¹

Moments later, the 3rd Maine, entering the woods and advancing into the thick coverts of oak and chestnut, formed to support the sharpshooters, who were advancing as skirmishers. Berdan's men had proceeded about fifteen rods (or about 83 yards) when they espied men in butternut and gray dodging among the trees.⁵² Sergeant Johnson with the 3rd Maine wrote, "We then advanced one-fourth of a mile through these woods, when our skirmishers became hotly engaged, driving the enemy's skirmishers and pickets before us."⁵³ Lieutenant Colonel Trepp was still upset about the route taken to enter the woods. In his official report he continued, "All this time we were marching or halting in plain view of the enemy. For this violation of rules of secret expeditions, we paid dearly."⁵⁴ He believed contact with the Confederate skirmish line shortly after entering the woods was due to the enemy seeing the sharpshooters on their way south from the Peach Orchard or while crossing the open field for almost a mile before entering the woods. However, the contact between the two opposing skirmish lines was just a meeting engagement between two forces that thought the other was there but did not know for sure, the reason they were both skirmishing through the same woods.

Advancing through the woods, the sharpshooters were almost immediately challenged by the Confederate skirmish line. The sharpshooters, taking the enemy entirely by surprise, dashed forward, firing rapidly. The rebels made but a short stand, and after one or two feeble volleys, the Confederate skirmish line retreated in confusion under heavy fire.⁵⁵ Bailey McClelen with the 10th Alabama wrote, "It was not

---

49. *OR*, 27, pt. 1, 515, 517.
50. Buchanan, "Oration by Lieut. Charles J. Buchanan," 1068.
51. Allen, "Berdan Sharpshooters," 3; Buchanan, "Oration by Lieut. Charles J. Buchanan," 1068.
52. *Maine at Gettysburg*, 128.
53. Johnson, *The Sword of Honor*, 10–11.
54. *OR*, 27, pt. 1, 516–517.
55. William Y.W. Ripley, *Vermont Riflemen in the War for the Union, 1861 to 1865: A History of Company F, First United States Sharp Shooters* (Rutland, VT, 1883), 115–116;

long until we heard the racket between our skirmishers and the enemy. The orders were to reserve our first shots until the enemy advanced close enough to make our shots effective. In a short time, the enemy moved our skirmishers back into retreat."[56]

Lieutenant John Hetherington with the 1st Sharpshooters, Company D, in a letter to his mother, stated, "We were ordered to make a reconnaissance with the 3d Maine regiment for a support. We deployed and entered a piece of woods. Advanced, driving their skirmishers in front of us till we came to a line of battle."[57] William W. Wilson, from Company F, stated that after they had driven in the enemy's skirmish line, Sergeant Lewis J. Allen, also of Company F, discovered a small force of rebels trying to get between their right flank and Emmitsburg Road.[58] Colonel Sanders's 11th Alabama regiment, moving to their assigned position, was the line of battle Hetherington described and the small force of rebels Allen discovered.

The sharpshooters turned their attention to Sanders's regiment and soon drove the 11th Alabama back in confusion.[59] Allen wrote,

> We had moved about a third of a mile through the woods, (the ground was rolling,) when, as I reached an elevation and looked toward our lines, I was astonished to see a line of rebel skirmishers swinging around us; they were nearly even with our line, going in the opposite direction. I sent word to Gen. Berdan to come to the right, and as he rode up asked: "How do you like that?" He gave orders to "Assemble on the right, double-quick!" and the next order was "Give them hell, boys!" I think they got it. I did not see a man of this skirmish line escape. Close behind it rode their Colonel (of the 10th Ala., I believe), sitting side saddle fashion on his horse. He and his horse went down at the first volley. Behind him were supports in echelon. They too melted away. Behind them were columns of companies, and 100 Sharp's rifles poured their "elixir of death" into the solid columns, which soon reeled and broke, going back to the shelter of the woods in dire confusion.[60]

Buchanan, "Oration by Lieut. Charles J. Buchanan," 1068; Stevens, *Berdan's United States Sharpshooters*, 304; Briscoe, "Capt. J.C. Briscoe's Report," 400; *OR*, 27, pt. 1, 482.

56. Rourke, *I Saw the Elephant*, 40.

57. R.L. Murray, ed., "John Hetherington to his mother, July 6, 1863," *Letters from Berdan's Sharpshooters* (Wolcott, NY, 2005), 131–132.

58. William W. Wilson, "From the Sharpshooters," *The Daily Green Mountain Freeman* (Montpelier, VT, 1863), 2. The author of the article by Wilson signed the article with the initials "W.W." The only W.W. from Co. F, First Sharpshooters Regiment is private William W. Wilson (see Tom Ledoux's *Vermont in the Civil War* website, specifically https://www.vermontcivilwar.org/units/ss/rostersf.php, accessed December 13, 2021).

59. Wilson, "From the Sharpshooters," 2.

60. Allen, "Berdan Sharpshooters," 3. The colonel was John C.C. Sanders, of the 11th Alabama, who received a severe wound in this action.

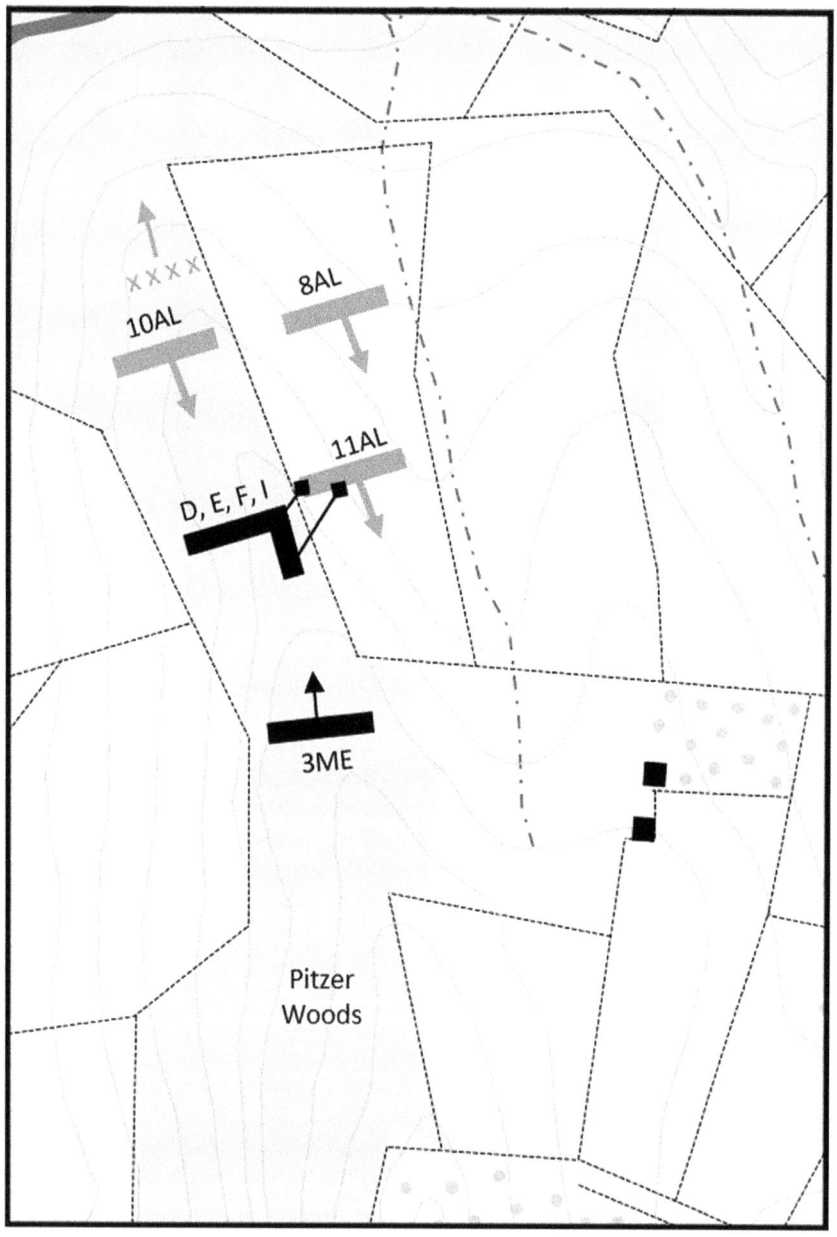

The sharpshooters, concealed in the woods, engage the 11th Alabama, which is in the open to the sharpshooters' right.

The 11th Alabama had advanced about 300 yards, moving diagonally across a field to take its intended position on the left of the 10th Alabama. When about halfway across the field, Colonel Sanders's regiment received a heavy volley of musketry on its right flank and rear from Berdan's men, concealed behind ledges of rocks and trees in the woods on the 11th Alabama's right. Sanders attempted to swing his regiment around facing the wall, but the fire was too severe. This produced some confusion, and the sudden attack upon its flank caused the 11th to fall back over the 8th, retreating to the fence. Meanwhile, the 8th Alabama was behind the 11th and moving by the right flank to a point still further to the left where it was to take position. When the firing began the 8th halted and formed a line parallel to the rock fence, and then Colonel Herbert ordered the 8th to lie down until the 11th passed to the rear of it.[61] Colonel John Sanders made a gallant personal effort to rally the men of the 11th Alabama, but fell from his horse immediately in front of 1st Sharpshooters, Company F. The rout of the enemy at this point was now complete. Trepp's men came upon the 11th Alabama unexpectedly, allowing the sharpshooters to close upon Sanders's regiment and inflict great damage upon them. This abrupt action threw the men of the 11th Alabama into confusion.[62]

The sharpshooters continued to advance when, through the trees and the smoke, suddenly there loomed in front of them three distinct lines of the enemy. William Wilson wrote that it "consisted of a whole division, forming three lines of battle." One behind another in close column, the enemy lines stretched almost 150 yards across.[63] This is when Berdan allegedly saw three columns of Confederate troops on the west slope of Seminary Ridge at or near Pitzer Run. He wrote, "We soon came upon the enemy, and drove them sufficiently to discover three columns in motion in rear of the woods, changing direction, as it were, by the right flank."[64] Berdan assumed these Confederate forces were making a move to the Union left. *The National Tribune* reported that once Berdan saw the Confederate lines, he sent Captain Briscoe back to General Sickles to report on the situation and "immediately ordered his small force to attack the enemy, in order to gain time for a counter movement to repel this contemplated attack of the enemy."[65] Stevens wrote that

---

61. *OR*, 27, pt. 2, 617; Clark, "Wilcox's Alabama Brigade," 229; Fortin, "Colonel Hilary A. Herbert," 114; Ladd and Ladd, *The Batchelder Papers: Volume 23*, 1056.
62. Ripley, *Vermont Riflemen*, 116. Colonel Sanders was hit in his knee and survived his wound.
63. Wilson, "From the Sharpshooters," 2; *Maine at Gettysburg*, 128.
64. *OR*, 27, pt. 1, 515; Stevens, *Berdan's United States Sharpshooters*, 304.
65. Editor, "Berdan's Reconnaissance," *The National Tribune* (Washington, D.C., July 12, 1888), 8.

Berdan "dispatched Capt. Briscoe to our generals, Birney and Sickles, a mile away, to warn them of the danger." He then ordered his men to "advance firing."[66] However, Briscoe wrote, "During this affair, from the roof of a blacksmith's shop on the Millerstown Road I saw the enemy's artillery and infantry in rear of the woods, evidently preparing for a demonstration on our left." Briscoe then stated he returned to headquarters to report to Birney with information about the reconnaissance, but he made no mention of Berdan ordering him to do so.[67]

Pressing their advantage to the utmost, the sharpshooters drove the 11th Alabama back nearly 300 yards to the tree line in Spangler Woods, where they made a stand behind a rail fence.[68] "Supported by the rest of Wilcox's brigade, the 11th Alabama dug in, and the sharpshooters could push them no farther."[69] But just at this time, the 10th Alabama moved forward promptly and encountered the advancing sharpshooters in the woods.[70] With the 10th Alabama standing its ground on the right, Bailey McClelen wrote, "The enemy charged up and shooting at us all they could until they got within 30 or 40 yards of our line before we arose from the ground and gave them a sound volley."[71] Sharpshooter Lewis Allen said, "Our men were 'mad with slaughter,' and rushed across the corner of cleared ground after the shattered column of the enemy as if an army were at their backs. We followed them into the thicket perhaps 30 to 40 rods, where one crashing volley struck 20 men out of our 100." The firing now became very vigorous, and the sharpshooters "found it very warm work, but held our ground till the 3d Me. Regiment was sent to our support."[72]

As the sharpshooters became hotly engaged, Colonel Berdan ordered Colonel Moses Lakeman to advance the 3rd Maine at the double-quick to the line the sharpshooters occupied. Lakeman moved forward and instantly formed his regiment under heavy fire from the enemy. He later wrote in his official report, "Here I labored under a decided disadvantage, which will account for my heavy loss. The skirmishers were well secured behind trees, while my battalion filled the intervals."[73] Sergeant Lewis Allen proved Lakeman's point by writing that "our supports, the men from Maine, came up even with our line. Four of them fell so close to my cover, a tree, that I could touch

---

66. Stevens, *Berdan's United States Sharpshooters*, 304.
67. Briscoe, "Capt. J.C. Briscoe's Report of Gettysburg," 400.
68. *OR*, 27, pt. 1, 517.
69. Buchanan, "Oration by Lieut. Charles J. Buchanan," 1068.
70. *OR*, 27, pt. 2, 617; Clark, "Wilcox's Alabama Brigade at Gettysburg," 229.
71. Rourke, *I Saw the Elephant*, 41; Fortin, "Colonel Hilary A. Herbert," 114.
72. Allen, "Berdan Sharpshooters," 3. The distance of 30–40 rods is 165–220 yards.
73. *OR*, 27, pt. 1, 507.

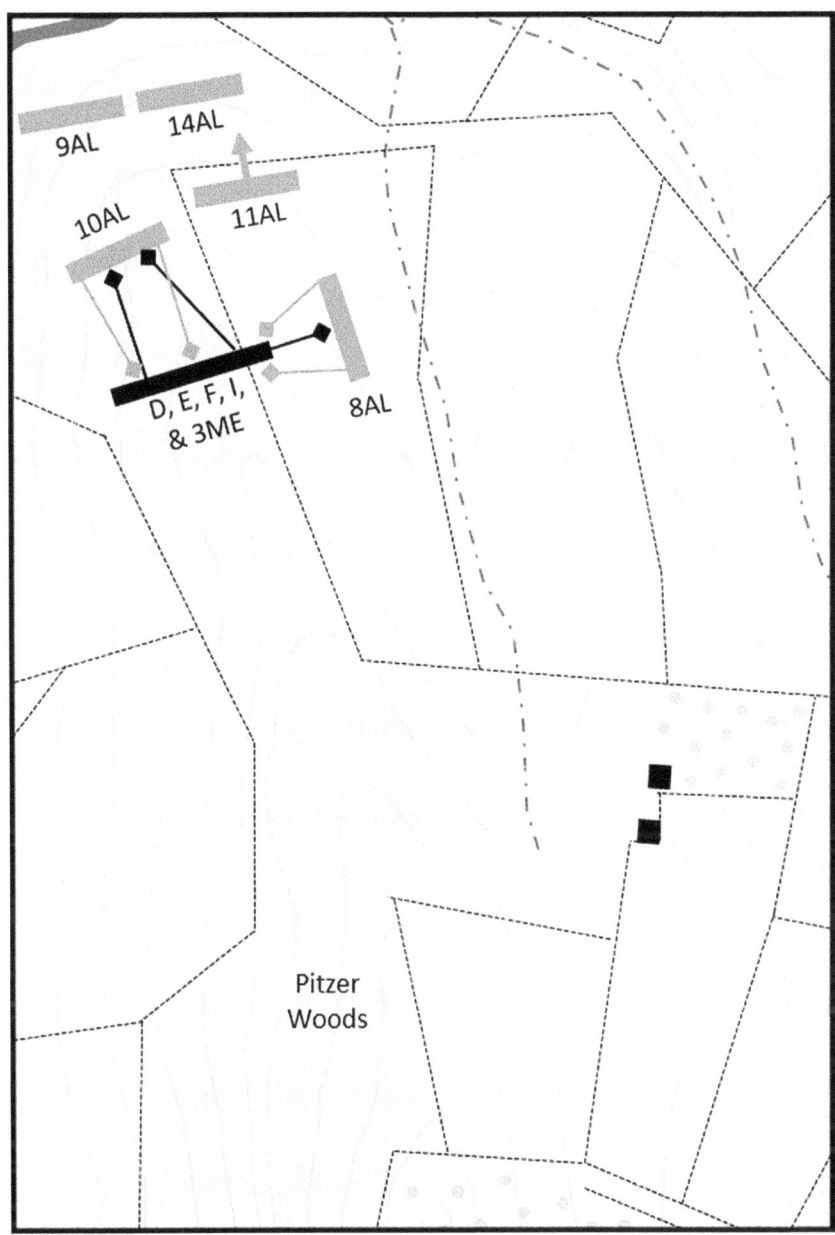

The sharpshooters stumble upon the 10th and 11th Alabama, who attack Berdan's men. The 3rd Maine promptly moves forward in support and begins firing.

all four without leaving its shelter."[74] The sharpshooters did, however, appreciate Colonel Lakeman and his 3rd Maine. "[They] supported us handsomely, and seeing the odds against which we were contending, came nobly up and strengthened our skirmish line, and helped us to the best of their ability. Many Confederates fell before our unerring breech-loading rifles."[75]

The engagement was short but severe. The firing now became very brisk for about 10 minutes while the 1st Sharpshooters and the 3rd Maine maintained their positions.[76] Lieutenant Hetherington, when writing his mother, said, "We had to fight their awhile as usual, which of course, was absurd (a few skirmishers fighting a line of battle). We have done so much of late that they expect wonders of us. Our reserve came up and we had a hard fight, a very serious one for Co. D."[77] The 3rd Maine, on the right, soon engaged the enemy in force. Sergeant Hannibal Johnson said the enemy "commenced to take us on the flank as well as front, attempting to cut us off from our line of retreat." He was witnessing the 8th Alabama advancing upon Johnson's position. Colonel Herbert, once the 11th Alabama had moved past, advanced his regiment forward, intending to drive the Union skirmishers from the stone wall.[78]

A spirited musketry fight between the 10th Alabama and Berdan's skirmish line went on for 10 to 15 minutes. Colonel Forney finally gave the command to charge, leading the 10th Alabama in person.[79] This, combined with the 8th Alabama approaching from the right, broke the sharpshooters' and 3rd Maine's line. Corporal Charles Buchanan of Company D believed that "as soon as the Rebels recovered from the confusion and fright into which our vigorous attack threw them, saw that our small skirmish line was entirely unsupported, and had the audacity to try to dispute the possession of these woods with their solid columns, they took in the almost ridiculousness of the situation, and assumed the aggressive."[80]

Berdan saw that the enemy had rallied and was now attacking his troops. Feeling he accomplished the object of the reconnaissance, Berdan gave the order to fall back, firing, and withdrew under cover of the woods, bringing off some of his wounded.[81] The Alabama regiments pursued a short distance as the Union skirmishers fled precipitously

---

74. Allen, "Berdan Sharpshooters," 3.
75. Buchanan, "Oration by Lieut. Charles J. Buchanan," 1068.
76. *OR*, 27, pt. 1, 517.
77. Murray, "John Hetherington to his mother," 132.
78. Johnson, *The Sword of Honor*, 10; Fortin, "Colonel Hilary A. Herbert," 114.
79. *OR*, 27, pt. 2, 617.
80. Buchanan, "Oration by Lieut. Charles J. Buchanan," 1068.
81. *OR*, 27, pt. 1, 515, 517.

from the woods, leaving their dead and wounded behind.[82] McClelen with the 10th Alabama wrote, "With a rebel yell we pursued them some distance and then fell back to near where we were lying in line of battle."[83] Buchanan admitted the 10th Alabama "hustled us out of this timber without ceremony." However, he also said that they were "badly scared, and came on slowly, for we had taught them a serious lesson and they were disposed to take no chances."[84]

Lieutenant Colonel Trepp reported that the Union men fell back in good order, but that was not necessarily the case. When the bugle called the retreat, Colonel Berdan's order was to fall back double-quick to the Peach Orchard. However, others received orders to retreat to the Wheatfield.[85] Additionally, others were not even aware that Berdan ordered the retreat. Sergeant Lewis Allen was unaware of Berdan's order to fall back, firing, and was still in position with dead or wounded 3rd Maine men around him. Allen wrote,

> The hammer was shot from my rifle, and I exchanged it with a wounded man who was using his for a crutch. The enemy must have been in great force, as their firing was informal. I felt our fire slacken, and looking, saw only a few men of my own company, who were regarding me with anxious looks. The nearest one managed, in answer to my questions, to tell me that the General ordered a retreat a little before. I asked, "Why in hell didn't you retreat, then?" He replied, "Oh, we thought we could stand it as long as you." I said, "I would gladly have left here an hour ago if I had known I could. Now git!"[86]

At 11:55 a.m., signal officer First Lieutenant Jerome sent another dispatch to General Butterfield that "the rebels are in force, and our skirmishers give way. One mile west of Round Top signal station, the woods are full of them."[87] Based on signal officer Jerome's reported times, the fight lasted only about 10 minutes, that is, from the time he spotted the advancing Confederate skirmishers at 11:45 a.m. to when he reported that Berdan's reconnaissance started to retreat at 11:55 a.m. The Confederates had rallied, advanced, and then overwhelmed Berdan's skirmishers. The sharpshooters and 3rd Maine retreated swiftly through the woods in what Jerome labeled "our skirmishers give way."[88]

---

82. *OR*, 27, pt. 2, 617.
83. Rourke, *I Saw the Elephant*, 41.
84. Buchanan, "Oration by Lieut. Charles J. Buchanan," 1068.
85. *OR*, 27, pt. 1, 515; Johnson, *The Sword of Honor*, 10; Gregory A. Coco, *Killed in Action: Eyewitness Accounts of the Last Moments of 100 Union Soldiers Who Died at Gettysburg* (Gettysburg, PA, 1992), 34; Wilson, "From the Sharpshooters," 2.
86. Allen, "Berdan Sharpshooters," 3.
87. *OR*, 27, pt. 3, 488. Round Top Mountain Signal Station, July 2, 1863, at 11:55 a.m.
88. *OR*, 27, pt. 2, 617.

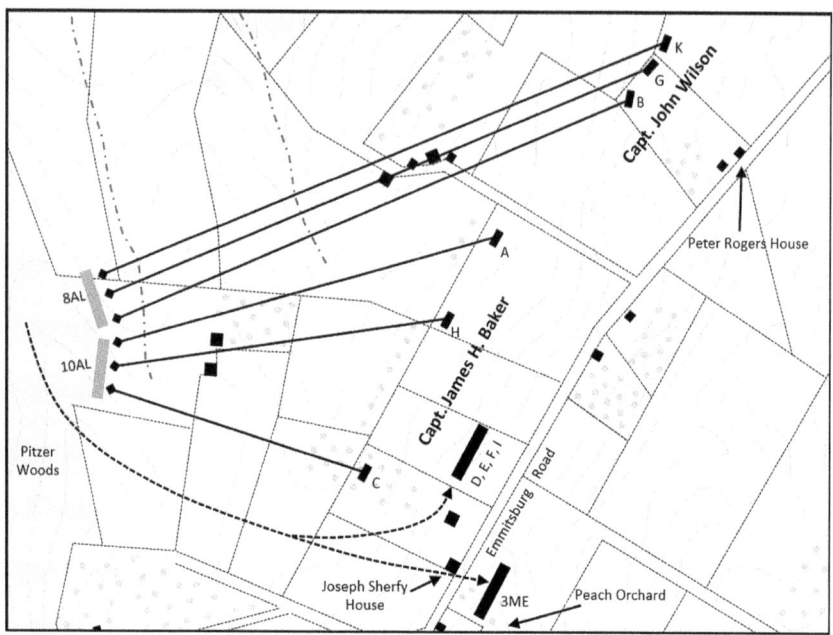

The two Alabama regiments quickly overwhelm Berdan's reconnaissance, the remnants of which retreat with heavy loss. As the retreating Union men exit the woods, fire from the 1st Sharpshooters skirmish line stops the Confederate pursuit.

The retreat was anything but easy, with pursuing Confederate regiments close behind, firing at the retreating men. Sergeant Hannibal Johnson with the 3rd Maine said, "When the bugle called the retreat, we fought our way back foot by foot."[89] Colonel Lakeman would order an occasional volley to check the enemy's advance, which seemed to be getting faster.[90]

The remaining men from Berdan's reconnaissance retreated from tree to tree, loading as they ran and stopping behind trees to fire. They reached the edge of the woods below a house, probably the Joseph Sherfy house, on the hill.[91] The Alabama regiments followed close behind. Allen remembers calling on the boys to "take trees, fire a half-dozen shots apiece, and shoot to kill." Soon there were no enemy skirmishers in sight.[92] The Confederates ceased their fire at the edge of the woods and abandoned their advance, as they were now visible and in range of

---

89. Johnson, *The Sword of Honor*, 10.
90. *OR*, 27, pt. 1, 507.
91. Allen, "Berdan Sharpshooters," 3.
92. *Ibid.*

the sharpshooters' skirmish line west of Emmitsburg Road, the same one Trepp established earlier that morning.

According to aide-de-camp William Price Shreve, "The ground descended beyond the [Peter Rogers] house, was perfectly open and cleared for perhaps a quarter of a mile, when it began to ascend again." Shreve said, "This [the retreat] brought on a fire all along the skirmish line as far as 'my' front and for a time it was very lively, producing no results."[93] Shreve's front was in the immediate area of the Rogers house. What he did not know was that Captain James H. Baker, in command of companies A, C, and H, to Shreve's left, had moved forward, coming in line with Shreve's front.

Captain John Wilson's skirmish line, consisting of companies B, G, and K, had maintained its position near the Rogers house. Companies A, C, and H were in position along Emmitsburg Road to the right of the Peach Orchard. Captain Baker moved these three companies forward, "where they had a splendid chance for execution, the enemy coming forward in heavy lines." Trepp, in his official report, wrote that Baker "took his [advanced] position without order, following the instincts of the true soldier, the sound of the firing ... he charged with part of his command on the enemy, driving them across the field."[94]

From the Peter Rogers house, south to the Joseph Sherfy house, 100 sharpshooters added considerable firepower in support of Berdan's reconnaissance and retreat.

Allen and the remaining sharpshooters then ran to a fence, pushed the top rails off, and over they went.[95] The 3rd Maine, retreating over the open field unmolested, took a position in the Peach Orchard. The remnants of the four

Captain James H. Baker, commanding Company C, 1st U.S. Sharpshooters. Courtesy the Brian T. White Collection.

---

93. Shreve, *William Price Shreve Papers*.
94. *OR*, 27, pt. 1, 515, 517.
95. Allen, "Berdan Sharpshooters," 3.

companies of Sharpshooters continued eastward into a wheat field, taking a position as support for Captain Baker's skirmish line. At this time, Trepp examined the ammunition of his detachment and found that they had not more than about five rounds per man. The 1st Sharpshooters regiment held this position until becoming exposed to artillery fire, when Berdan ordered Trepp to have the regiment fall back to the position of the morning, taking no more active part in the battle that day.[96]

Captain John Wilson, commanding Company B, 1st U.S. Sharpshooters. Courtesy the Brian T. White Collection.

According to Corporal Charles Buchanan of Company D, they had accomplished all that Sickles had assigned to them, and more than their orders required. Their instructions were to push into these woods as far as they could, determine the number of Rebels concealed there, and find out what they were doing. All this they did, but at a fearful cost to their regiment, which, though deployed and fighting as skirmishers, lost one-fifth of the number engaged in just a few minutes.[97] The 1st Sharpshooters suffered one commissioned officer killed, two officers wounded, and 16 enlisted men killed, wounded, or missing. The 3rd Maine sustained a loss of 48 killed, wounded, or missing.[98]

The contents of signal officer Jerome's dispatch apparently made it to Sickles by way of Butterfield and Birney soon after Jerome sent it. Birney communicated the discovery, location, and apparent movement of Confederate troops to General Sickles, who then observed the enemy massing large bodies of troops on the Confederate right. "The enemy's columns were moving rapidly around to our left and rear. These facts were again reported to headquarters but brought no response."[99] Sickles

---

96. *OR*, 27, pt. 1, 517; *Maine at Gettysburg*, 129; Wilson, "From the Sharpshooters," 2.
97. Buchanan, "Oration by Lieut. Charles J. Buchanan," 1068.
98. *OR*, 27, pt. 1, 507, 517.
99. *OR*, 27, pt. 1, 482; 130–131.

determined to "wait no longer the absence of orders, and proceeded to make my dispositions on the advanced line."[100]

For Sickles, the critical moment had arrived. He believed Confederate movements indicated their intent to seize the Round Tops, and with the high ground in their possession, Longstreet would easily cut up Sickles's left wing. Birney's report prompted Sickles to move the III Corps forward to Emmitsburg Road, seeing the need to occupy the high ground in his front and to extend his lines left to Big Round Top. To prevent this anticipated disaster, Sickles acted on his own initiative, directing General Ward's Division and Captain James E. Smith's 4th New York Battery to secure vital defensive positions, and Sickles had Birney change his front to meet the expected attack.[101]

When Captain Briscoe returned to offer his report on the reconnaissance, he wrote, "I found that General Birney, in anticipation of the attack, was about changing his line, by advancing the left five hundred yards and swinging round the right so as to rest on Emmettsburg Road at the Peach Orchard." Birney was working on changing his line in a way to hold the crest in his front while extending his left, including Major Stoughton's 2nd Sharpshooters, to support Ward and cover the rear of the army.[102] Interestingly, Berdan claimed to report back to General Birney at about 2:00 p.m. with the results and discoveries of the reconnaissance.[103] But Sickles and his subordinates were already making plans to adjust the Union line well before 2:00 p.m., and it is likely Sickles sent out his orders to advance sometime between 12:15 p.m. and 12:30 p.m., not long after receiving signal officer Jerome's message.

Colonel E. Porter Alexander wrote that the Confederates noticed an important change had occurred in the Union's position. Until noon, the main Union line had run nearly due south from Cemetery Hill to Little Round Top, while a strong skirmish line was out upon the Emmitsburg Road.[104] About noon or shortly thereafter, Sickles advanced the III Corps to hold the ground near the Peach Orchard.

Many early historians were unanimous in writing that Sickles advanced because of the lure of high ground to his front and made no mention of the Berdan–Wilcox skirmish as the specific catalyst for the advance of the III Corps.[105] Sickles, worried about the high ground in

---

100. United States, *Report of the Joint Committee*, 298.
101. *OR*, 27, pt. 1, 131.
102. Briscoe, "Capt. J.C. Briscoe's Report of Gettysburg," 400; *OR*, 27, pt. 1, 131.
103. *OR*, 27, pt. 1, 515; United States, *Report of the Joint Committee*, 366.
104. Alexander, *Military Memoirs*, 392–393.
105. Richard A. Sauers, *Gettysburg: The Meade-Sickles Controversy* (Lincoln, NE, 2003), 110.

his front as soon as he saw it, had no orders from Meade to advance and take it, and it was unlikely Meade would permit Sickles to do so. However, there seems to be some perceived vagueness in Meade's orders that gave Sickles the wiggle room he needed to move his corps. Meade said, "He then said to me that there was in the neighborhood of where his corps was some very good ground for artillery, and that he should like to have some staff officer of mine go out there and see as to the posting of artillery. He also asked me whether he was not authorized to post his corps in such manner as, in his judgment, he should deem the most suitable. I answered General Sickles, 'Certainly, within the limits of the general instructions I have given to you; any ground within those limits you choose to occupy I leave to you.'"[106] Sickles wanted the high ground at the Peach Orchard, and it seems he used First Lieutenant Jerome's 11:55 a.m. message "the rebels are in force … the woods are full of them" as motive to advance his corps, since he and his staff were already planning to advance the III Corps before either Briscoe or Berdan had officially reported back to Birney.

Colonel E. Porter Alexander, General Longstreet's Chief of Artillery. Library of Congress.

At 12:50 p.m., General Butterfield sent a dispatch to Captain George E. Randolph, Commanding Officer Artillery Reserve, indicating Sickles wanted Randolph to move a battery to General Sickles's left.[107] Randolph ordered Captain Smith to place two sections of his battery on a rocky hill (Houck's Ridge) near the extreme left of the Union line. This position overlooked a long valley running toward Emmitsburg Road. Smith could not place more than four guns on the crest. Behind this ridge the ground descended sharply to the east, leaving no room for the limbers on the crest. Smith posted the guns as close as the nature of the ground permitted, placing the remaining two guns, with caissons

---

106. United States, *Report of the Joint Committee*, 331.
107. *OR*, 27, pt. 3, 1086.

and horses, together in the valley to the rear about 75 to 150 yards away where they could cover the Plum Run Valley passage.[108]

Two regiments of infantry, the 4th Maine, Colonel Elijah Walker commanding, and the 124th New York, Colonel Van Horne Ellis commanding, deployed to cover the open space between the woods and base of Big Round Top. The 4th Maine was on the extreme left, while the 124th New York was on Houck's Ridge, directly to the rear of Smith's four guns.[109]

Longstreet, observing the summit of Little Round Top, noticed Union troops waving signal flags. Since Lee gave formal instructions to disguise the march of the First Corps, General McLaws halted his division while waiting for orders. To remain undetected, Longstreet decided on a retrograde movement to the north. This new route caused a deviation of about five miles, further delaying Longstreet's arrival on the southern end of the battlefield.[110] The movement did not go undetected because at 1:30 p.m., signal officer Captain James S. Hall on Little Round Top spotted Longstreet's movement and sent a dispatch to General Butterfield, stating, "A heavy column of enemy's infantry, about 10,000 strong, is moving from opposite our extreme left toward our right."[111]

As Longstreet's column switched directions again to the south, Longstreet ordered Hood to send scouts in advance and give information about the enemy and determine the location of the Union's left flank. Hood instructed the scouts to go through the woodlands and, in the absence of cavalry, act as vedettes.[112] The scouts left, returning

Colonel Van Horne Ellis, commanding the 124th New York Infantry. Library of Congress.

---

108. *OR*, 27, pt. 1, 581–582, 588; James E. Smith, *A Famous Battery and Its Campaigns, 1864–64* (Washington, D.C., 1892), 101–102.
109. Smith, *A Famous Battery*, 102.
110. The Comte De Paris, *History of the Civil War*, 607.
111. *OR*, 27, pt. 3, 488.
112. Longstreet, *From Manassas to Appomattox*, 367.

sometime later, reporting to Hood that the Union left rested upon Round Top Mountain. The country was open, and Hood could march through an open woodland pasture around Round Top and assault the enemy in the flank and rear. Union wagon trains were in the rear of their line and badly exposed to an attack in that direction.[113]

General Evander Law wondered how far up the slope of Round Top the Union left extended, but no answer was forthcoming as the woods effectually concealed from view everything in that quarter. To gain information about this important point, Law sent out his scouting party of six picked men. Law instructed the men to move rapidly to the summit of Round Top and locate the left of the Federal line. Law further instructed the scouts that when they reached the summit they should carefully observe the situation on the other side and send a runner back to report their observations. The scouts moved off at a trot. The entire absence of Federal cavalry on the Union left convinced Law that the Federals were relying upon the protection of the mountain. They would consider their left flank secure, and this location would therefore be their most vulnerable point.[114]

Longstreet's corps proceeded to the extreme right of the Confederate line for an attack up the Emmitsburg Road. McLaws moved his division southward, with Hood's division following close behind. Before reaching their destination, Longstreet ordered Hood to quicken the march of his division and to pass to the front of McLaws. Hood sent forward men to tear down fences, clearing the way and speeding up his advance to the Confederate right.[115]

As the Confederate line continued to move to their right, Major Stoughton reported to General Ward with the 2nd Sharpshooters. Ward, after placing his brigade in the position assigned by Birney, directed Stoughton to advance his regiment as skirmishers across the field in front of his line for half a mile and await further orders.[116] For Stoughton and his men, their five-hour deployment between Little Round Top and Houck's Ridge was almost over. Stoughton was to extend the Union line to the south and then advance westward toward Emmitsburg Road, pushing the regiment across the farmland of John Slyder. The understrength regiment, with eight companies and about 170 men, would be all that stood between the Round Tops and the massing Confederate troops to the west.

---

113. Hood, *Advance and Retreat*, 73.
114. Law, "Round Top," 299.
115. Hood, *Advance and Retreat*, 57.
116. *OR*, 27, pt. 1, 493.

Three

Outguessing the Opponent
Positioning of Troops in the Early Afternoon
(2:00 p.m. to 4:00 p.m.)

> *In war, obscurity and confusion are normal. Late, exaggerated, or misleading information, surprise situations, and counterorders are to be expected.*[1]

General Butterfield received a dispatch at 2:10 p.m. from signal officer Captain Hall stating, "Those troops were passing on a by-road from Dr. Hall's house to Herr's tavern, on Chambersburg Pike. A train of ambulances is following them."[2] Opposite Sickles on the west side of the Emmitsburg Road, General Longstreet had his columns moving rapidly around to the Union left. Sickles was countering Longstreet's movement by occupying the high ground in front of Little Round Top and advancing his line to the Peach Orchard, hoping to meet a flank attack with a line of battle. General Meade looked for the attack on the Union right at Cemetery Hill and Culp's Hill, leading Meade to neglect his left, including the Round Tops.[3] It is feasible that Longstreet could have massed 17,000 men in the woods on the Union flank without their presence being known. Longstreet's movement was a surprise to General Meade. Although several of Meade's staff, including Sickles, sent information to Meade regarding the assumed Confederate move to the Union left, he paid little attention to his left until he found that his left was under attack, and then he expressed surprise at the position of the III Corps.[4]

---

1. George C. Marshall, *Infantry in Battle, 3rd Edition* (Richmond, VA, 1986), 16.
2. *OR*, 27, pt. 3, 488. From the Round Top Mountain Signal Station at 2:10 p.m. on July 2, 1863.
3. Cowell, *Tactics at Gettysburg*, 40, 43–44.
4. Fox, "New York at Gettysburg," 94.

Union troops were moving into their new positions as Sickles had put his defensive plan in motion somewhere around 12:30 p.m. and possibly earlier. General Ward's Second Brigade held the left of General Birney's line, with Captain Smith's 4th New York Battery posted on the south end of Houck's Ridge. Ward's left-most regiment, the 4th Maine, placed one company on the brow of the hill next to Smith's Battery, and the rest of the regiment stretched across Plum Run Valley, with the left of the 4th Maine's line resting on Big Round Top's western slope.[5] To the right of Smith's Battery and extending through the timber to the Wheatfield were the 124th and 86th New York, the 20th Indiana, and the 99th Pennsylvania.[6] To the right and west of Ward lay Colonel Régis De Trobriand's Brigade. Ward and De Trobriand formed their lines on high ground near the eastern edge of Rose Woods with a commanding view of the open fields beyond.[7] By 2:00 p.m., Sickles's advance was fully underway. Birney's left moved forward a quarter of a mile to the rocky ground directly in front of Little Round Top. Meanwhile, his right swung around facing nearly southward, and at a right angle to Emmitsburg Road at the Peach Orchard.[8]

Major Stoughton and the 2nd Sharpshooters remained in their position in the Plum Run Valley until about 2:00 p.m. when Stoughton executed Ward's order to form up his companies and deploy his regiment across the ravine and through the woods on the right. Once formed, the sharpshooters would advance.[9] However, the nature of the ground prevented Stoughton from forming up his regiment across the ravine. Instead, Stoughton moved his regiment in a southwesterly direction to the Slyder farm road and formed up his regiment there. Corporal Curtis Abbott of Company H confirms this, writing, "Company H moved from Little Round Top along the west slope of the hill, to the lane running across its south base. Other companies of their regiment joined them here by deploying in due order along the lane."[10] Just to reiterate, as it will be important later, Company H arrived coming from the east side of Plum Run, whereas the other seven companies arrived from the north moving southward through the Plum Run Valley.

General Hood's Division, still moving southward, was west of and gradually approaching Emmitsburg Road. Hood's objective was to

---

5. Fox, "New York at Gettysburg," 39; Briscoe, "Capt. J.C. Briscoe's Report of Gettysburg," 400–401; *OR*, 27, pt. 1, 509.
6. *Maine at Gettysburg*, 160.
7. Fox, "New York at Gettysburg," 39; Briscoe, "Capt. J.C. Briscoe's Report of Gettysburg," 401.
8. Meade, *The Life and Letters of George Gordon Meade, Volume II*, 77.
9. *Maine at Gettysburg*, 349–350; *OR*, 27, pt. 1, 518.
10. Kellogg and Kellogg, *The Curtis Abbott Papers*, 256–257.

THREE—Outguessing the Opponent

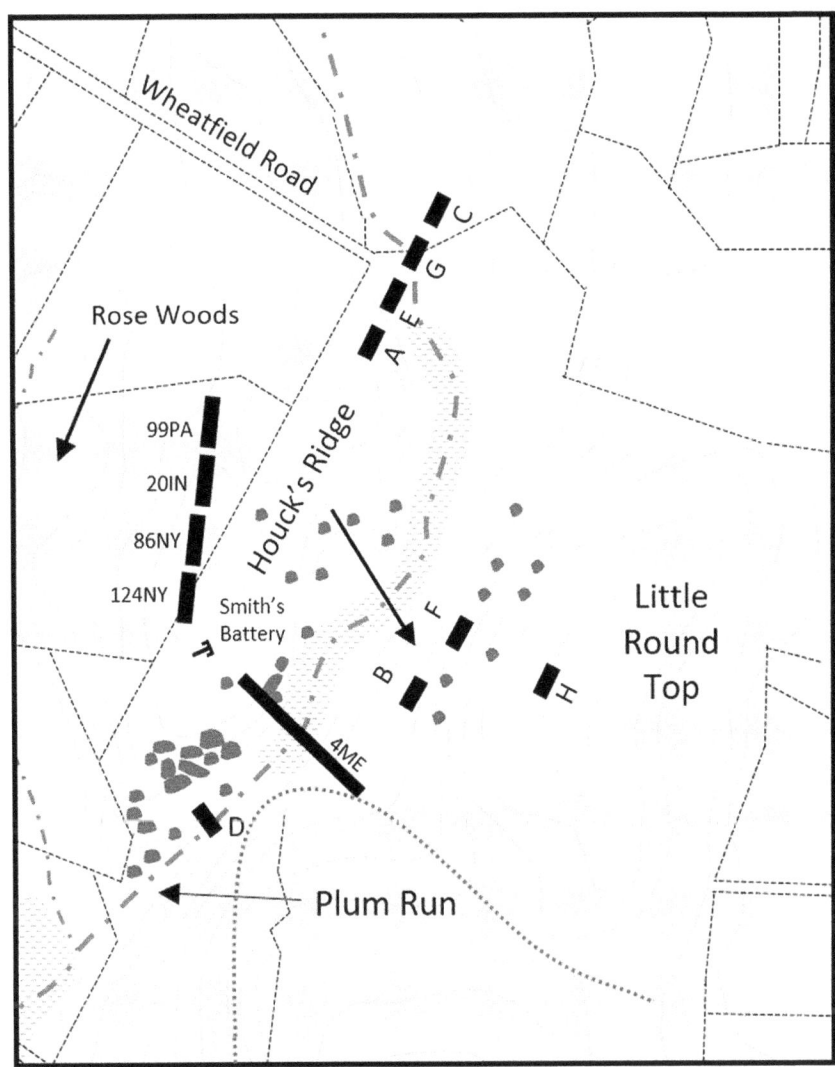

The left of the Union line around 2:00 p.m. showing positions of III Corps, Second Brigade regiments, except for the 1st Sharpshooters and 3rd Maine, who are still out by Emmitsburg Road after their reconnaissance. Companies B and F likely moved into the valley once Houck's Ridge became otherwise occupied.

strike from a position beyond the Union's left. The 2nd Sharpshooters was to watch for Hood's arrival, engage the enemy if necessary, and do everything possible to delay their approach to the Round Tops. General Sickles's plan required the 2nd Sharpshooters, 20th Indiana, and 99th

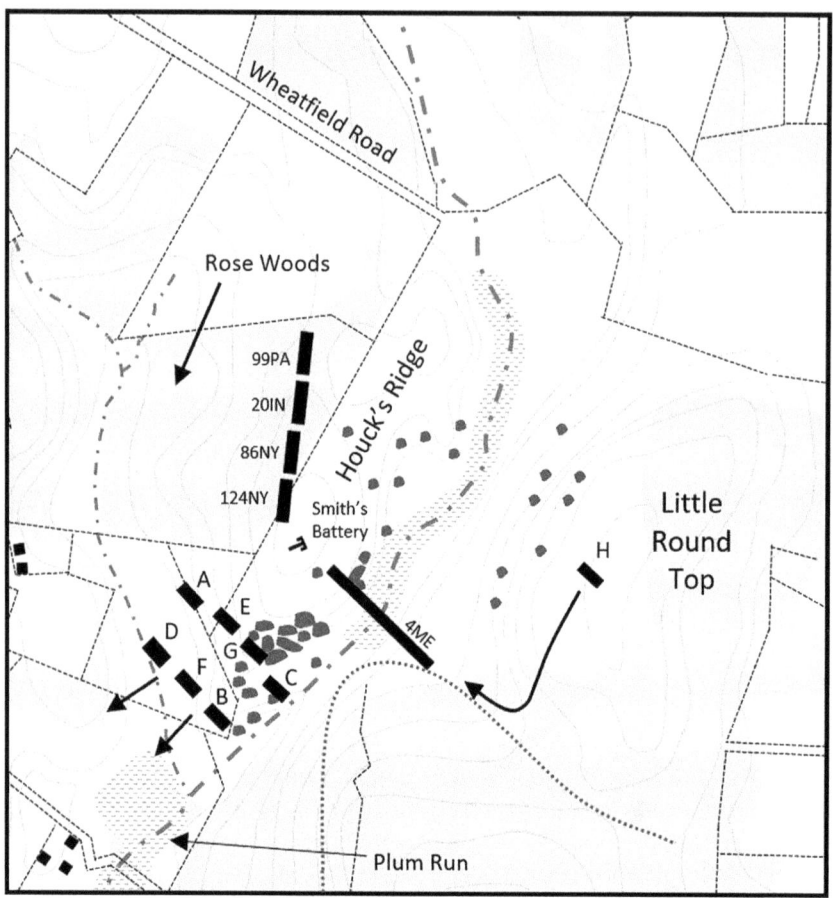

Major Stoughton tries to form a line across the Plum Run Valley from Devil's Den eastward to the Round Tops in preparation for their move. Due to the rocky and uneven ground, the regiment waits to form up when reaching the Slyder farm road. Company H moves down the west slope of Little Round Top, joining the regiment by following a logging trail or farm road around the base of Big Round Top.

Pennsylvania to advance in predetermined directions as a skirmish line.[11] Although Major Stoughton, and Private Wyman White of Company F, would both comment about being unsupported, it seems that initially Stoughton's right was to connect with the 20th Indiana's left in Rose Woods, but the two regiments became separated during Stoughton's advance to the southwest.

---

11. *OR*, 27, pt. 2, 358; *Maine at Gettysburg*, 160.

Three—Outguessing the Opponent

As Stoughton began his southwestward advance, an important meeting occurred among General Lee's staff. Private William Youngblood, recently with the 15th Alabama and reassigned as a courier for General Longstreet, sat on his horse within earshot of generals Lee, Longstreet, and Hood. Lee was standing as an orderly held his horse nearby; the other two were in their saddles. General Hood said to Lee, "My scouts report to me that there is a wagon road around Round Top, at its foot, which has been used by farmers in getting out timber, over which I can move troops. I believe I can take one of my brigades, go around this mountain and simultaneously attack from the flank or rear, with the men in front, and capture Round Top." Lee asked Longstreet's opinion. Longstreet said, "I have great faith in General Hood's opinions and his ability to do whatever he plans to do." This was all the reply Longstreet made. Lee stood with head bowed, looking upon the ground in deep thought for a long time. When he raised his face to look at Longstreet and Hood, Lee said, "Gentlemen, I cannot risk the loss of a brigade; our men are in fine spirits, and with great confidence will go into this battle. I believe we can win upon a direct attack." Extending his hand to Longstreet, Lee said, "Goodbye, General, and may God bless you." Lee turned, shaking Hood's hand in farewell, and said, "God bless you, General Hood; drive them away from you, take Round Top and the day is ours." With tears in his eyes, Lee turned, mounted his horse, and rode away.[12]

Longstreet's orders were still a direct attack on the Peach Orchard, but Lee changed Hood's orders to a direct attack on the Round Tops. The decision would cause chaos and confusion for Hood's troops advancing from Warfield Ridge. For the 2nd Sharpshooters, this decision would put them in a position to affect the outcome of the day's battle. Private Wyman White noted that while the sharpshooters advanced, "troops seemed to be getting into position, and that the enemy seemed very interested in our left flank."[13] White's statement likely refers either

---

12. William Youngblood, "Unwritten History of the Gettysburg Campaign," *Southern Historical Society Papers* 38 (1910), 314–315. James Cameron mentioned that "during a presentation on early photography of the battlefield, former park ranger Kathy Georg Harrison described a "local circulatory system" of paths and wagon tracks running between farms and to and from the more established roads. Most of this never found its way onto maps of the field" (James Cameron, personal communication, November 12, 2021). The "wagon road around Round Top" described in Youngblood's account was part of this "local circulatory system" that Ranger Harrison referred to. Company H followed a lane at the south base of Little Round Top, also part of this road network. Chapter Five contains additional evidence for this road and its location.

13. Charles Hamlin, C.T. Stevens, S.W. Thaxter, G.W. Verrill, and C.E. Nash, "Company D, Second U.S. Sharpshooters," *Maine at Gettysburg* (Portland, ME, 1898), 349; White, *Civil War Diary*, 163.

to the 4th Maine getting into position in the ravine, to the troops on Houck's Ridge, or both, as their deployment would have been visible to the sharpshooters stationed in Plum Run Valley. A fight was coming, and Stoughton's men could sense it.

Stoughton moved his regiment to the southwest, advancing until reaching a second crossroad, known as the Slyder farm road. This road ran past the Slyder house and farm, intersecting Emmitsburg Road farther west.[14] Stoughton's men reached the Slyder farm road at about 2:15 p.m. when all eight companies stopped and formed up on this road. Stoughton then right-wheeled the regiment to be nearly parallel with Emmitsburg Road. It was at this time that Captain Albert Buxton of Company H called for scouts to reconnoiter the area in their front.

Sergeant Grove Scribner of Company H and Corporal Henry C. Congdon of Company E, with 15 picked men from Companies E and H, led a patrol beyond the 2nd Sharpshooters skirmish line. According to Curtis Abbott, Captain Buxton ordered Sergeant Scribner "over the ridge in front and by a detour to the right strike the Emmetsburg Road and pass down it far enough to sight the enemy and then return through the wood that protects it toward our line." Adjutant Seymour F. Norton accompanied them, and the patrol advanced in a westerly direction across the intervening farmland to Emmitsburg Road.[15] Major Stoughton's official report does not mention this patrol, but it is quite likely he gave the task to Captain Buxton, who delegated the assignment to Sergeant Scribner.[16]

Scribner's patrol was an "offensive patrol" aimed at gaining

---

14. *OR*, 27, pt. 1 518; Benedict, *Vermont in the Civil War*, 766. The "first" crossroad was the Wheatfield Road that led past the Peach Orchard and across which Stoughton deployed companies A, E, G, and C earlier in the morning.

15. Kellogg and Kellogg, *The Curtis Abbott Papers*, 214, 256; Benedict, *Vermont in the Civil War*, 766; Seymour Norton, *Civil War Papers—Company E Sharpshooters* (Gettysburg, PA, date unknown), 7. Norton claimed it was about 3:00 p.m. when he took the men out on patrol. However, he also states that within the course of an hour or so from the time the patrol came back the "painful silence of the long afternoon" was abruptly broken by the appearance of an enemy's battery that wheeled into position directly in front of the line of skirmishers in the angle to the left of the crossroad and this side the Pike. The Rebel artillery appeared around 3:30 p.m. So either Norton's patrol left closer to 2:15 p.m., which matches other time events, or he is wrong about the time between his return and the start of the artillery duel at 3:30 p.m.

16. Buxton gave command of the patrol to Scribner. Even though Adjutant Norton would later state that the scouts were under his command, his claim would come years after the war, when many veterans would, later in life, exaggerate their actions. As the day unfolds, an action by Scribner, described in Chapter Six, will verify who was in command of the squad of scouts. Corporal Curtis Abbott, friend and tentmate of Scribner, always wrote as if Scribner commanded the scouts, never mentioning Norton. Additionally, G.G. Benedict wrote that Norton only accompanied the patrol, never stating he led it.

THREE—*Outguessing the Opponent* 85

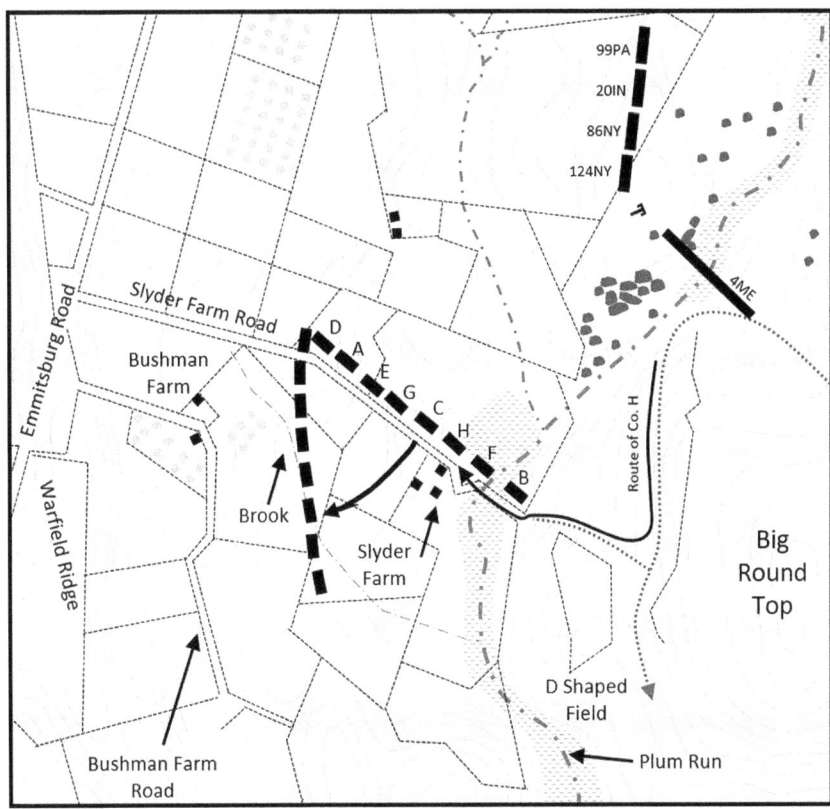

Major Stoughton, with his regiment forming up along the Slyder farm road, performs a right wheel across the Slyder farmland to align parallel with Emmitsburg Road.

intelligence of the enemy's whereabouts. Offensive patrols contain more men than defensive patrols, with the number being proportional to the distance traveled and the extent of the front examined. The main duties of an offensive patrol are to determine whether the enemy is nearby, gain a good idea of his position and strength, make out his movements, and bring an accurate account of his distance from their own forces.[17]

As Scribner and his men moved out, Stoughton continued his advance westward another 200 yards to a brook west of Slyder Farm.[18]

---

17. D.H. Mahan, *An Elementary Treatise on Advanced-Guard, Out-Post, and Detachment Service of Troops, and the Manner of Posting and Handling Them* (New York, 1861), 113–114.
18. *OR*, 27, pt. 1, 518. There is a drainage (i.e., brook) beyond the Slyder farm road to the south. Therefore, Stoughton moved south-southwest beyond the Slyder farm road around 200 yards. This drainage is not on the Warren map but is visible on the

The regiment was now about halfway between the Slyder and Bushman farms, with their skirmish line conforming to the natural shape of the country. C.W. Tolles, chief quartermaster with the VI Corps, wrote that "the shape of lines of battle is invariably governed by the characteristics of the ground." Brigadier General Silas Casey's 1863 *Infantry Tactics* contains the operating procedures for infantry when contact with the enemy is imminent or has occurred. He states that "skirmishers ought generally to preserve their alignment, but no advantages which the ground may present should be sacrificed to attain their regularity."[19] Stoughton's skirmish line took advantage of natural irregularities of the farmland ground, forming a skirmish line that was not necessarily straight as it conformed to the terrain.

Sergeant Grove Scribner, Company H, 2nd U.S. Sharpshooters. Courtesy the Brian T. White Collection.

Once on Emmitsburg Road, Scribner turned the patrol to the right and scouted along the road toward Gettysburg without discovering the enemy. Coming to the Slyder farm road, he advanced his squad eastward and rejoined the regiment in their advanced position near the brook. Adjutant John M. Cooney rode out to discuss the patrol with Scribner and Norton, asking where they went and what they saw. Norton described the route taken and that he had seen nothing of the enemy.

Elliott map (see Appendix C). The brook normally does not have water in it; therefore, it is an ephemeral stream, which is a temporary stream that only flows for a brief period as a direct result of precipitation. The day before, Wednesday, July 1, was described as "rainy" (Pullen, *Soldiers in Green*, 160), "rain in the morning" (White, *Civil War Diary*, 161), "cloudy with signs of rain" (Hays, *Under the Red Patch*, 191), and "raining hard" (Kate M. Scott, *History of the One Hundred and Fifth Regiment of Pennsylvania Volunteers* (Philadelphia, PA, 1877, 81), and the brook was flowing on July 2, 1863.

19. *Maine at Gettysburg*, 349–350; Tolles, "Army Movements," 541; Silas Casey, *Infantry Tactics, for the Instruction, Exercise, and Manœuvres of the Soldier, a Company, Line of Skirmishers, Battalion, Brigade, or Corps D'Armée, Volume 1* (New York, 1863), 185, 188.

Norton believed that the enemy (who were in the woods beyond Emmitsburg Road) saw his patrol but made no demonstration for fear of disclosing the Confederate position.[20] One thing to note that will be clarified later: The men in Scribner's patrol, including Adjutant Norton, did not return to their respective companies (E and H) but stayed together with Scribner on the Slyder farm road and eventually to the immediate right of Company H.

First Lieutenant Seymour F. Norton, adjutant, 2nd U.S. Sharpshooters. Courtesy the Brian T. White Collection.

About 2:30 p.m., as Scribner's patrol returned to the regiment, Stoughton called for several smaller patrols, using the term "scouts," to advance out in front of the skirmish line and reconnoiter the ground. These four-man defensive patrols were to move forward and identify points that might present cover to the enemy's scouts and draw the enemy's fire, thus revealing their whereabouts, as the sharpshooters could see nothing of the enemy in their front.[21]

Stoughton picked 16 sharpshooters from four companies and assigned them to four four-man scout teams.[22] Of the 16 men sent, the Confederates captured 11, killed two, and two others went missing. Just one returned to the regiment. Only four of the 16 men sent provided any detail of these patrols: First Sergeant Dyer B. Pettijohn[23] and Private Edwin Aldritt, both from Company A, and privates Charles Fairbanks and Ira Carr, both from Company E. Charles Fairbanks wrote

---

20. Norton, *War Papers*, 6–12; Benedict, *Vermont in the Civil War*, 766.
21. *OR*, 27, pt. 1, 518; Burnham, *Notes of Army and Prison Life*, 49–51; Mahan, *An Elementary Treatise on Advanced-Guard*, 113. Stoughton calling for scouts is a separate event from Scribner's patrol, as the Confederates captured none of Scribner's men but did capture some of the scouts, as described next.
22. Stoughton seems to be following Brigadier General Silas Casey's *Infantry Tactics*, which dictates when skirmishing, men should deploy in four-man teams (Casey, *Infantry Tactics*, 184).
23. Pettijohn, just before the Gettysburg battle, received a Second Lieutenant's commission but was unable to muster; therefore, when captured he was still a First Sergeant (Stevens, *Berdan's United States Sharpshooters*, 345).

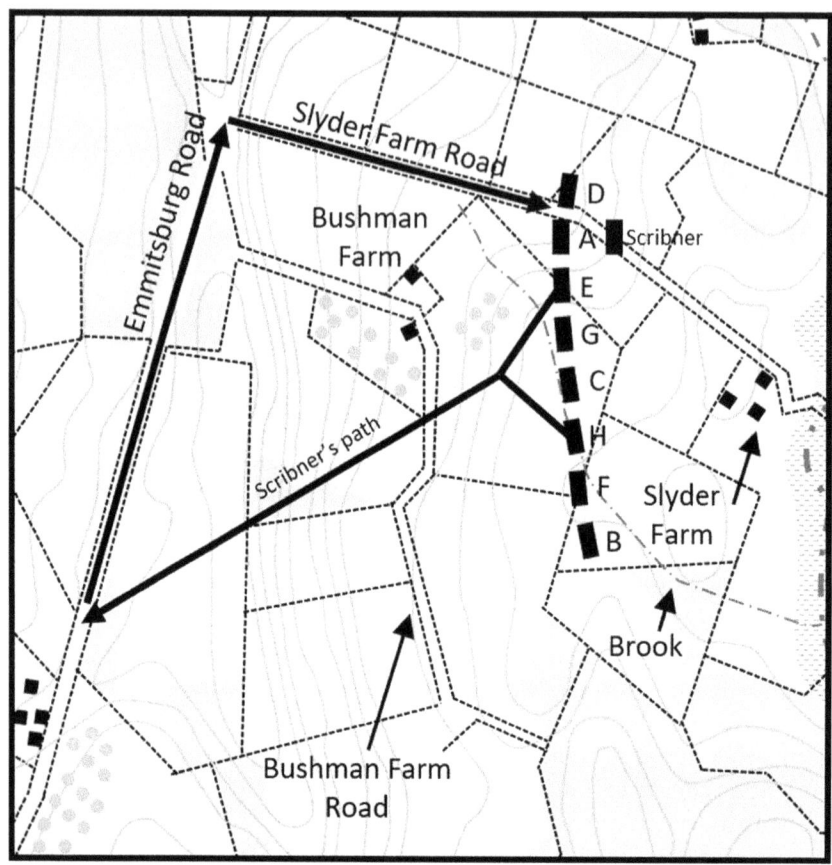

Route of Sergeant Grove Scribner's offensive patrol with men from companies E and H. Scribner's position in the rear of Company A is the estimated location of his reconnaissance party after the patrol, as Stoughton was toward the right of his line. See Appendix C for Adjutant Norton's actual hand-drawn map.

that the detail totaled 11 men including himself. Fairbanks said, "I took the cakes and all of the eleven prisoners who belonged to my regiment, gathered around me ... I had broken the cakes into eleven pieces and they were devoured."[24] The Confederates did capture 11 men from this detail, but Fairbanks did not account for the men killed or missing or for Aldritt, who returned to the regiment. Based on the available information,[25] these scout teams most likely consisted of the following:

---

24. Burnham, *Notes of Army and Prison Life*, 57.
25. Status of each man in these patrols: l = captured, (k) = killed, (m) = missing, (r) = returned to the regiment, compiled from Burnham, *Notes of Army and Prison Life*,

THREE—*Outguessing the Opponent* 89

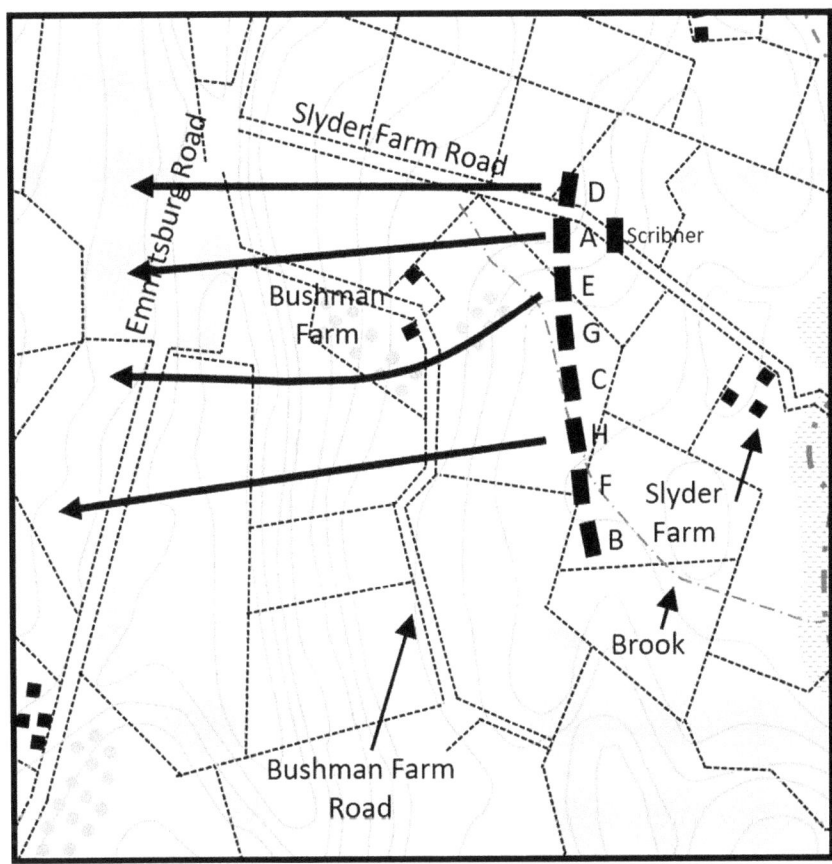

Estimated paths of the four four-man defensive patrols carried out by men from companies D, A, E, and H.

- *Company A*: First Sergeant Dyer B. Pettijohn (c), Corporal Benjamin O. Hamblet (k), Private Edwin Aldritt (r), Private John O. Dolson (k).
- *Company D*: Corporal Richard C. Boynton (c), Corporal Argyl D. Morse (c), Corporal John H. Rounds (c), Private Francis W. Ladd (c).
- *Company E*: Corporal Henry C. Congdon (c), Private Charles Fairbanks (c), Private Ledrue M. Rollins (c), Private Ira Carr (c).
- *Company H*: Corporal George W. Diamond (c), Private Wilman

49–51; Ira Carr, "A Sharpshooter at Gettysburg," *The National Tribune* (Washington, D.C., 1886), 3; Travis W. Busey and John W. Busey, *Union Casualties at Gettysburg: A Comprehensive Record* (Jefferson, NC, 2011), 1068–1070. Curtis Abbott of Company H stated Congdon and one of the other captured men (he did not identify whom it was) participated in both reconnaissances (Kellogg and Kellogg, *The Curtis Abbott Papers*, 257).

D. Allard (c), Private Elisa Harrington (m), Private Albert S. Healey (m).

The patrol from Company E passed south of the Bushman farm. Advancing about one-third of a mile, the patrol came to some woods on a knoll and then went down into a ravine putting them just west of Emmitsburg Road. Private Carr stated that at about 3:00 p.m., Adjutant John M. Cooney rode up, still out in the lines gathering information. Cooney apparently continued toward Emmitsburg Road after meeting with Norton, and then to his left, seeking out the patrols for their report. Corporal Congdon told Cooney that the rebels were massing troops in the woods at their right. Cooney said that he would report to General Birney and rode off. Soon after, Congdon decided to go back and report the massing, as he thought the "Adjutant might have been captured." Congdon went northward on the Emmitsburg Road, which was likely close to the rebel line. Confederate skirmishers soon captured Private Carr, as he remained in position when the Confederate charge commenced. Fairbanks wrote that it was at this point "Longstreet's Corps, began their desperate charge ... three lines of battle appeared in his front and left flank so suddenly that all of us that had been detailed were captured."[26] At the location specified by Fairbanks, the time was about 3:00 p.m., the same time when Longstreet's men began to deploy along Emmitsburg Road. Hood's Division of Longstreet's Corps had two brigades in front with two brigades 200 yards behind. The third line was probably the Confederate skirmish line.

The patrol from Company A was north of Company E near the Slyder farm road. The men of this scout team advanced westward toward Emmitsburg Road and soon came to a clearing where a woman was sitting on the porch at the Bushman farm.[27] As Private Edwin Aldritt stood reconnoitering, he saw a boy running from the opposite side of the clearing, yelling at his mother, claiming the woods behind him were full of "men in gray." Aldritt did not wait for clarification and ran across the clearing, not paying any more attention to the woman and the boy. Behind the house, he saw a stone smokehouse on top of a small hill at the base of which, not 50 yards away, was the Confederate skirmish line. A little to his left, toward Emmitsburg Road, was the main body of their infantry. A group of mounted officers was looking at a map in front of the Confederate infantry.[28]

---

26. Burnham, *Notes of Army and Prison Life*, 49–51; Carr, "A Sharpshooter at Gettysburg," 3; Busey and Busey, *Union Casualties*, 1068–1070.
27. Hoisington, "I Never Saw Such Shooting," 47.
28. *Ibid.*

As Aldritt was assessing the situation, First Sergeant Pettijohn fired at the mounted officers, and the man holding the map tumbled from his horse. Aldritt joined Pettijohn in "blazing away" at the group of officers.[29] The Confederate skirmishers soon advanced and Aldritt, Pettijohn, Hamblet, and Dolson were soon actively engaged, being in the enemy's immediate front. The advancing rebel line resembled a haphazard-looking zigzag formation but steadily moved forward. While the four sharpshooters from Company A were paying attention to the enemy troops in their immediate front and left, another Confederate regiment advanced on the sharpshooters' right through a grove of timber, remaining undetected until Pettijohn noticed their presence, already within easy pistol range.[30]

The advancing Confederate skirmish line continued forward, cutting off Pettijohn's path of retreat to his regiment. He soon realized his position was hopeless, and thinking that discretion was the better part of valor, he jumped into a low spot of ground behind a large rock. Hamblet and Dolson, who were with Pettijohn at the time, tried to escape to their line by running. Pettijohn heard the commander of the rebel regiment call out to them to "halt," which they failed to do. The commander then ordered his men to fire, and a "rattle of musketry" was the response.[31]

Aldritt, farther away from the Confederate skirmish line than the other three sharpshooters, turned and ran back across the clearing toward the Bushman farm. As the Confederate skirmishers fired a volley, Aldritt heard the bullets "smash up against the smokehouse." Aldritt's claim of hearing the bullets "smash up against the smokehouse" is probably from the "rattle of musketry" described by Pettijohn. By the time the first Confederate skirmishers reached the top of the hill, Aldritt was across the clearing, hiding behind some big rocks. He fired several shots at them before they could locate his position and then Aldritt said he "dusted for our lines." Of the four-man squad from Company A, Hamblet and Dolson died from their wounds, and Aldritt successfully made it back to his regiment's skirmish line at the brook, but Pettijohn ended up a prisoner and sent to Richmond.[32] Pettijohn would later write, "I learned after coming back from the South that on the next day when our army reoccupied that part of the battlefield, those boys were found at that place—one was dead and the other badly wounded. Although a dozen bullets had struck him, hopes were first entertained

---

29. *Ibid.*
30. Pettijohn and Pettijohn, "Something of the Pettijohn (Pettyjohn) Family."
31. *Ibid.*
32. Hoisington, "I Never Saw Such Shooting," 47–48.

for his recovery, but he dies in about a week."[33] Confederate soldiers shot both men on July 2; Hamblet, shot in the leg, died the next day and Dolson, receiving three wounds in his shoulder and side, died on September 3. The men from companies D and H did not leave a record of their patrols; however, they likely met a similar fate, as all eight men were either captured or listed as missing.

By 3:00 p.m., Confederate troops were massing in the sharpshooters' front.[34] After much marching and countermarching in attempting to conceal their movements from the signal station on Little Round Top, Hood arrived at Emmitsburg Road and formed his division on a wooded ridge facing Birney's line.[35] Hood would later realize that his position did not fully envelop the Union left. The guides and scouts that Hood had sent around the Union left earlier that morning were confused upon their return and failed to lead the column far enough to the Confederate right. By the time Hood discovered he was not far enough south to envelop the Union line, it was too late as his troops were "heavily engaged."[36]

While organizing his men to attack up Emmitsburg Road, Hood changed his lines per General Lee's instructions for a direct attack on the Round Tops. It was not feasible to align his brigades to cross the road at nearly right angles, as Lee had initially planned, since that formation would leave his right flank open to attack from Union artillery on Little Round Top.[37] While Hood changed his lines, General Law met a returning runner from the scout team sent out earlier. The runner reported that the scouts reached the crest of Big Round Top and discovered there were no Federal forces on the summit.[38]

Earlier, Hood's scouts discovered that the Round Tops were unoccupied and that a path lay open to the rear of the Union Army, either through the gap between the two hills or by a roundabout course south of Big Round Top. There, Hood believed, was the place to plant a mortal blow. A route existed by which he could endanger the Union supply trains and smite with panic the reserve artillery parked in the region just behind the two heights.[39] Hood's scouts also reported the defenseless condition of Little Round Top, and the apparent ease with which

---

33. Pettijohn and Pettijohn, "Something of the Pettijohn (Pettyjohn) Family."
34. Pullen, *Soldiers in Green*, 160.
35. Norton, *Attack and Defense*, 253–254; Alexander, *Military Memoirs*, 394.
36. Lafayette McLaws, "Gettysburg," *Southern Historical Society Papers* 7, no. 2 (February 1879), 73.
37. Jesse B. Young, *The Battle of Gettysburg, A Comprehensive Narrative* (New York and London, 1913), 245–246.
38. Alexander, *Military Memoirs*, 394; Law, "Round Top and the Confederate Right," 299–300.
39. Young, *The Battle of Gettysburg*, 245–246.

THREE—Outguessing the Opponent

Confederate troops could attack the rear of the Federal army by passing completely around the larger mountain.[40]

In addition to the convincing information brought back by Law's and Hood's scouts, Law captured several Federal soldiers who, upon questioning, confirmed the intelligence brought back by the scout teams. A few moments after Law's scouts departed on their mission, Law observed several dark figures crossing the fields from the rear of Round Top and moving toward Emmitsburg Road. Upon capture, these men proved to be Union soldiers, who seemed surprised at Law's sudden appearance in that quarter. Law questioned the prisoners, who stated they had surgeon's certificates and were going to the rear, pointing in the direction of Emmitsburg. From these prisoners, Law obtained information that the "medical and ordnance trains around the mountain were insecurely guarded as no attack being expected at that point. The other side of the mountain could easily be reached by a good farm road along which they had traveled, the distance being a little more than a mile."[41] The "good farm road" was certainly the Slyder farm road.

The only figures Law would have seen moving through the fields that day and at that time were the scouts from Stoughton's sharpshooters. Private Charles Fairbanks, one of the sharpshooters captured while scouting, tells a slightly different story. He said, "The rebels had kept us, after taking our rifles and ammunition, in the thickest of the shelling. Our shot and shell were bursting and doing havoc all the while for nearly an hour when the prisoners were taken to the rear ... where we were questioned by staff officers as to the arrangements within our lines. They did not get much reliable information, as we were all 'yankees' and knew how to deceive our enemy, which we did."[42] Fairbanks did not say what else the prisoners divulged, but by reading between the lines, it seems the captured sharpshooters had provided information that was not as accurate as the Confederates believed. Private Fairbanks, from Company E, gives the only detailed account of the men captured from the four four-man scout teams. The staff officer doing the questioning was undoubtedly General Law or someone from his staff. Additionally, when Fairbanks refers to "our shot and shell," it is a reference to General Ward's order for Captain George Winslow's and Captain James Smith's batteries to fire upon the advancing columns of the enemy infantry.[43]

---

40. Samuel Toombs, *New Jersey Troops in the Gettysburg Campaign from June 5 to July 31, 1863* (Orange, NJ, 1888), 200.
41. Law, "Round Top," 299–300; John Purifoy, "The Lost Opportunity at Gettysburg," *Confederate Veteran* 31, no. 6 (June 1923), 216.
42. Burnham, *Notes of Army and Prison Life*, 51–53.
43. OR, 27, pt. 1, 493.

At about 3:30 p.m. the Confederate artillery opened fire on Captain Smith's 4th New York Battery's right and front, directing a portion of their fire upon his position. One of General Ward's aides ordered Smith to return fire, an order he readily followed. Soon after, the Confederates brought forward a battery of six guns from the woods beyond Emmitsburg Road. A spirited duel, as described by Fairbanks, immediately began between this battery and Smith's battery, lasting nearly 20 minutes.[44]

General Law communicated to General Hood the information obtained from the captured Union soldiers, pointing out the ease of getting to the rear of the Round Tops. Hood concurred fully with Law's views but stated that his orders were to attack in front as soon as Longstreet's Corps were in position. Law, therefore, entered a formal protest against a direct attack, on the grounds (1) that the great natural strength of the enemy's position in the Confederate front rendered the result of a direct assault extremely uncertain; (2) that, even if successful, the victory would be purchased at too great a sacrifice of life; (3) that a frontal attack was unnecessary; and (4) that a flank movement would compel a change of front on the part of the enemy, the abandonment of his strong position on the heights, and force him to attack Hood's Division in position.[45]

Hood dispatched a staff officer to Longstreet with a message requesting permission to pass to the south of Big Round Top and thereby turn the position. Longstreet replied that Lee's orders were to attack up Emmitsburg Road. Hood renewed his request to turn Round Top two more times, but each time he received the same reply. Longstreet did not forward Hood's request to Lee because Longstreet had already urged upon Lee the advisability of the same movement, but without success. Additionally, Lee had carefully considered the move to the right and rejected it in favor of Hood's present orders.[46] Longstreet could not reopen the argument without appearing insubordinate. As a result, Lee was unaware of the true position of the enemy's flank.[47] During the interim between the second and third petitions, Hood continued using his artillery upon the enemy, becoming more

---

44. *Ibid.*, 588.
45. Law, "Round Top," 300–301. Law and Hood both confirm that Hood's division was to make a direct assault on the Round Tops. The argument here is that Law wants to go around Big Round Top and attack the flank and rear of the Union line. Hood likes the idea but says his orders are for a direct attack and he does not have the authority to change them.
46. Another reference to Hood's orders for a direct assault upon the Round Tops.
47. Cowell, *Tactics at Gettysburg*, 52; Longstreet, *From Manassas to Appomattox*, 368.

THREE—Outguessing the Opponent

convinced the Union line extended to Big Round Top. Hood, feeling the direct attack as ordered would not accomplish much, concluded that "the enemy occupied a position by nature so strong, or impregnable, that independently of their flank fire, they could easily repel our attack by merely throwing and rolling stones down the mountain side, as we approached."[48]

Hood and Law understood the attack was upon the Round Tops, However, both men felt that at that time, and from their viewpoint, Union forces occupied both hills and they regarded the position as too strong for a frontal attack. Hood and Law made one last plea to Longstreet to abandon the direct attack and pass around the Union left, seize Big Round Top, and fall upon the supply and ordnance trains. Longstreet replied that Lee's orders were for the direct attack, and it must begin without delay. After Hood protested a third time against the direct attack, he ordered his line to advance and make the assault, claiming that this was the first and only protest he ever made during his entire military career.[49]

After many frustrating delays, Longstreet reached the desired position opposite the Round Tops. The Confederate line of battle occupied a partially wooded ridge, with a valley between the ridge and the heights held by the Union troops. Law, seeing the position occupied by the Federal left wing in front of him, believed it was one of the most formidable positions he had ever confronted. Big Round Top rose like a huge sentinel guarding the Federal left flank, while the spurs and ridges trending off to the north afforded unrivaled positions for the use of artillery. As the Federal batteries fired at the Confederates, puffs of smoke rising at intervals along the line of hills clearly indicated that Federal troops had not neglected these advantages. Thick woods covered the sides of Big Round Top and the adjacent hills, concealing from view the rugged nature of the ground, which increased fourfold the difficulties of the attack.[50]

Around 3:30 p.m., Hood's division pushed forward, reaching Emmitsburg Road opposite the Round Tops. Here Longstreet formed his line of battle at an acute angle with the road, the right advancing between the road and the mountain, and the left extending across and in rear of the road. The formation was in two lines, General Evander M. Law's Alabama and General Jerome B. Robertson's Texas brigades

---

48. Hood, *Advance and Retreat*, 58–59.
49. C.A. Jones, "Longstreet at Gettysburg," *Confederate Veteran* 23, no. 12 (December 1915), 551–552; Alexander, *Military Memoirs*, 394; Hood, *Advance and Retreat*, 58–59.
50. Law, "Round Top," 299.

in front, supported at about 200 yards by the Georgia brigades of generals Henry L. Benning and George T. Anderson. The Artillery Battalion, composed of 20 guns from the batteries of Captain James Reilly, Captain Alexander C. Latham, Captain Hugh R. Garden, and Captain William K. Bachman, moved to advantageous points upon the Warfield Ridge alongside the line of infantry. There were no signs of Federal cavalry or troops of any kind on the Confederate right.[51]

Robertson's brigade consisted of one Arkansas and three Texas regiments, arranged in the following order from left to right: 3rd Arkansas (Colonel Van H. Manning), 1st Texas (Colonel Phillip A. Work), 4th Texas (Colonel John C.G. Key), and 5th Texas (Colonel Robert M. Powell). Law's brigade consisted of five Alabama regiments in the following order from left to right: 4th Alabama (Colonel Lawrence H. Scruggs), 47th Alabama (Colonel James W. Jackson), 15th Alabama (Colonel William C. Oates), 44th Alabama (Colonel William F. Perry), and 48th Alabama (Colonel James L. Sheffield).

Law and Robertson sent several companies from the 1st and 4th Texas regiments and the 47th and 48th Alabama regiments out in front of the Confederate line as skirmishers.[52] It was now almost 4:00 p.m. and Hood's troops were in position for the attack. If there had previously been any question regarding the policy of a frontal attack, not a "shadow of a doubt" remained that the true strategic point was Round Top, from where the Confederate right wing could extend toward the Taneytown and Baltimore roads on the Federal left and rear.[53]

Earlier in the afternoon, as the four sharpshooters four-man patrols advanced westward from their skirmish line, Major Stoughton rode out about half a mile in advance of his line and to the right, along the Slyder farm road. While in this position, he discovered Confederate skirmishers advancing from the woods to his front and right. Stoughton believed his right was unsupported and decided to withdraw to protect his flank.[54] He moved the regiment back 200 yards opposite the direction they had advanced and took up defensive positions in and around the Slyder Farm and farm road. However, around 2:00 p.m., Colonel De Trobriand, per General Ward's order, detached the 3rd Michigan to support Stoughton's right. The 3rd Michigan, under the command of Colonel Byron R. Pierce, moved to the Peach Orchard and then advanced as skirmishers to support the sharpshooters, who were to Pierce's left.

---

51. *Ibid.*, 297.
52. Hood, *Advance and Retreat*, 57–58; *OR*, 27, pt. 2, 391, 395; Young, *The Battle of Gettysburg*, 249.
53. Law, "Round Top," 299–300.
54. *OR*, 27, pt. 1, 493, 518.

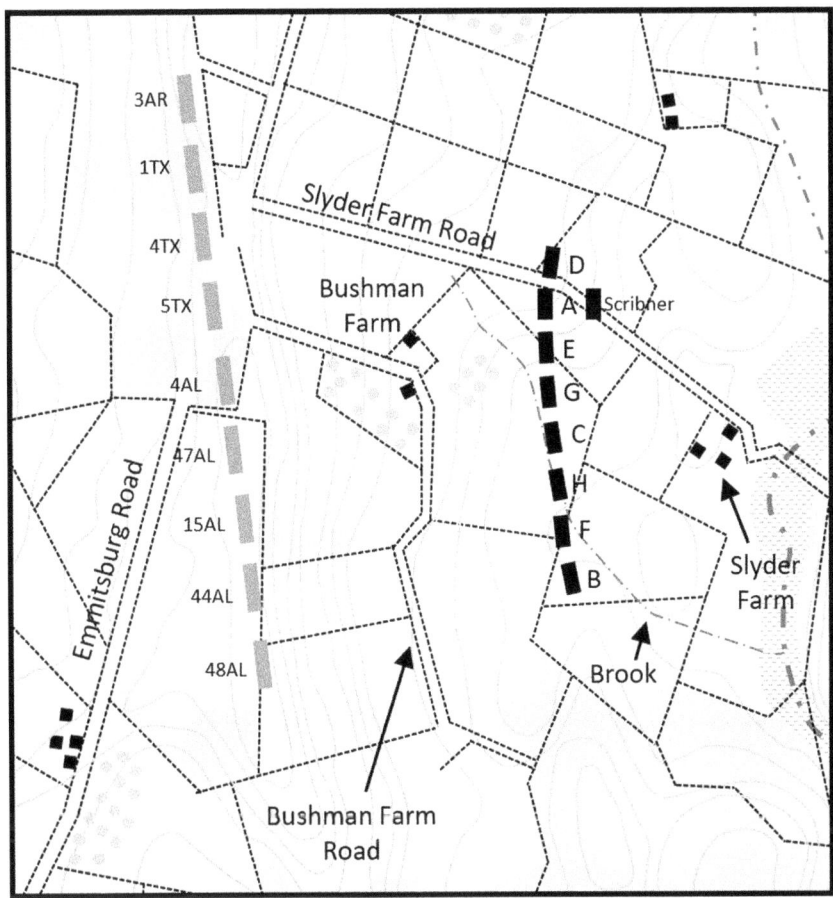

Hood's battle line in position just before stepping off Warfield Ridge.

The 3rd Michigan deployed across the Rose Farm, east of Emmitsburg Road.[55] Major John W. Moore of the 99th Pennsylvania wrote that "during the afternoon my regiment, with the Twentieth Indiana, was ordered forward through the woods to support Berdan's Sharpshooters." Lieutenant Colonel William C.L. Taylor of the 20th Indiana wrote, "Early in the day the whole brigade moved forward. The Twentieth Indiana moved to the front, and formed line of battle in a grove, its right connecting with the Ninety-ninth Pennsylvania."[56]

Stoughton's belief of being unsupported is easy to understand.

---

55. *OR*, 27, pt. 1, 519–520, 524; A.S. Shattuck, "Address of A.S. Shattuck," *Michigan at Gettysburg, July 1st, 2nd and 3rd, 1863* (Detroit, MI, 1889), 76.
56. *OR*, 27, pt. 1, 513, 506.

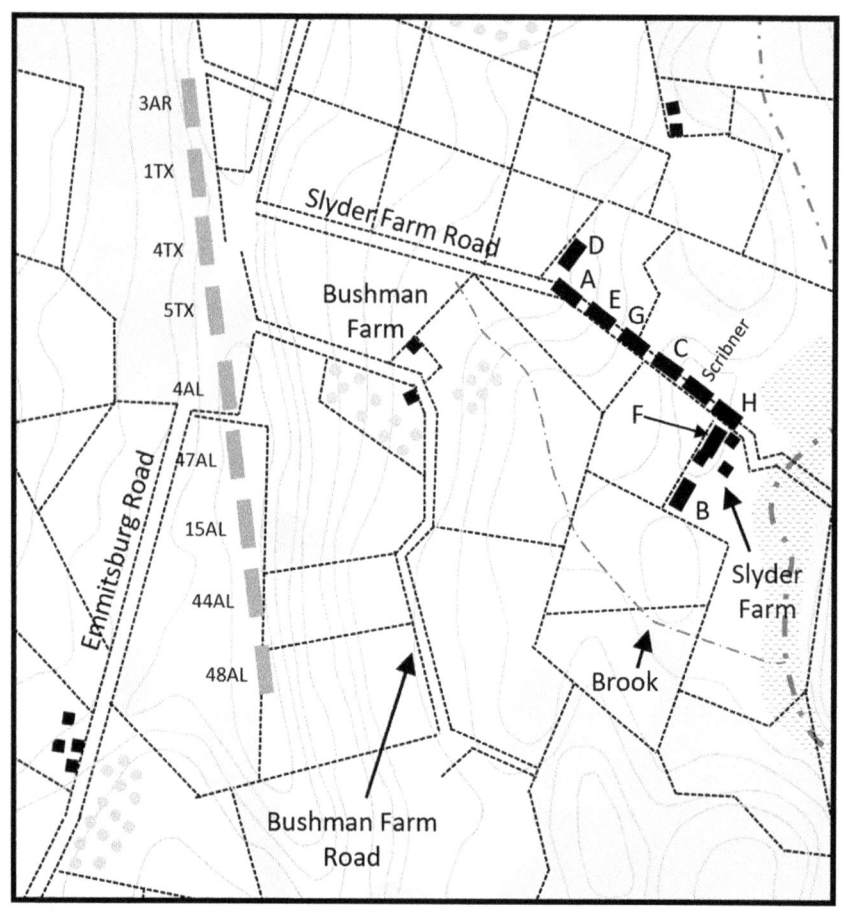

Major Stoughton moves the regiment back to a defensive position in and around Slyder Farm.

From the time the sharpshooters moved beyond Plum Run Valley, where Stoughton's right was to connect with the 20th Indiana's left in Rose Woods, until just before the Confederate advance, Stoughton did not see infantry in a supporting position.[57] The 2nd Sharpshooters was on the extreme left of the Union line and General Ward had made no moves to support Stoughton's left. However, Ward did order the 20th Indiana, 99th Pennsylvania, and 3rd Michigan forward as support, but they failed to link up with Company D, Stoughton's rightmost company. From his position, Stoughton could not see any of the supporting regiments.[58]

---

57. White, *Civil War Diary*, 164.
58. *Maine at Gettysburg*, 349–350. Timothy Orr states, "Ward had told him

Three—Outguessing the Opponent

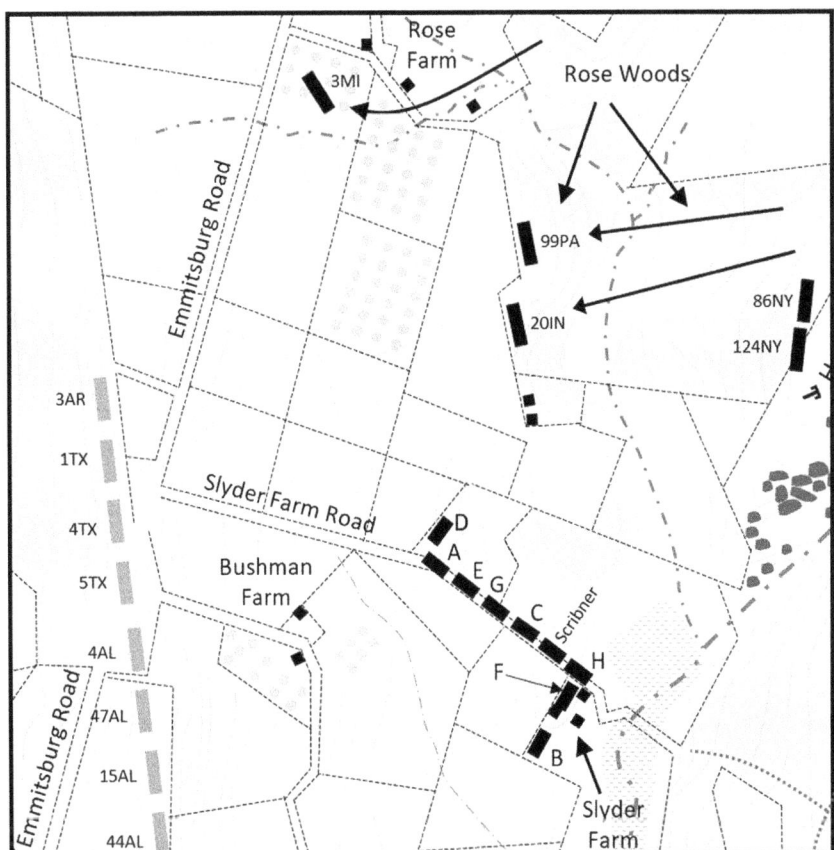

Supporting regiments on Major Stoughton's right move forward into position.

Just before 4:00 p.m., the 2nd Sharpshooters had taken up defensive positions, falling back to the Slyder Farm area. Private Wyman White of Company F was between the Slyder house and barn and knew they did not have long to wait before the rebels would spill over the ridge to

---

[Stoughton] that skirmishers from the main line of battle posted back on Houck's Ridge would deploy additional skirmishers—one company from the 99th Pennsylvania and one from the 20th Indiana—and eventually connect to Company D." Orr does not cite a reference for this statement between Ward and Stoughton (Timothy J. Orr, "On Such Slender Threads does the Fate of Nations Depend: The Second United States Sharpshooters Defend the Union Left," *The Most Shocking Battle I Have Ever Witnessed: The Second Day at Gettysburg*, ed. Chris Little (Gettysburg, PA, 2008), 129). The *Official Records* states that General Ward ordered the 20th Indiana and 99th Pennsylvania regiments, not companies from these regiments, forward in support of the sharpshooters. Support was there, but the 3rd Michigan was too far away to see, and Rose Woods masked the 20th Indiana and 99th Pennsylvania.

their front across Emmitsburg Road. He felt very certain that when the fight opened, it would be on his regiment's front at the left of the Union Army's line. Corporal Curtis Abbott of Company H, positioned in the Slyder farm road, assessed the situation, writing, "The right of the line being refused toward Ward's brigade, and the left resting at the south base of Round Top. There, diagonally across the opening of Plumb Run Gorge, and on the extreme left flank of the army, they awaited developments. The sharpshooters, in the lane, were two hundred, about fifty infantry men were in the gorge as their support, and on the cliff above Devil's Den were three pieces of artillery. Under these conditions they received the Confederate charge."[59]

Longstreet ordered the attack to begin when the two divisions of his corps came into position. Hood's division was to attack first, by crossing Emmitsburg Road and advancing along the line, taking the left of the Union line in flank and rear. Law's brigade on the right flank would start the advance, with the other commands falling in successively toward the left. McLaws would next deploy across the road in two lines of battle and drive the Federals from the Peach Orchard. According to Private Samuel Toombs of Company F, 13th New Jersey, "these instructions were not carried out in the manner designed, and the battle was fought on a plan which developed itself."[60]

The artillery on both sides were actively engaging each other and would continue to fire heavily until Confederate troops engaged Union infantry.[61] Longstreet rode up as Hood's troops were moving forward into position and, passing through the line, took position about 50 yards in front. A few minutes later Hood came down from the right, and a short conversation ensued. Hood again called Longstreet's attention to the strength of the Union line and asked permission to move his command to the right and take the enemy in the flank. Longstreet's reply was somewhat curt: "Hood, go where you are ordered. General Lee directs me to attack here. We must obey the orders of General Lee." As he turned off, Hood said, "Very well, General, but I'll get all my people killed."[62] Hood, after his last attempt to change Longstreet's mind, rode a little nearer to his line and, standing in his stirrups and lifting his hat, gave the command, "Forward!," and advanced with his line under heavy fire.[63]

---

59. White, *Civil War Diary*, 163–164; Kellogg and Kellogg, *The Curtis Abbott Papers*, 256.
60. Law, "Round Top," 301; Toombs, *New Jersey Troops*, 200.
61. Law, "Round Top," 301–302.
62. Jones, "Longstreet at Gettysburg," 552; Hood, *Advance and Retreat*, 58–59.
63. Jones, "Longstreet at Gettysburg," 552.

Four

Stepping Off and Rifles Blazing

The Attack and Defense of Slyder Farm

(4:00 p.m. to 4:30 p.m.)

> *Even a small regiment of practical riflemen, armed with Sharp's breech-loading rifles, and supplied with one hundred rounds of ammunition to each man, is a fearful engine of destruction in such a position.*[1]

About 4:00 p.m., Stoughton, looking in the direction of Emmitsburg Road, saw Confederate skirmishers emerge from the woods, followed by Robertson's and Law's brigades of Hood's Division. Stoughton wrote, "The enemy then advanced a line of battle covering our entire front and flank." General Ward described Hood's advance as "in line and *en masse*, yelling and shouting." Robertson's brigade advanced as Ward described; however, Law's brigade proceeded in a more disciplined and somewhat quieter manner.[2]

The 2nd Sharpshooters kept the same deployment order while retreating to a more defendable position. Company D, on the right flank, was at the intersection of Slyder farm road and a stone wall running northward from the road.[3] Company B was on the extreme left of the line with Company F to its right.[4] Company F was near the Slyder house with Company H on its right.[5] Company H, immediately west of the Slyder house, took position behind a low stone wall topped with

---

1. Peteler, "Narrative of the First Company," 508.
2. *OR*, 27, pt. 1, 493, 518; *Maine at Gettysburg*, 161.
3. *Maine at Gettysburg*, 349–350.
4. Michigan Gettysburg Battlefield Commission, "Sharpshooters," *Michigan at Gettysburg, July 1st, 2nd and 3rd, 1863* (Detroit, MI, 1889), 113.
5. White, *Civil War Diary*, 164.

rails that bordered the south side of the road. Company E was a short distance to the right of Company H.[6] Going by the deployment order described by Stoughton while in the Plum Run Valley (A-E-G-C and B-F), the logical assumption is that since D was already in the ravine, that company took the rightmost position on the line. A-E-G-C, in that order, fell in next to D, with H coming down from Little Round Top and falling in next to C. B and F fell in next, with B going to the leftmost position of the line and F falling in line between B and H. The order from left to right facing forward would be B-F-H-C-G-E-A-D. As for Sergeant Scribner and his scouts, his actual position was to the immediate right of Company H.

During the general retreat described in the next chapter, Scribner and his men followed Captain Buxton and Company H eastward on the Slyder farm road, toward Big Round Top. Based on his direction of escape, east instead of north, and the location of Captain Buxton based on accounts by Corporal Curtis Abbott, upon completion of their patrol, Scribner and his scouts ended up to the right of Company H just west of the Slyder farmhouse, behind the fence bordering the south side of Slyder farm road.

It was now about 4:00 p.m. and Major Stoughton placed the 2nd Sharpshooters in defensive positions on and around Slyder Farm. Stoughton wrote, "In this position we had but little time to wait. The enemy's skirmishers advanced to the top of the hill in our front, and immediately after they placed a battery directly in our front, and being too far for our range, I sent forward a few men under cover of woods on the left, and silenced one piece nearest us."[7] The only Confederate battery that makes sense is the Rowan Artillery of Reilly's battery of Henry's battalion, situated on the right flank of the Confederate line. The Rowan guns were directly west of Company B and a tree line on their left flank would have given them the cover Stoughton mentions. During the evening, the exact time unknown, one three-inch rifle belonging to Captain Reilly's battery burst.[8] Confederate official reports do not mention this silencing of the guns, and whether the cannon bursting was the result of the Company B assault is unknown.

After a short preliminary engagement with Union skirmishers, the heavy Confederate battle lines appeared across the entire Union front. General Ward had barely established his line of battle when Hood's division emerged from the narrow belt of woods along

---

6. Kellogg and Kellogg, *The Curtis Abbott Papers*, 256; Benedict, *Vermont in the Civil War*, 766.
7. *OR*, 27, pt. 1, 518.
8. *OR*, 27, pt. 2, 428.

Four—Stepping Off and Rifles Blazing

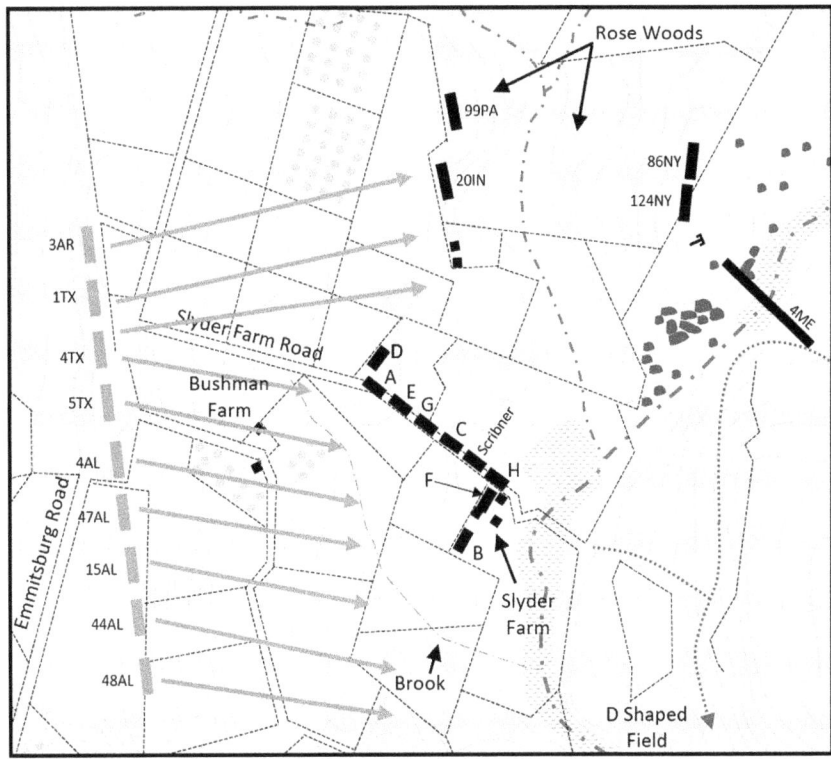

The 2nd Sharpshooters in position at Slyder Farm awaiting the Confederate advance from Warfield Ridge.

Warfield Ridge. Beyond the western side of Big Round Top, the land descends in a gentle slope of cleared and cultivated land about a quarter of a mile or more. After crossing Plum Run, the ground rises slightly until reaching Emmitsburg Road on Warfield Ridge. The country between Big Round Top and Emmitsburg Road is open, with principal obstacles to free movement being fences that surround the numerous fields. The part of the battlefield containing the Bushman and Slyder farms is undulating ground, rocky and very rugged, and interspersed with groves of timber and an occasional rock as large as a haystack. Even with a gentle slope, the ground was not ideal for advancing infantry. The Confederate lines moved down the sloping fields and forward to the attack, bearing down on the Union left. Preceded by their skirmishers, Law's and Robertson's brigades swept rapidly across the intervening farms and advanced toward Houck's Ridge and the Round Tops.[9] Curtis Abbott noted that Stoughton, with Captain Cooney of General Ward's staff, had made a somewhat perilous ride to headquarters. Having just returned, Stoughton dismounted his horse and directed the right of his line.[10]

The Confederate advance, however, did not start as planned. Colonel William C. Oates recounted later that "the advance was not skillfully made in all respects."[11] While advancing, five companies covering Law's front as skirmishers had moved directly toward the center, only to later change direction to the right. These five companies (two from the 48th Alabama and three from the 47th Alabama) went around to the eastern side of the Big Round Top and completely missed the battle on July 2. The Confederate advance was not simple, as the skirmishers doubtless believed. Instead, it was a left half-wheel; essentially the main battle line went left as the skirmishers went right. Oates later claimed that if these five companies had joined his column on the north side of Big Round Top, he would have captured the Union ordnance train, enabling him to have captured Little Round Top.[12] Major James Campbell of the 47th Alabama wrote that before the Confederate line formed, "three companies were detached from my regiment, and placed in rear of our right, to guard a road," and that they remained on this part of the field until the regiment fell back on the morning of the 4th. The other seven companies went into the fight in line with the brigade.[13] Gary Bruner suggests that Major Campbell knew that someone detached three companies, but simply got the reason wrong as he was not in command at that time.[14] Incidentally, it was the 7th Georgia that moved to the right flank to watch for movements of Union cavalry.[15]

Another issue was when the Confederate battle line formed just before the advance. Oates directed a two-man detail from each of the 11 companies in the 15th Alabama to take all the canteens to a well about 100 yards in the rear and fill them with cool water. However, before this detail could fill the canteens, General Hood ordered the advance. Oates says that the water detail followed with the canteens of water,

---

9. Briscoe, "Capt. J.C. Briscoe's Report of Gettysburg," 401; *Maine at Gettysburg*, 350; Fox, "New York at Gettysburg," 44–45; *OR*, 27, pt. 1, 483; Rafferty, "Gettysburg," 6; Hunt, "The Second Day at Gettysburg," 282–283; Norton, *Attack and Defense*, 255.
10. Kellogg and Kellogg, *The Curtis Abbott Papers*, 257.
11. William C. Oates, *The War Between the Union and the Confederacy* (New York and Washington, D.C., 1905), 207.
12. *Ibid.*, 207–208.
13. *OR*, 27, pt. 2, 395.
14. Gary P. Bruner, "Up Over Big Round Top: The Forgotten 47th Alabama," *Gettysburg Magazine*, issue 22 (July 2000), 15.
15. *OR*, 27, pt. 2, 396.

Four—Stepping Off and Rifles Blazing

but when they got into the woods, they missed Oates and walked right into the Union lines, who captured them, canteens and all. Oates would later claim that the loss of those 22 men and lack of water contributed largely to his failure to take Little Round Top later that afternoon.[16]

Colonel William C. Oates, commanding the 15th Alabama Infantry. Alabama Department of Archives and History.

Additionally, the farmland in Hood's front was a huge obstacle to the advancement of infantry. The undulating ground, interspersed with groves of timber, was very rough and rocky, and numerous stone fences and other obstructions divided the land. Law's Brigade moved forward over as "rough ground as was ever passed over by troops." Hood observed during his objection to the direct attack that at the base and along the slope of the mountain, advancing infantry would confront immense boulders so massed together as to form only narrow openings. He deemed it almost an impossibility to clamber along the boulders up this steep and rugged mountain.[17] These obstacles would eventually divert, divide, and segment the advancing Confederate forces.

By all accounts, the Confederate advance was anything but orderly. When Hood ordered the advance, the whole division made a mad rush

---

16. Oates, *The War*, 212.
17. Pettijohn and Pettijohn, "Something of the Pettijohn (Pettyjohn) Family"; Longstreet, *From Manassas to Appomattox*, 367; Norton, *Attack and Defense*, 255; Hood, *Advance and Retreat*, 58–59; John M. Vanderslice, *Gettysburg Then and Now* (New York, 1897), 148.

down through the wheat, firing and yelling like demons. The Confederate line advanced in quick time, with some running neck and neck, each striving to be first at the stone fences that protected the Union line of skirmishers, who were firing into the faces of the advancing Confederates.[18] Other descriptions of the advance include "advancing rapidly across the valley," "our line advanced in quick time," and "the order was then given to move forward, which we did at a double-quick."[19] Moreover, once the Confederate infantry was moving forward, the Union artillery turned their fire from the Confederate artillery toward the advancing Confederate line, making it nearly impossible for the advancing infantry to maintain good order.

Parts of Brigadier General Jerome B. Robertson's orders were to rest his left on Emmitsburg Road and to keep his right well closed on Brigadier General Evander M. Law's left. Robertson's brigade had advanced a short distance when he discovered that his brigade would not fill the space between Law's left and the road, due mostly to Law's movement to the right. Robertson needed to leave the road or disconnect his brigade from Law's brigade. He chose to abandon the road but only his two right-most regiments closed on Law's left. This shift caused a separation of Robertson's regiments as Law continued his angled advance to the right.[20]

Historians commonly place the separation in Robertson's brigade between the 1st Texas and the 4th Texas, with the 3rd Arkansas and 1st Texas going left and the 4th and 5th Texas going right. However, the split occurred in the ranks of the 4th Texas, with part of that regiment going left toward Houck's Ridge and the other part going right toward Big Round Top. Excerpts from the personal accounts of John C. West (Company E), James M. Polk (Company I), and Lieutenant Colonel Benjamin F. Carter (Company B), all from the 4th Texas, illustrate this. West wrote, "When the command was given to charge, we moved forward as fast as we could towards the battery." Likewise, Polk stated, "We were right in front of the battery." This is Smith's battery on Houck's

---

18. Oates, *The War*, 207; William C. Oates, "Gettysburg—The Battle on the Right," *Southern Historical Society Papers* 6 (July–December 1878), 174; Jeffrey D. Stocker, ed., *From Huntsville to Appomattox, R.T. Cole's History of 4th Regiment, Alabama Volunteer Infantry, C.S.A., Army of Northern Virginia* (Knoxville, TN, 1996), 104; John C. West, "Incidents at Gettysburg—Recollections of a Soldier Who Fought with Hood in This Battle," *Unveiling and Dedication of Monument to Hood's Texas Brigade* ed. Frank B Chilton (Houston, TX, 1911), 347.

19. John Purifoy, "Longstreet's Attack at Gettysburg, July 2, 1863," *Confederate Veteran* 32, no. 8 (August 1923), 292; Oates, *The War*, 207; Oates, "Battle on the Right," 174; *OR*, 27, pt. 2, 391.

20. Alexander, *Military Memoirs*, 395–396.

Ridge. Additionally, Carter said, "Advancing up Big Round Top, the 4th engaged the 2nd U.S. Sharpshooters."[21] Also, Lieutenant Colonel Phillip A. Work, commanding the 1st Texas, wrote that Company I of the 4th Texas became separated from its regiment and attached itself to the 1st Texas, remaining with it throughout the evening and night.[22] These 4th Texas soldiers' accounts indicate the regiment was in two different locations because somewhere along their line, the regiment divided or separated, with at least two companies, E and I, going left, and the remaining companies going to the right with Law's brigade.

Taking a closer look at this separation shows that the 4th and 5th Texas followed Law's movement, keeping connected to the 4th Alabama. Robertson's other regiments, the 1st and 4th Texas and 3rd Arkansas, went straight on toward Devil's Den.[23] With Law moving to his right and hoping to turn the Union flank, a gap opened between the divisions of Robertson and Law. Per their orders, the 4th and 5th Texas on Robertson's right tried to stay connected to Law's left. In doing so, the two Texas regiments detached themselves from Robertson's brigade and attached themselves to Law's brigade. Robertson's brigade thus split into two bodies as the brigade traversed the rough ground.[24] Sergeant James Matthews, Company D, 2nd Sharpshooters, was on the right of the sharpshooter skirmish line and directly east of the two advancing Texas regiments. About 10 minutes into the advance, Matthews noted the enemy's movement to his left, stating, "The enemy obliged (obliqued) to our left which seem intended to out flank us."[25]

Robertson, in his official report, said the separation "was remedied as promptly as the numerous stone and rail fences that intersected the field through which we were advancing would allow." The 1st and 4th Texas and 3rd Arkansas, while heading straight for Devil's Den, had left a considerable interval between the two parts of Robertson's brigade, and ended up engaged with Union forces on the outskirts of Rose Woods. In the meantime, the 4th and 5th Texas continued eastward with Law's brigade and never corrected the separation as they

---

21. John C. West, *A Texan in Search of a Fight, Being the Diary and Letters of a Private Soldier in Hood's Texas Brigade* (Waco, TX, 1901), 85; J.M. Polk, *Memories of the Lost Cause: Stories and Adventures of a Confederate Soldier in General R.E. Lee's Army, 1861 to 1865* (Austin, TX, 1905), 17; Lana J. Henley, "Lt. Col. Benjamin F. Carter," *UDC Magazine* 73 (December 2010), p. 16.
22. *OR*, 27, pt. 2, 405.
23. Alexander, *Military Memoirs*, 395–396. Going forward, any reference to the 4th Texas will be with the understanding that this regiment split into two separate entities and is not the full regiment when discussed.
24. *Ibid.*
25. Pullen, *Soldiers in Green*, 160.

approached Big Round Top. Law would eventually move two Alabama regiments from his right to fill the gap.²⁶

Sergeant James M. Matthews, Company D, 2nd U.S. Sharpshooters. Courtesy the Brian T. White Collection.

The 3rd Arkansas and the 1st and 4th Texas moved across open fields, advancing under devastating artillery bombardment from Smith's rifled guns on Houck's Ridge. John C. West of Company E, 4th Texas, wrote, "When the command was given to charge, we moved forward as fast as we could towards the battery. It was between a half and three-quarters of a mile across an open field, over a marshy branch, over a stone fence, and up a very rugged and rocky hill, while Yankee sharp shooters were on the higher mountains, so as to have fairer shots at our officers. On we went yelling and whooping, and soon drove the Yankees from the first battery, but were too much worn out and exhausted to climb to the second."²⁷

James M. Polk of Company I, 4th Texas, described the advance, saying, "It was 300 or 400 yards to the foot of the hill, on which bordered a rock fence. When we were forty or fifty steps from this fence, the Federal batteries on the hill turned loose at the fence with solid shot, and rocks were flying in every direction. This scattered our men; many of them were killed, wounded, and captured. We were right in front of the battery. So great was the confusion that I have no recollection of passing over the fence. I can remember when I was about halfway up the hill, I stopped behind a big rock to load my gun; I could see Captain Reilly's battery a little to our right, and he was cleaning off the top of that hill. There was a solid blaze of fire in front of his battery. When we reached the battery at the top of the hill, the men had all left. Some dead were lying around, I don't remember how many."²⁸

The right of General Ward's line, the 20th Indiana and 99th

26. *OR*, 27, pt. 2, 404; Norton, *Attack and Defense*, 174, 255.
27. West, *A Texan in Search of a Fight*, 85–87.
28. Polk, *Memories of the Lost Cause*, 15–16.

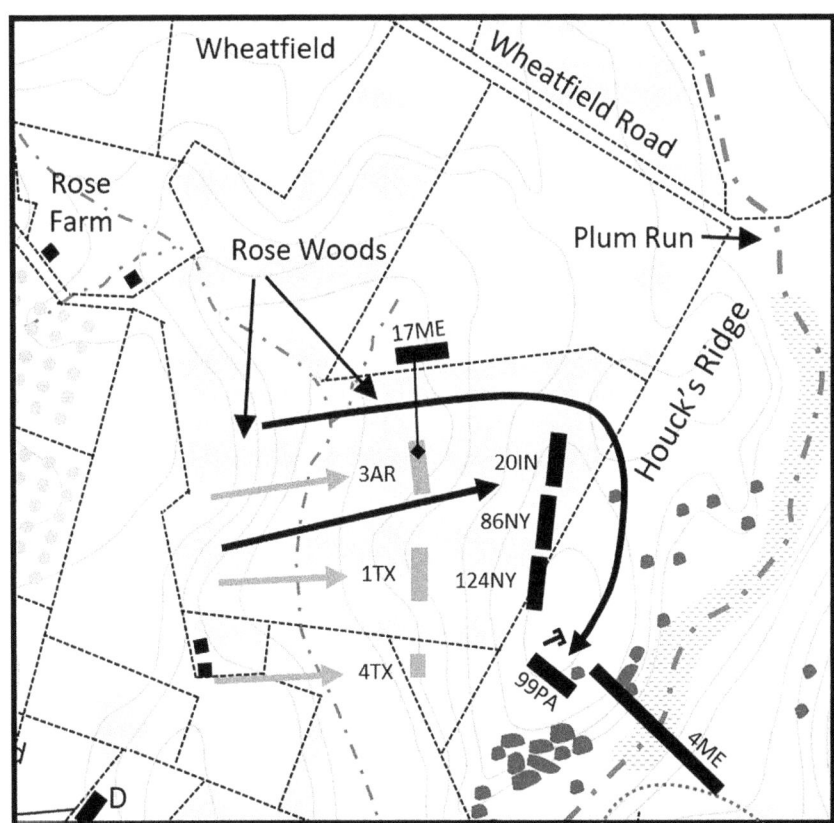

The 3rd Arkansas and the 1st and 4th Texas advance through Rose Woods.

Pennsylvania that Ward previously advanced into Rose Woods to support Stoughton's sharpshooters, was waiting for the Confederate troops to come into range. Ward's left, the 124th New York and 86th New York, remained on Houck's Ridge supporting Smith's battery, while the 4th Maine moved left of the battery and across Plum Run Valley, defending Ward's left flank and rear and the approaches to Little Round Top. The 17th Maine, Colonel Charles B. Merrill commanding, took a position behind a stone wall between Rose Woods and the Wheatfield, connecting with Ward's right.[29]

---

29. Samuel H. Leavitt, "Dedication of Monument. 86th Regiment Infantry Historical Sketch," *Final Report of the Battlefield of Gettysburg, Volume 2* (Albany, NY, 1900), 701; *OR*, 27, pt. 1, 511; Fasnacht, *Historical Sketch*, 9–11; Charles H. Weygant, *History of the One Hundred and Twenty-Fourth Regiment* (Newburgh, NY, 1877), 173; Charles H. Weygant, "What They Did Here," *Final Report of the Battlefield of Gettysburg, Volume 2* (Albany, NY, 1900), 868–869; *Maine at Gettysburg*, 162; *OR*, 27, pt. 2, 407.

The 3rd Arkansas and the 1st and 4th Texas advanced until arriving at a stone wall at the western edge of Rose Woods. The wall offered some protection from the hailstorm of shot and shell, plus afforded protection against the waiting 20th Indiana and 99th Pennsylvania, who were engaging the advancing Confederate regiments.[30] The 3rd Arkansas with the two Texas regiments on their right flank drifted to the right as the firing from the 20th Indiana and 99th Pennsylvania intensified. This shift to the right exposed the 3rd Arkansas's flank and rear to the 17th Maine's enfilading fire.[31] As the 3rd Arkansas engaged the 20th Indiana and 17th Maine, the 1st and 4th Texas continued to drift to the right while advancing toward Houck's Ridge. The first battle for possession of Smith's battery was mainly between the 1st Texas and the 124th New York, supported by the 86th New York. Around 4:15 p.m., Ward moved the 99th Pennsylvania from the right of his line to the left, to support Smith's battery as the battle for Smith's guns evolved into Ward's left against the advancing 1st and 4th Texas.[32]

Meanwhile, on the Confederate right, Law's brigade was the first to advance, but the two right regiments, the 44th and 48th Alabama, dropped back a short distance. Law would have given the order for the movement but provided no explanation; however, Oates suggested that Law was preparing to move these two regiments to the left to fill the gap between brigades. Oates wrote, "As we entered the valley the Forty-fourth Alabama was directed to the left to attack the Devil's Den, and the Forty-eighth continued as a reserve or second line, which made the Fifteenth a little in advance and on the extreme right of Longstreet's column of attack."[33] The 15th Alabama and the 2nd Sharpshooters were now at the extreme end of their respective lines.

With Robertson's left engaged in Rose Woods, the 4th and 5th Texas continued veering to the right with Law's Brigade. Major John P. Bane of the 4th Texas wrote, "We were ordered to advance on the enemy, who occupied the heights about 1½ miles distant, the Fifth Texas, the directing battalion, on my right, and the First Texas on my left. Advancing at double-quick, we soon met the enemy's skirmishers who occupied a skirt of thick undergrowth about one-quarter of a mile from the base of the cliffs, upon which the enemy had a battery playing upon us with

---

30. Craig L. Dunn, *Harvestfields of Death: The Twentieth Indiana Volunteers of Gettysburg* (Carmel, IN, 1999), 182; *OR*, 27, pt. 2, 408–410; Jones, "Longstreet at Gettysburg," 552.

31. Dunn, *Harvestfields of Death*, 183; *OR*, 27, pt. 2, 408; Jones, "Longstreet at Gettysburg," 552; *OR*, 27, pt. 1, 522.

32. *OR*, 27, pt. 1, 522; Edwin B. Houghton, *The Campaigns of the Seventeenth Maine* (Portland, ME, 1866), 92; *Maine at Gettysburg*, 162.

33. Oates, *The War*, 207.

the most deadly effect."³⁴ These enemy skirmishers were the men from Company D, 2nd Sharpshooters. Stoughton had positioned the right of his line behind a stone fence running almost parallel to Emmitsburg Road. Company D was about one-third of a mile in front of Smith's battery, located on Houck's ridge.

The 2nd Sharpshooters prepared to engage the advancing Confederate line that emerged from the trees along the crest of Warfield Ridge. Wyman White noted that "they came yelling and firing and struggling over fences and through the timber. Just in front of where I was, the land was open and, as they were mostly dressed in butternut colored clothes they had the appearance of a plowed field being closed in mass formation until they got within good fighting distance to our line, when they broke into line of battle formation three lines deep."³⁵

General Ward gave instructions to the 20th Indiana and 99th Pennsylvania deployed in Rose Woods not to fire until they could plainly see the enemy. Those in Ward's left, including Stoughton's sharpshooters, were not to fire at distances greater than 200 yards. Ward wrote, "My command did not fire a shot until the enemy came within the distance prescribed." When the 4th and 5th Texas and 4th Alabama were within the specified 200-yard range, the entire sharpshooters regiment fired a volley. This fire checked the enemy advance, allowing the sharpshooters to reload and fire another volley into the Confederate line.³⁶ The 4th and 5th Texas and the 4th Alabama were the primary opponents for Stoughton's sharpshooters near Slyder Farm and the advancing line required their immediate attention. For the time being, the 2nd Sharpshooters did not engage the rest of Law's brigade that was passing south of Slyder Farm.

General Robertson described the moment Union sharpshooters fired their first volley as the advancing Confederate line reached the 200-yard mark. He wrote, "As we approached the base of the mountain, General Law moved to the right, and I was moving obliquely to the right to close on him, when my whole line encountered the fire of the enemy's main line, posted behind rocks and a stone fence."³⁷ Robertson continued, "The Fourth and Fifth Texas regiments, while returning the fire and driving the enemy before them, continued to close on General Law, to their right. As we advanced through this field, for half a mile we were exposed to a heavy and destructive fire of canister, grape, and shell from six pieces of their artillery on the mountain alluded to, and the same

---

34. *OR*, 27, pt. 2, 410–411.
35. Benedict, *Vermont in the Civil War*, 766; White, *Civil War Diary*, 164.
36. *OR*, 27, pt. 1, 493.
37. *OR*, 27, pt. 2, 404.

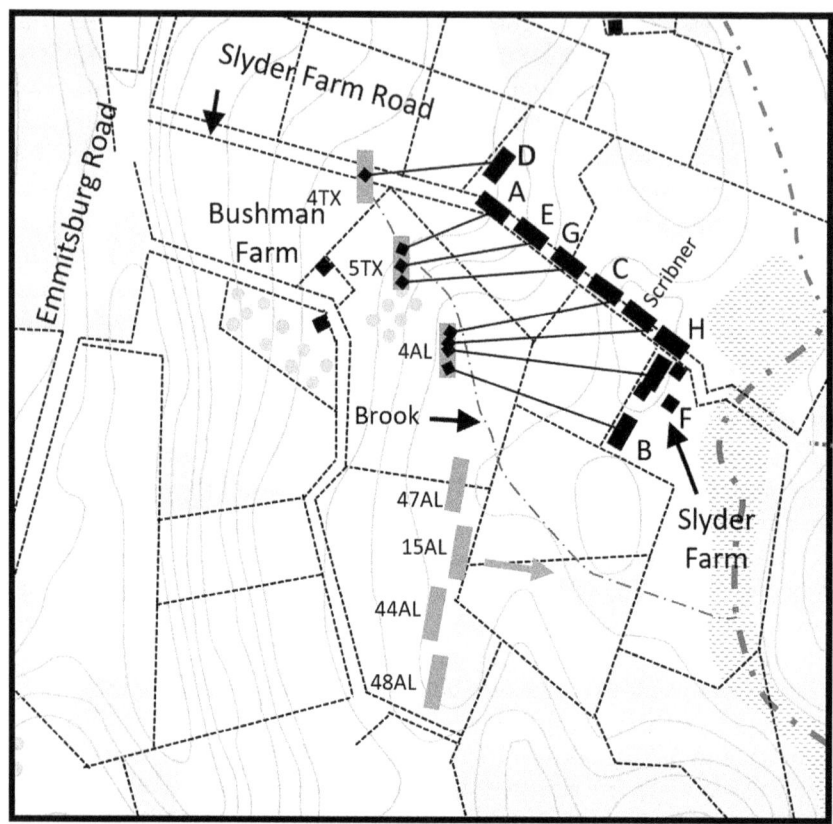

The 2nd Sharpshooters responds to the Confederate advance. Target lines are estimates. The right of Law's line did not engage the sharpshooters during the advance until reaching Big Round Top on the east side of Plum Run.

number on a commanding hill but a short distance to the left of the mountain, and from the enemy's sharpshooters from behind the numerous rocks, fences, and houses in the field."[38]

Robertson's official report stated that at the same time as the sharpshooter's first volley, the 1st Texas and 3rd Arkansas were hotly engaged with a greatly superior force, that being the 99th Pennsylvania and 20th Indiana. While engaged with those two regiments, the 17th Maine appeared and opened fire on the left flank of the 3rd Arkansas.[39] At about 4:15 p.m., Ward moved the 99th Pennsylvania to the left of

---

38. *Ibid.*
39. *Ibid.*

Four—Stepping Off and Rifles Blazing 113

Smith's battery to support the 124th New York and the battery itself.[40] Therefore, no later than 4:15 p.m., Robertson's two regiments were "hotly engaged" with the 20th Indiana and 17th Maine, indicating the sharpshooters' first volley was most likely between 4:15 and 4:20 p.m.

The 2nd Sharpshooters' precise and rapid shooting disrupted the advancing Confederate line, who rallied and again advanced, which only caused more men to fall from the sharpshooters' accurate fire, which grew ever deadlier as the Confederate line approached.[41] Private Edwin Aldritt, a sharpshooter from Company A, wrote, "We sharpshooters were behind a stone wall and we made a quick work of the skirmishers. They brought up a regiment but had no chance. They had come across a clearing of about 200 yards and we shot them to pieces. Their loss was terrible, and they didn't get half way before they broke and ran back for the woods." Curtis Abbott from Company H wrote, "[The enemy] emerged from the fringe of trees along the crest, the sharpshooters opened fire, and its first line was checked and broken while descending the slope. It gathered and came on and was soon reinforced."[42]

Although Hood's division covered the sharpshooters' entire front and flank, the 2nd Sharpshooters assailed the Confederate line valiantly, and their fire was so severe that one Confederate regiment broke three times before it would advance. Stoughton summed up their performance succinctly when stating, "While they [the enemy] were advancing, the Second Regiment did splendid execution, killing and wounding a great many."[43] Wyman White, describing the initial assault, gave credit to his weapon and training, saying, "For we were armed with breech loaders and, as we took the matter very coolly, many a brave Southron threw up his arms and fell. But on they came, shouting and yelling their peculiar yell."[44]

Fighting on the defensive, the 2nd Sharpshooters held an early advantage because Hood's division crossed mostly open ground, fields, and farmland while under fire.[45] It was now about 4:25 p.m. Stoughton wrote in his official report that he held his position until the Confederate line of battle, primarily the 4th Alabama, and the 4th and 5th Texas, was within 100 yards of his position. However, Captain Abraham Wright of Company A and Francis Peteler suggested the sharpshooters

---

40. *OR*, 27, pt. 1, 513; *Maine at Gettysburg*, 162; Fasnacht, *Historical Sketch*, 10.
41. Benedict, *Vermont in the Civil War*, 766; *OR*, 27, pt. 1, 493.
42. Hoisington, "I Never Saw Such Shooting," 48; Kellogg and Kellogg, *The Curtis Abbott Papers*, 256.
43. *Maine at Gettysburg*, 350; *OR*, 27, pt. 1, 518.
44. White, *Civil War Diary*, 164.
45. Oates, *The War*, 207.

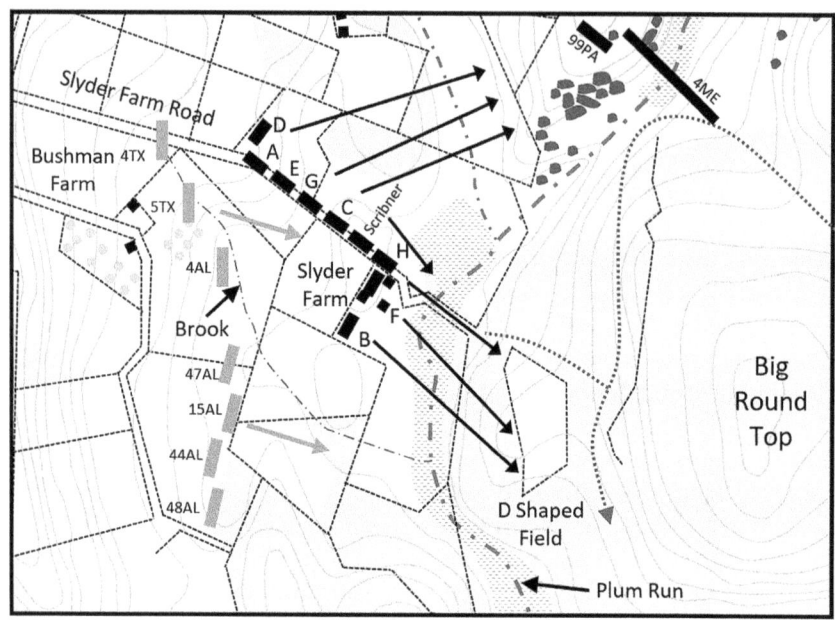

The 2nd Sharpshooters falls back, some northward into Plum Run Valley, and others eastward across Plum Run and up the western side of Big Round Top.

continued to fire until the advancing Confederates were within 50 yards of their position.[46] As Confederate skirmishers approached Stoughton's right flank, he ordered the regiment to "fall back, firing as they retreated."[47]

Fall back, firing, is a tactical withdrawal that generally means retreating forces fall back while maintaining contact with the enemy. A tactical withdrawal is a managed retreat rather than an all-out rout, with forces withdrawing in good order to fight another day. Troops falling back may have completed their assigned task (e.g., a delaying action), and a move like this could, if done correctly, be almost as effective as a battle victory, at least in terms of damage to the opponent's morale. Indeed, the attacking soldiers, hyped for battle, will often find themselves confused and frustrated if their intended target is not where they expected it to be. A tactical withdrawal can possibly force the enemy to change parts of their strategy or disregard it entirely. More importantly, an orderly retreat is always less costly than a rout. The routed force is

---

46. *OR*, 27, pt. 1, 518; A. Wright and F. Peteler, *History of First Company Sharpshooters of Minnesota* (Minneapolis, MN, 1889), 3; *Maine at Gettysburg*, 350.
47. *OR*, 27, pt. 1, 518–519.

Four—Stepping Off and Rifles Blazing

broken. A retreating force is merely leaving and often has reasonable hopes to fight again.[48]

The sharpshooters inflicted serious damage to the advancing Confederate troops, but the advancing enemy line was about to overrun Stoughton's position. Some sharpshooters retreated northward through the 4th Maine line in Plum Run Valley. Others retreated eastward to the western slope of Big Round Top. Even in retreat, Stoughton's regiment effectively used their skills. General Longstreet recognized their abilities, writing, "Stoughton's well-seasoned troops knew how to utilize the advantage of the ground and put back their dreadful fires from rocks, depressions, and stone fences, as they went for shelter near Devil's Den or on Big Round Top."[49] As the sharpshooters performed their tactical withdrawal, the men in Hood's division were going to discover that the 2nd Sharpshooters were far from finished creating problems for the advancing Confederate line. These problems would greatly affect the outcome of the day's contest.

---

48. Tactical Withdrawal, https://tvtropes.org/pmwiki/pmwiki.php/Main/Tactical-Withdrawal (accessed February 8, 2019).
49. Longstreet, *From Manassas to Appomattox*, 370.

Five

Fall Back or Be Killed

The 2nd Regiment Retreats

(4:30 p.m. to 6:00 p.m.)

A masterly retreat is in itself a victory.[1]

The 2nd Sharpshooters' well-directed fire checked the Confederate advance for a time, but Hood's division greatly outnumbered the understrength sharpshooters regiment.[2] Private Wyman White, of Company F, described the scene, writing, "Our line being only a skirmish line, that means five paces distance between the men, we were obliged to fall back or be either killed or taken prisoner. The enemy force in our front was at least ninety men to our one."[3] The sharpshooters held their position until the Confederate line was between 50 and 100 yards away. Major Stoughton then ordered, "Fall back, firing!" As the sharpshooters fell back, they kept up a continuous fire upon the advancing Confederate line.[4]

At this juncture, Captain Buxton, standing to the right of his company, shouted the order to retreat, and the line on both sides of him began falling back. Company H and the men to its right, being Norton and Scribner with his squad of scouts, fell back in the direction they had advanced along the east side of the Plum Run, that is, eastward toward Big Round Top. The "bull-dogs" of the line lingered for a last shot, before being crowded in by the pursuing Confederates. The regiment retreated in detached parties.[5] These actions were the first step of a tactical with-

---

1. Norman Vincent Peale, https://www.brainyquote.com/quotes/norman_vincent_peale_159732 (accessed May 27, 2020).
2. Norton, *Attack and Defense*, 256.
3. White, *Civil War Diary*, 164.
4. *Maine at Gettysburg*, 350.
5. Kellogg and Kellogg, *The Curtis Abbott Papers*, 257; Benedict, *Vermont in the Civil War*, 767.

drawal. The "bull-dogs" were the front-rank men who, when the retreat began, faced the enemy and fired while the rear-rank men fell back.

As an illustration of the "fall back, firing" method of a retreating line, Brigadier General Silas Casey's *Infantry Tactics* states that "the front-rank man of every file will halt, face to the enemy, fire, and then reload whilst moving to the rear; the rear-rank man of the same file will continue to march and halt ten or twelve paces beyond his front-rank man, face about, come to a ready, and fire, when his front rank-man has passed him in retreat and loaded; after which, he will move to the rear, reloading while so moving. The front-rank man in his turn, after marching briskly to the rear, will halt at ten or twelve paces from the rear-rank, face the enemy, finish loading his piece, and fire, conforming to what has just been prescribed for the rear-rank man; the firing will thus be continued."[6] As Wyman White stated, the 2nd Sharpshooters' skirmish line was one line with the men about five paces apart and they did not have front or rear-rank men. Although not stated, there was likely a contingency or adaptation of this maneuver allowing for half the regiment to fire (i.e., the "bull-dogs") as the other half fell back 10 to 12 paces, reloading if necessary. This second half would then fire and the first half, who fired first, would retreat 10 to 12 paces, reloading as they move, so they could fire again.

As the 4th and 5th Texas flanked the sharpshooter's right, Stoughton realized capture was imminent and had his right wing, companies D, A, E, G, and C, fall back, where they soon passed through the 4th Maine line in Plum Run Valley. Sharpshooter Sergeant Joseph Brown of Company C wrote that "we had to fall back slowly to our support" while executing the tactical withdrawal.[7] Some sharpshooters from the right wing remained with the 4th Maine, filling vacant places in their thin line; the rest continued to the western base of Little Round Top, taking positions behind fences and boulders.[8] Major Stoughton, Adjutant Norton, and Scribner with his scouts, along with left-wing companies H, B, and F, retired to the east, crossed Plum Run, and entered the woods at the base of Big Round Top. Lieutenant Colonel Bryan of

---

6. Casey, *Infantry Tactics*, 203–204.
7. *OR*, 27, pt. 1, 519; Joseph B. Brown, "Letter to Matilda Crandall, July 29, 1863." Crandall Family Papers, https://altchive.org/node/13657 (accessed December 1, 2021). Brown is a cousin of Corporal George Crandall, also of Company C. Confederate troops captured Crandall on July 2, 1863, sending him to Belle Island at Richmond, Virginia.
8. Warren L. Goss, *Recollections of a Private: A Story of the Army of the Potomac* (New York, 1890), 204; Charles Hamlin, "The Battle of Gettysburg," *Maine at Gettysburg* (Portland, ME, 1898), 11; *Maine at Gettysburg*, 162; Benedict, *Vermont in the Civil War*, 767; Hamlin, Stevens, Thaxter, Verrill, and Nash, "Company D, Second U.S. Sharpshooters," 350.

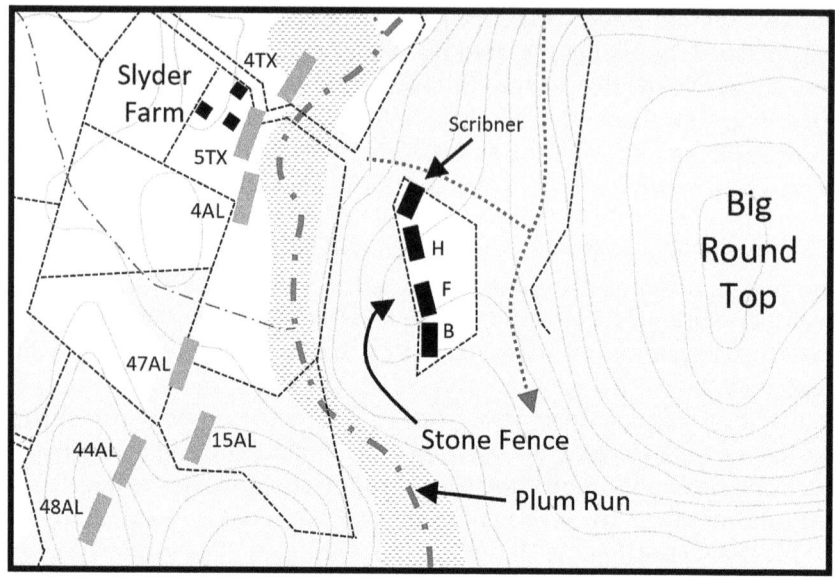

The 2nd Sharpshooters retreats to new positions. Companies B, F, and H and Scribner's squad of scouts are behind a stone fence in the D-shaped field. The remaining companies fall back into Plum Run Valley.

the 5th Texas said, "The enemy had a line of sharpshooters at the foot of the first height, behind a stone fence, about three-fourths of a mile from our starting point, which distance was passed over by our line at a double-quick and a run. At our approach [to the Slyder Farm], the enemy retired to the top of the first height, protected by a ledge of rocks [the stone fence]."[9] This fence marked the west edge of Slyder Farm's D-shaped field, located on slightly elevated ground, just east of Plum Run and at the western foot of Big Round Top.

As the sharpshooters fell back firing, the Confederate line continued advancing. Colonel Scruggs of the 4th Alabama wrote, "The order was then given to move forward, which we did at a double-quick across a plowed field for half a mile, the enemy's batteries playing upon us with great effect until we arrived at a stone fence, behind which the Union's first line of infantry [sharpshooters] was posted, which position we soon succeeded in carrying with the bayonet." William A. Fletcher of the 5th Texas made a similar claim: "We were soon forward and near on the opposite side of the valley. We routed pickets and scaled rock fences, and worked our way to the front rapidly, with pickets giving away before us,

---

9. *OR*, 27, pt. 2, 412.

firing but little."[10] Fletcher's claim of the sharpshooters "firing but little" is an accurate observation. The volume of fire during the tactical withdrawal was probably half of what it was when the sharpshooters were firing while in position at Slyder Farm. The tactical withdrawal would have half the sharpshooters falling back while the other half fired, only to have the second group fall back while the first group turned and fired. Additionally, only about half the regiment was now in front of the 5th Texas, as the others had retreated northward.

Law's brigade, with Robertson's two detached Texas regiments, was quickly moving eastward in the direction of Big Round Top; Robertson's other two regiments with a few detached companies from the 4th Texas were advancing toward the artillery on Houck's Ridge. The gap between the two brigades was increasing; however, General Law would soon correct this by redirecting the 44th and 48th Alabama regiments northward to fill the gap.

General Longstreet's official report noted that "the enemy was soon dislodged and driven back upon a commanding hill, which is so precipitous and rough as to render it difficult of ascent. Numerous stone fences about its base added greatly to its strength. The enemy, taking shelter behind these, held them, one after another, with great pertinacity."[11] As Stoughton's left wing retreated eastward through Plum Run, Private Wyman White of Company F stated, "The country that my company fell back over was first a low swampy intervale."[12] The sharpshooters crossed the swampy intervale associated with Plum Run and started up the western side of Big Round Top. However, they soon stopped and took a defensive position behind a stone fence along the western edge of Slyder Farm's D-shaped field.[13] Tactically, this was a good defensive position. The sharpshooters had cover behind the stone fence and forced the advancing Confederates to cross a marshy stream before fighting an uphill battle. The exact reason for forming a line at this location, other than it being a good defensive position, is unknown, as Stoughton in his official report, Wyman White in his diary, and Charles Stevens in his regimental history do not mention the action at this stone fence. What we do know is that Company H, with Scribner and his squad of scouts in tow, "assembled on the first acclivity of Round Top among the trees." Stoughton was trailing the retreating left-wing companies and

---

10. *OR*, 27, pt. 2, 391; William A. Fletcher, *Rebel Private Front and Rear* (Beaumont, TX, 1908), 73.
11. *OR*, 27, pt. 2, 358. Pertinacity means they were stubbornly tenacious.
12. White, *Civil War Diary*, 164. An intervale is a low-lying tract of land along a river, in this case, Plum Run.
13. *OR*, 27, pt. 1, 519.

reached the wooded prominence from the right, coming upon the stone wall where the left of his line had rallied. At this point, he began directing his men into position.[14]

Adjutant Seymour Norton, Scribner and his scouts, and Company H did in fact retreat toward Big Round Top, taking a position to the right of Company F on Stoughton's new line. Norton wrote, "The Second Regiment did not long dispute the advance from the Pike down into the little valley. I kept to the left, down the cross road towards Little Round Top, with my small squad of scouts. In the woods (into which this cross road ran) I was surprised by seeing a line of battle of the enemy suddenly appear on our left."[15] The crossroad Norton references is the Slyder farm road, which enters the woods east of Plum Run. Norton, with Scribner and his scouts, numbering between 12 and 15 men from companies E and H, took defensive positions on the right of Stoughton's new line. During the tactical withdrawal, Benedict wrote that *"most of Company H fell back along the east side of the gorge"* (emphasis added).[16] The rest of Company H was still attached to Scribner. To get to the east side of the gorge, better known as Plum Run Valley, Company H would have retreated eastward on the Slyder farm road. Since Scribner and his squad of scouts were to the right of Company H at Slyder Farm, Norton and Scribner would have likely followed Company H while retreating. Norton, Scribner and his scouts, and Company H ended up near Stoughton's second position at the D-shaped field, extending his new line to the right (north) with Company H on the left of Scribner.

A letter from Stoughton to Abbott, dated October 31, 1887, verifies this positioning. Stoughton wrote, "You recollect our men were deployed in the Lane running from the Emmettsburg Pike to the big round top passing the Slyder house just before coming to the little run near where Maj. Powell was wounded, and the left ran round onto the Stone Wall enclosing the little plateau at the foot of the mountain and where you all made so stubborn a stand Co. F & B at your left and the others more or less of them congregated along there & gave some sharp resistance as testified to by Col. Oates of 15th Alabama."[17] Companies B and F were to the left of Company H and the others, that is, Scribner and his men, were to the right of Company H, all congregated behind the stone fence.

---

14. Kellogg and Kellogg, *The Curtis Abbott Papers*, 257.
15. Norton, *War Papers*.
16. Benedict, *Vermont in the Civil War*, 767. As a reminder, Curtis Abbott said Company H retreated in the direction from which they had advanced, that is, to the east toward the Round Tops, following a logging trail that ran south of Little Round Top.
17. Kellogg and Kellogg, *The Curtis Abbott Papers*, 214.

Five—Fall Back or Be Killed 121

Oliver Norton, who was with the 83rd Pennsylvania on Little Round Top, wrote that from his perspective, there were only three companies with Stoughton in front of Big Round Top.[18] Unfortunately, Oliver Norton does not identify the three companies, but he was likely referring just to 2nd Sharpshooters companies B, F, and H, since Scribner and his scouts were members of a patrol and not a recognized company. However, Confederate colonel William C. Oates, in a March 28, 1898, letter to Dr. F.A. Dearborn, verifies that there were four companies along the stone fence at the western base of Big Round Top. Oates wrote, "I have talked with Col Stoughton who was Lt Col & in command of the 4 companies of sharpshooters of the 2nd U S whom we incountered at the foot of the mountain on the south side [i.e., the west slope of Big Round Top]."[19] Additionally, a newspaper article states that after a stubborn resistance, strewing the field with dead and wounded in the meadow west of the Slyder house, Stoughton and *four companies* of sharpshooters had to retire over the hill in their rear (Big Round Top) but rallied and made a stand in a smooth field (Slyder's D-shaped field) on a table land a quarter way up the slope.[20] Stoughton, in his official report, never says how many companies fell back to Big Round Top, only that his left wing fell back. Company H fought alongside and to the right of companies B and F. Factoring in Scribner's scouts (with Norton attached), Stoughton's new line could be described as being comprised of four companies, and these are likely the four companies Oates is referring to in his letter, as no other Union troops were in that location at that time.

Although Stoughton did not mention Scribner and Company H in his official report, much later he acknowledged their contribution to the defense of his second position, stating, "In the engagement on the 2d of July, when Longstreet attacked us, these two companies, E and H, were in the thickest of the fight, and when the Fifteenth Alabama struck us they stood their ground and entered into that fight with great zeal."[21] Technically, Company E fell back to the north through the 4th Maine line in Plum Run Valley. Norton was from Company E and the squad of scouts contained men from companies E and H, so Stoughton stating

---

18. Norton, *Attack and Defense*, 256.
19. Glenn W. LaFantasie, "William C. Oates Remembers Little Round Top," *Gettysburg Magazine* 21 (July 1999), 61.
20. Editor, "Fights of the Sharpshooters," *The Rutland Weekly Herald and Globe* (Rutland, VT, 1887), 2.
21. Homer R. Stoughton, "Companies E and H, Second United States Sharpshooters," *Revised Roster of Vermont Volunteers, 1861–1866*, compiled by Theodore S. Peck (Montpelier, VT, 1892), 607. In the original quote, Stoughton had the date as 3rd of July. I have changed it to the correct date.

both companies were there was somewhat accurate. Also, the only place the 15th Alabama could strike Scribner and Company H was at this stone fence, as the 15th Alabama was too far south of Slyder Farm to engage these companies. Scribner and Company H most likely faced the 4th Alabama and/or the 5th Texas during the initial Confederate advance near Slyder Farm and engaged those same regiments plus the 4th Texas at the stone fence. It was unlikely, however, that Scribner or Company H engaged the 15th Alabama at the stone fence, as the regiment was still too far south to engage either company at this time.

As the Confederate line advanced through Slyder Farm and toward Plum Run Valley, General Law detached the 44th Alabama to fill the gap in Robertson's Brigade. Law ordered Colonel William F. Perry to move across to the left and attack Smith's Battery on Houck's Ridge. Perry writes, "Having advanced with the brigade down the long slope and through the intervening meadow, it was detached from its place in the line, by order of General Law, and by a flank movement was brought to the extreme left of the brigade. When at a short distance from the stone fence near the base of the mountain General Law informed me that he expected my regiment to take a battery which had been playing on our line from the moment the advance began."[22]

General Law next ordered the 48th Alabama, Colonel James L. Sheffield commanding, to support the 44th Alabama. At about 4:35 p.m., the 44th Alabama, shortly followed by the 48th Alabama, started their move to the left. Law then ordered Oates to change directions. Oates said that he "looked to the rear for the 48th Alabama, and saw it going, under General Law's order, across the rear of our line to the left, it was said, to reinforce the Texas Brigade, which was hotly engaged."[23] Following Law's instructions, the 44th and 48th Alabama continued their flank movement to the left until they passed the 4th and 5th Texas regiments.[24] General Law rode up to Colonel Oates as they were advancing and informed Oates that the 15th and 47th Alabama were on the extreme right of the Confederate line. At this time, Law told Oates to hug the base of Big Round Top going up the valley between the two mountains until he found the Union left, and then Oates was to turn the Union line and do all the damage he could. Law also ordered Lieutenant

---

22. *OR*, 27, pt. 2, 393.
23. Oates, *The War*, 210. There is no official record of Law's order to Colonel James L. Sheffield, directing the 48th Alabama to attack the battery or support the 44th Alabama. Neither Law nor Sheffield references that order in their reports; only Oates verifies Law's order to Sheffield. The Texas Brigade mentioned is Robertson's 1st Texas and 3rd Arkansas near Houck's Ridge.
24. *Maine at Gettysburg*, 162–163; W.F. Perry, "The Devil's Den," *Confederate Veteran* 9, no. 4 (April 1901), 161; *OR*, 27, pt. 2, 394.

Colonel Bulger to keep the 47th close to the 15th Alabama, and if separated from Law's brigade, Bulger would act under Oates's orders.[25]

When Law ordered the 48th Alabama to the left, the 4th and 5th Texas and the 4th Alabama were approaching Big Round Top. The innumerable obstacles and harassment from Union weaponry quickly disorganized the Confederate lines as the Texas and Alabama regiments advanced across the open ground of Slyder Farm. Val Giles of the 4th Texas said, "We were now about 400 yards from the timber. The fire from the enemy, both artillery and musketry, was fearful. In making that long charge, our brigade got jammed. Regiments lapped over each other, and when we reached the woods and climbed the mountains as far as we could go, we were a badly mixed crowd." Additionally, William A. Fletcher of the 5th Texas wrote that when they struck the foot of Big Round Top, they found it "rough and rocky, with large boulders now and then, so their lines were not at all times well closed."[26]

The early advantage was again clearly with the sharpshooters. The disorganized Confederate line prevented the three regiments from making a coordinated attack on the sharpshooters' position. Furthermore, Scribner's squad and Company H were on tactically advantageous high ground behind the stone fence and were well prepared to engage the approaching Confederate regiments. During the Confederate advance from Emmitsburg Road, the sharpshooters had already "killed and wounded a great many."[27] When the Confederate line arrived at Plum Run, Company H and Scribner's squad of scouts again plied their deadly skills.

Several Confederate participants described the action as they approached Big Round Top. Mark Smither of the 5th Texas wrote to his wife, saying, "We advanced through a field about half a mile before we reached the timber at the foot of the mountain. Our men tumbling out of ranks at every step, knocked over by the enemy's sharpshooters who lined the side of the mountain."[28] Colonel Lawrence H. Scruggs of the 4th Alabama said, "We advanced up the mountain under a galling fire."[29] William Fletcher with the 5th Texas commented, "We soon were near enough the enemy's line for them to open fire. We had but a poor chance to retaliate with much effect. Our men near me commenced

---

25. Oates, *The War*, 210; *OR*, 27, pt. 2, 392.
26. Mary Lasswell, *Rags and Hope: The Recollections of Val C. Giles, Four Years with Hood's Brigade, Fourth Texas Infantry, 1861–1865* (New York, 1961), 179; Fletcher, *Rebel Private*, 73.
27. *OR*, 27, pt. 1, 518.
28. Joseph L. Owen and Randy S. Drais, eds., "Private John Marquis 'Mark' Smither—Fifth Texas Infantry," *Texans at Gettysburg* (Croydon, England, 2016), 130.
29. *OR*, 27, pt. 2, 391.

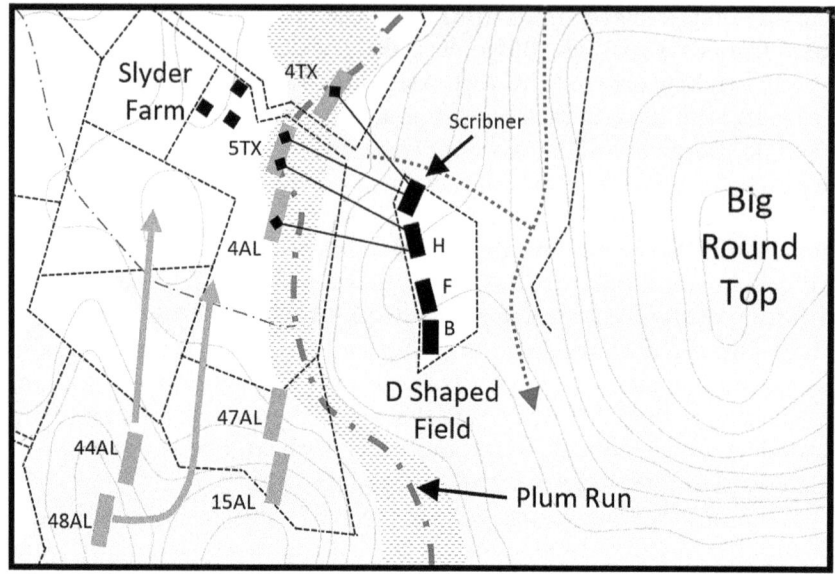

The 4th and 5th Texas and the 4th Alabama start taking fire from the 2nd Sharpshooters, while the 44th and 48th Alabama change direction to the north to assist Robertson's Texas Brigade near Devil's Den.

falling rapidly."[30] Major John P. Bane of the 4th Texas described the engagement as a "sharp contest," suggesting a violent encounter. He wrote, "I met the enemy in full force in a heavy, wooded ground sheltering themselves behind rocks, from which, after a sharp contest, he was driven to the heights beyond in our front and in close proximity to the mountain."[31] From the Sharpshooters' viewpoint, Corporal Curtis Abbott wrote, "The enemy's further advance upon Round Top was slow. No surprised and panic-stricken host fled before them—the surprise was to themselves that their numbers were diminishing before a mere skirmish line, which receded as they advanced. Yet they pressed forward cautiously from rock to rock."[32]

The marshy ground of Plum Run and the enticement of the stream itself presented additional problems for the advancing Confederates. Besides being a physical obstacle that slowed down the advance, the lure of cool water to thirsty soldiers was a big distraction. Men slowed down or stopped, unwittingly presenting the sharpshooters with ideal targets. W.C. Ward with the 4th Alabama wrote, "As we dashed into the

---

30. Fletcher, *Rebel Private*, 73.
31. *OR*, 27, pt. 2, 411.
32. Kellogg and Kellogg, *The Curtis Abbott Papers*, 257.

slow-running water. Billy [Marshall] stooped, supporting himself on his left hand, without kneeling, holding his musket in his right hand, and drank as an animal might have done. I never saw him afterwards. Without doubt, he was killed before he reached the mountain."[33] The sharpshooters' gunfire further thinned the Confederate ranks as they crossed the swampy marsh of Plum Run.

The 4th Texas plunged through Plum Run into the woods of Big Round Top and advanced straight to the stone fence. Captain Decimus Barziza of Company C, 4th Texas said, "On we go ... jumping over and plunging through creeks, pulling through mud, struggling through underbrush, still keeping up the loud, irregular and terrible Confederate yell. Suddenly we find ourselves at the base of a range of hills—a rough, woody, rocky country. Here the great severity of the Federal Infantry stopped our progress, and then commenced a rapid, continuous, and murderous musketry fight; we at the base, they on the sides of the hill. From behind trees and huge rocks we poured in our fiery discharges; the din was incessant and deafening."[34] J.B. Polley, also with the 4th Texas, wrote, "The enemy stood their ground bravely, until we were close on them, but did not await the bayonet." Polley continued, "We closed in with a rush and a wild rebel yell."[35]

Scribner's scouts and Company H were both understrength, and as the Texas regiments got closer the contest became quite uneven as two small companies of about 40 sharpshooters engaged three regiments totaling over 900 men.[36] Furthermore, the sharpshooters, likely seeing in the distance the 48th Alabama moving northward, may have assumed that the Alabama regiment was moving to flank the sharpshooters, as opposed to their actual mission of continuing northward to support the 44th Alabama.

The 4th Alabama reached the foot of the mountain and halted for a few minutes to reform the line. Likewise, the 5th Texas stopped further up the mountain at the stone fence, allowing those who had fallen behind to regain their places in line.[37] These two regiments stop-

---

33. W.C. Ward, "Incidents and Personal Experiences on the Battlefield at Gettysburg," *Confederate Veteran* 8, no. 8 (August 1900), 347.
34. Henley, "Benjamin F. Carter," 16; R. Henderson Shuffler, ed., *The Adventures of a Prisoner of War 1863–1864* (Austin, TX, 1964), 45.
35. J.B. Polley, *Hood's Texas Brigade, Its Marches, Its Battles, Its Achievements* (New York and Washington, D.C., 1910), 168–169.
36. Scribner's squad of scouts numbered about 15 men. Company H consisted of approximately 25 men. The combined engaged strength of the three Confederate regiments was approximately 1,150 men. Factoring in losses up that that point, 900 seems like a reasonable estimate.
37. *OR*, 27, pt. 2, 391, 412; Stocker, *From Huntsville*, 104.

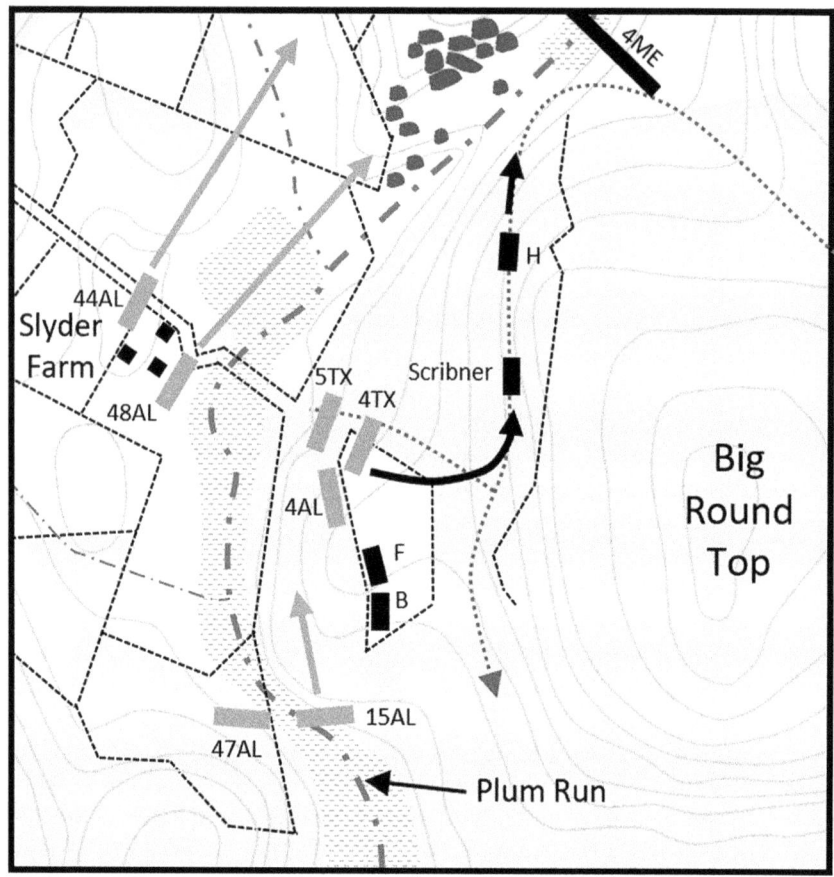

Scribner and Company H retreat eastward toward Big Round Top; the 44th and 48th Alabama continue their advance northward. Oates with the 15th and 47th Alabama left wheels to begin their advance north along the base of Big Round Top.

ping to reform their lines allowed the 4th Texas to reach and cross the stone fence first; however, the enemy was not behind the fence. Sharpshooter Corporal Curtis Abbott of Company H wrote, "Captain Buxton who should have obeyed rather than commanded shouted the order 'Retreat!' which [caused] our regiment to fall back from its strong position. A young man of his company, not above 3d Sargeant in rank, criticized his captain freely saying you are opening those hills to the enemy but the stonewall had been deserted."[38]

While crossing the fence the 4th Texas took devastating flank

---

38. Kellogg and Kellogg, *The Curtis Abbott Papers*, 214.

Five—Fall Back or Be Killed

fire.[39] With the 4th Alabama and 5th Texas yet to cross the stone fence, the 4th Texas caught the full attention of the sharpshooters. It is unknown where the flank fire came from, but the only logical source would be from Scribner's squad of scouts to the left of the advancing 4th Texas. By the time the Texas and Alabama regiments crossed the fence, Captain Buxton with Company H had retreated eastward across the D-shaped field, toward Big Round Top. Scribner might not have initially noticed that Buxton had retreated. Alexander Rose illustrated this, writing, "Combat, in any battle, is inherently chaotic, and most of the time the soldiers fighting on the ground have little or no idea what is happening even fifty yards away."[40] Upon seeing the 4th Texas cross the fence, Scribner's squad likely fired one volley into the advancing enemy and then retreated themselves. Both Buxton and Scribner crossed the D-shaped field and then moved along the farm road as it veered northward, essentially following the road back toward Little Round Top, that is, the same farm road Company H advanced on earlier that afternoon.

It is also quite possible that Company F did not know that the right of their line retreated and that the 4th Texas had cleared the stone fence. Company F, with Company B on their left, was on the far side of a slight rise of ground and slightly pointed away from the 4th Texas. None of the three Confederate regiments tried to attack Company F, so it is likely the rise of ground in conjunction with the stone fence and smoke from the engagement that just ended concealed Stoughton's two left companies. It would not be surprising for a soldier to miss the enemy completely under these circumstances.

As the 4th Alabama reformed their line and rushed up to the stone fence, the men dropped to their knees to fix bayonets and then jumped the fence, expecting bullets to riddle them. W.C. Ward of the 4th Alabama said this action "was the act of a moment, not minutes. Looking around, this soldier saw his comrades quickly coming over the wall and forming into a line of battle. The enemy had retreated up the sides of the mountain."[41] R.T. Cole wrote, "The 4th Alabama at the point of the bayonet routed the enemy from behind a stone fence upon reaching the foot of the mountain."[42] Cole's statement is questionable because by the time the 4th Alabama reached the wall, as Ward pointed out, the sharpshooters in their front (Scribner and Company H) were already gone, and no other accounts indicate the 4th Alabama attacked Company F to their

---

39. Henley, "Benjamin F. Carter," 16.
40. Alexander Rose, *Men of War: The American Soldier in Combat at Bunker Hill, Gettysburg, and Iwo Jima* (New York, 2015), 7.
41. Ward, "Incidents," 347.
42. Stocker, *From Huntsville*, 104.

right. Lieutenant Colonel King Bryan of Company F, 5th Texas, wrote in his official report that "every man leaped the fence, and advanced rapidly up the hillside. The enemy again fled at our approach, sheltering himself behind his fortified position on the top of the second height, about 200 yards distant from the first."[43] The 4th Alabama and the 4th and 5th Texas crossed the western slope of Big Round Top, reformed their lines, and marched in columns into the valley between the two Round Tops. Their next objective was to seize Little Round Top.[44]

Major Stoughton's line is now somewhat fragmented. On the left of his line, companies B and F are still behind the stone fence, eyeing the approaching Confederate line comprised of the 15th and 47th Alabama. The right of his line has retreated with Company H and Scribner, heading northward on the east side of Plum Run Valley, following the Slyder farm road as it veered to the north. On the east end of the field, Norton wrote, they came upon a wagon road that they followed northward into the wooded depression between the Round Tops.[45] This road belongs to the same network of wagon roads as the one described by Hood's scouts (see Chapter Three). Youngblood wrote that the scouts described the road as "a wagon road *around* Round Top, at its foot, which has been used by farmers getting out timber"[46] (emphasis added).

Norton described the road they followed when Scribner and Norton retreated from Slyder Farm, stating, "I kept to the left, down the cross road [Slyder farm road] towards Little Round Top, with my small squad of scouts. In the woods (into which this cross road ran) between Little Round Top and Big Round Top."[47] Norton was on a road, in the woods, between the Round Tops, and his description is that of a continuous road. This wagon road does not appear on the Warren map, suggesting that either that between the time of the battle and the creation of the map, vegetation reclaimed the landscape and the wagon road essentially disappeared, or that the wagon trail was a minor road and was intentionally left off the map.

However, three other sources described the road Norton followed, two from H.C. Parsons with the 1st Vermont Cavalry and one editorial submission describing cavalry actions on July 3, 1863. In summarizing, the authors state that in the intervening valley is the Slyder Farm. Projecting from Round Top was a hill, perhaps 100 feet high, on the top of which was a field (Slyder D-shaped field) surrounded by high stone

---

43. OR, 27, pt. 2, 412. The second height is Little Round Top.
44. Norton, *Attack and Defense*, 173–174; Stocker, *From Huntsville*, 104.
45. Norton, *War Papers*, 13.
46. Youngblood, "Unwritten History," 314.
47. Norton, *War Papers*, 12–13.

FIVE—*Fall Back or Be Killed*

walls. A road or lane (Slyder farm road) extended from the Emmitsburg Pike to its base (hill projecting from Round Top) *and then turned to the left toward Devil's Den and thence between the Round Tops.* They went on to say the road "stretched southward along the side of Round Top, east of the plateau [Slyder D-shaped field] and that beyond this road was a *high rail fence*," a fence that is visible on the Warren map[48] (emphasis added). This is the same road that Corporal Curtis Abbott described at the south base of Little Round Top, and the one upon which Company H advanced, connecting with the Slyder farm road as the regiment formed up earlier that afternoon.

Two accounts from 5th Texas soldiers also mention this fence. A soldier with Company H, writing anonymously, said, "They attempted to rally behind this barrier [the stone fence], but we never stopped, and, with a rush, pressed them onward till we came to a *stake-and-rider fence* at the foot of Sugar Loaf Mountain, beyond which was heavy timber and rocks. Over the fence once we swept on up the mountain, climbing with great difficulty, occasionally pulling each other up on account of the rocks" (emphasis added).[49] J.W. Stevens wrote, "There was a stone fence [on the west side of the D-shaped field] 500 or 600 yards in our front, behind which we expected to find the enemy. Onto it we rushed, no Yankees there. Then 400 or 500 yards further [the east side of the D-shaped field] there is a *rail fence, just in the edge of the timber.* We expect to find the enemy there. Onto it we move at a charge, but, no Yankee there. Over the fence we go, and through this timber, 200 or 300 yards, and we came to the foot of the mountain [Little Round Top]" (emphasis added).[50] The fence was there, and the road was there. Knowing their locations, an estimate of Scribner's movement on the battlefield is possible, which will be important for two upcoming interactions.

While the three regiments on Law's left attacked Stoughton's right, Colonel William C. Oates, commanding the 15th Alabama, changed the direction of the 15th and 47th Alabama in accordance with General Law's directive. As previously mentioned, Stoughton, Wyman White, and Charles Stevens do not mention the action at this stone fence. Fortunately, Colonel Oates wrote at length about this encounter.

---

48. H.C. Parsons, "Farnsworth's Charge and Death," *Battles and Leaders of the Civil War: Volume 3, The Tide Shifts* (Secaucus, NJ, 2010), 393; H.C. Parsons, "A Cavalry Charge," *National Tribune* (Washington, D.C., 1890), 1; Editor, "The Famous Cavalry Charge," *The Rutland Weekly Herald and Globe* (Rutland, VT, 1887), 2.
49. Anonymous, "Pickett's and Hood's Charges at Gettysburg," *The Southern Bivouac* 3, no. 2 (October 1884), 76–77. The hill was Big Round Top, not "Sugar Loaf Mountain."
50. J.W. Stevens, *Reminiscences of the Civil War: A Soldier in Hood's Texas Brigade, Army of Northern Virginia* (Hillsboro, TX, 1902), 114.

Combining Oates's commentary with accounts from other participants allows one to piece the engagement together.

Soon after receiving updated orders from General Law, Oates left-wheeled his two regiments and began moving to the north with the 15th Alabama on the right, crossing Plum Run. He called it a "small muddy, meandering stream," the muddy nature the consequence of three Confederate regiments crossing the run upstream from Oates just moments earlier. The 15th Alabama now approached the foot of Big Round Top.[51] At this point, sharpshooter companies B and F, behind the stone fence on Stoughton's left, fired into the 15th Alabama's right and flank.[52]

Stoughton's only comment in his official report is, "My left wing retreated up the hill and allowed the enemy to pass up the ravine, when they poured a destructive fire into his flank and rear."[53] Stoughton's attack point, "flank and rear," differs from where Oates says Stoughton's men hit his line, "right and flank." Oates wrote in a letter to Stoughton after the war and said, "Our advance of 150 yards further without change of direction would have presented my right flank to your left, had your line been parallel; but as your right was retired in conformity to the ground, you had partly a front and partly a right oblique fire on me.[54] Stoughton's men hit the right front and flank of Oates' line, but not the rear." So, what is Stoughton referring to?

Stoughton also said that the enemy went up the ravine and then fired into their flank and rear, which was a separate, second attack and happened later in the day, after the encounter at the stone fence. When Stoughton attacks Oates for a second time that day, as described in Chapter Six, Stoughton attacks the flank and rear of Oates's line. Stoughton, in his official report, skipped the stone fence fight and went right to the next encounter later that afternoon.

Receiving no orders, Oates did not vary his course until he received the second fire, which wounded several of his men.[55] The woods to Oates's right concealed the sharpshooters. Oates said, "I could not know what force was there and I knew that it would not do to go on and leave a force, I knew not how large, in my rear and the 48th our reserve which

---

51. Oates, *The War*, 210; Oates, "Battle on the Right," 174; William C. Oates, "Letter to Col. H.R. Stoughton, Nov. 22, 1888," *Berdan's United States Sharpshooters in the Army of the Potomac, 1861–1865* (St. Paul, MN, 1892), 327.

52. Oates, *The War*, 210; *OR*, 27, pt. 2, 392; William C. Oates, *Letter to J.L. Chamberlain, 8 March 1897* (Gettysburg, PA, 1897).

53. *OR*, 27, pt. 1, 519.

54. Oates, "Letter to Col. H.R. Stoughton," 327.

55. Oates, "Letter to Col. H.R. Stoughton," 326–327; Oates, *The War*, 210–211; Oates, *Letter to J.L. Chamberlain*.

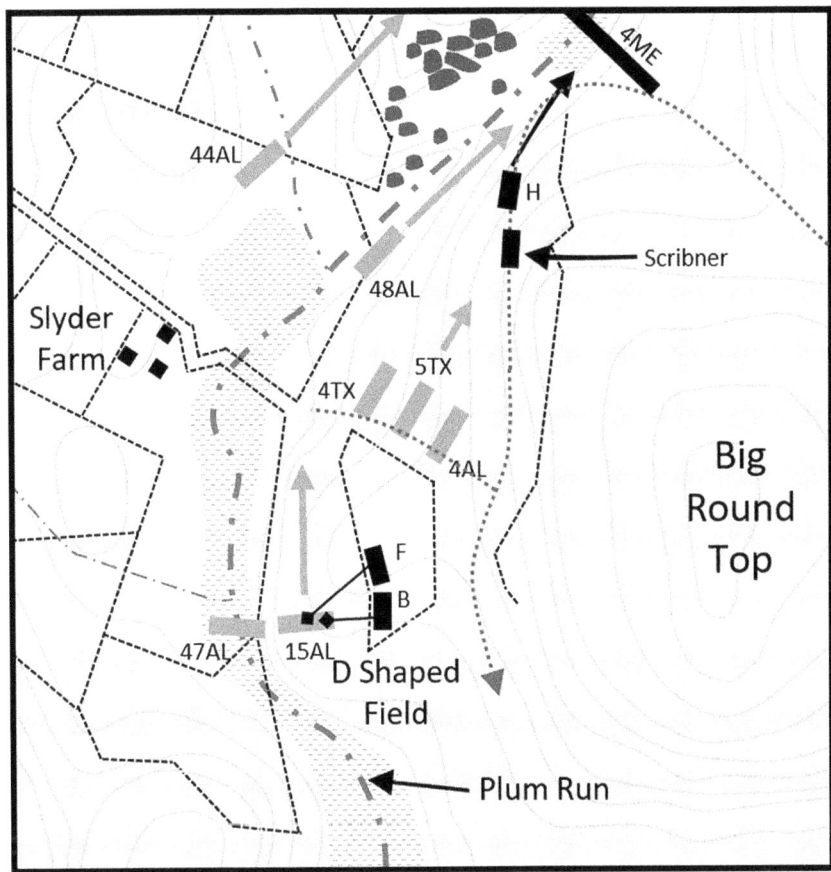

The 15th and 47th Alabama receive fire from companies B and F hidden behind the stone fence. Scribner and Company H continue their northward retreat along the old logging road.

started behind me to meet just such contingencies had been carried across our rear to the left and that left no one in my rear or on my right to meet this foe."[56] Under these circumstances Oates changed direction by wheeling to the right, swinging around far enough to advance on companies B and F at the stone fence, and advanced with the 15th and 47th Alabama. The seven companies of the 47th swung around with the 15th and kept in line with it.[57]

The two Alabama regiments advanced toward the stone fence,

---

56. Oates, *Letter to J.L. Chamberlain*; Oates, *The War*, 210.
57. Oates, "Letter to Col. H.R. Stoughton," 326–327; Oates, *The War*, 210–211; Oates, *Letter to J.L. Chamberlain*; Peteler, "Narrative of the First Company," 508.

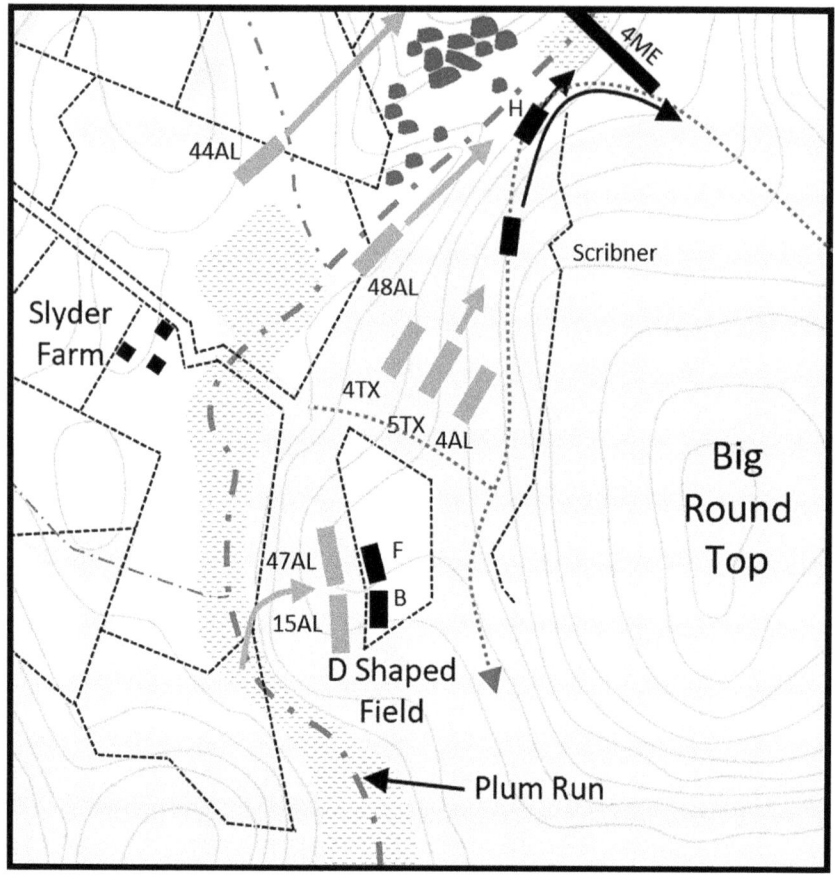

After taking a second volley from the sharpshooters, Oates changes direction to the east and engages the sharpshooters behind the stone fence.

behind which stood the two understrength sharpshooter companies. Even so, companies B and F put up a stubborn resistance.[58] Major Stoughton wrote, "The left of my line swung back onto the mountain among the rocks where the regiment did splendid execution ... of the advancing Rebels."[59] William Jordan with Company B, 15th Alabama, described the action, writing, "In the charge a great many were killed and wounded, many did not get over the stone fence, or through the valley to the base of the next ridge."[60] In a letter to his wife, Colonel James

---

58. Norton, *Attack and Defense*, 174.
59. Ladd and Ladd, *The Batchelder Papers: Volume 2*, 767. The original has "The *right* of my line," which is incorrect and should be "The *left* of my line."
60. William C. Jordan, *Some Events and Incidents During the Civil War* (Montgomery, AL, 1909), 42.

W. Jackson of the 47th Alabama described the sharpshooter's fire, writing, "We stopped for a moment behind a stone fence, the only covering from the place we had started to the foot of the mountain. I gave them only a moment to rest and gave the order to advance. Then the slaughter commenced in earnest. We were in good range of the sharp shooters, but we could get no crack at them from the fact they were entrenched behind stone fences. We got in about a hundred yards of the first line when the men gave a shout and charged it at double quick. The Yanks waited until we came in forty or fifty paces and gave way and fled." Colonel Jackson, in another letter written to the Montgomery Daily Mail, described the carnage left in the wake of the sharpshooter's retreat, writing, "The dark and bloody ground told wither they had gone."[61]

Sharpshooter companies B and F retreated through the woods and up the west side of Big Round Top, closely followed by the 15th and 47th Alabama. The sharpshooters kept up a lively fire on the advancing Confederate line, which returned fire but without much success. Oates claimed their ineffectiveness was due to the sharpshooters "being trained sharpshooters and skirmishers, [that] kept well under cover, taking advantage of the bowlders which line the mountain side."[62]

After crossing the stone fence, General Law ordered Oates to left wheel his two regiments and move toward Little Round Top on his left. Oates failed to obey this order since he was rapidly advancing up Big Round Top and heavily engaged with two companies of sharpshooters. Moreover, Oates would have had great difficulty turning his line as the 47th Alabama on his left was crowding and running into the 15th Alabama, causing considerable confusion. Oates, therefore, continued to press forward.[63] Stoughton's two companies continued up the west side of Big Round Top, firing down just enough to lure Oates on, as he could only catch glimpses of the sharpshooters dodging from boulder to boulder. Midway up the hill, the sharpshooters disappeared. Oates could not tell which way they went in the dense timber and foliage, so he advanced his two regiments toward the top of Big Round Top.[64]

As companies B and F retreated up Big Round Top's west side, Company H continued northward on the east side of Plum Run, continuing to retreat in the direction from which they advanced, and soon approached the 4th Maine line. Scribner, his scouts, and Norton were still on the old wagon road that had turned eastward running between

---

61. James W. Jackson, "Letter to wife, July 7, 1863" (Gettysburg, PA, 1863), 2; James W. Jackson, "Letter to Montgomery Daily Mail, July 26, 1863" (Gettysburg, PA, 1863), 1.
62. Oates, "Letter to Stoughton," 327.
63. *OR*, 27, pt. 2, 392.
64. Oates, *Letter to J.L. Chamberlain*, 5.

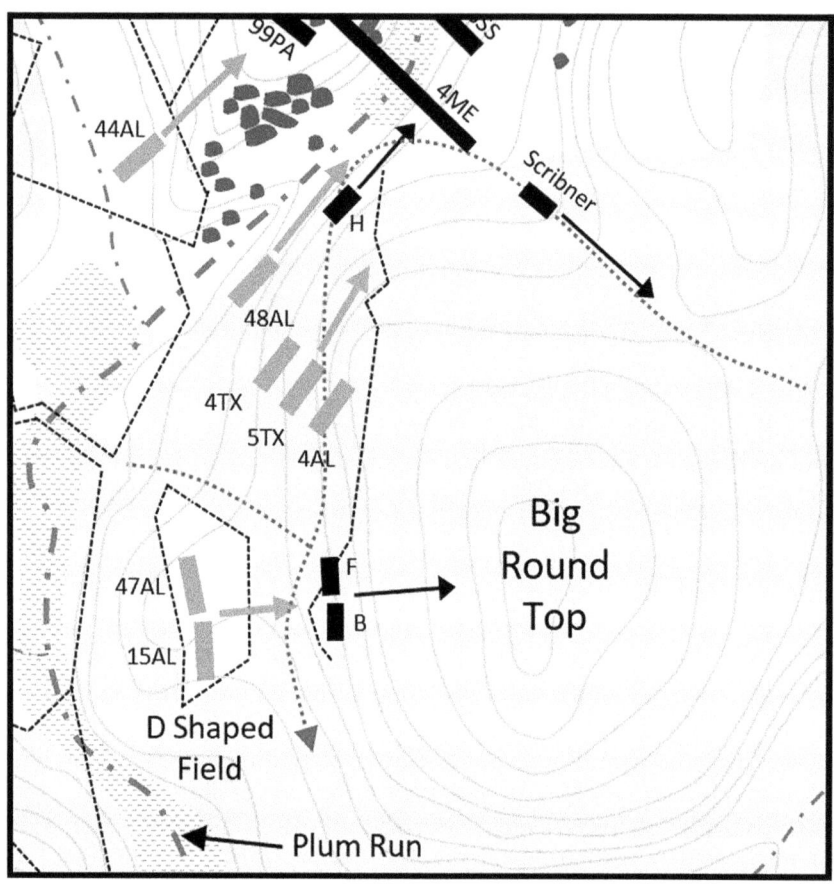

Scribner and Company H become separated in the woods. Company H continues to retreat in the direction from which it advanced earlier in the afternoon, while Scribner and his squad of scouts follow the logging trail in between the Round Tops. Companies B and F retreat up Big Round Top, pursued by the 15th and 47th Alabama.

the Round Tops.[65] As Scribner reached this position, Norton wrote that they stumbled upon some men from the left wing of his regiment, apparently lost and separated from their company. These men joined up with Scribner's squad. Norton described later, "These scouts under my command, and some few others from the left of our Regiment which we then ran across took a position on the side of Big Round Top."[66] These

---

65. Norton, *War Papers*, 13.
66. *Ibid.*, 14–15. Again, the 15 sharpshooters were under the command of Sergeant Scribner, as previously described.

"some few others from the left of our regiment" that Norton "ran across" were men from Company H, since companies F and B were still on the west side of Big Round Top, retreating from the 15th and 47th Alabama regiments. These Company H men joined Scribner's scouts after becoming separated in the woods as their company retreated along the east side of Plum Run.

Oates continued to advance straight up Big Round Top as the sharpshooters took every advantage afforded by the nature of the ground to hinder and break the force of the attack.[67] Private Wyman White of Company F described the retreat, writing, "then up over the western slope of the Big Round Top. It was mostly wooded, and large boulders and granite were thickly set in so they gave us a splendid cover from which to oppose the enemy's advance. But with all our advantage, our loss was considerable for the enemy kept up a terrible fire and we fell back no faster than we were obliged to, so when we skipped from one boulder to another the rebels had very good opportunities to get in their murderous work. An occasional lull in the fire would be followed by a terrific volley and the bullets would snap on the rocks and spat on the trunks of the trees and glance off with a peculiar screech that a rifle or musket ball is famous for when it comes in contact with something hard and glances off."[68]

As the two Alabama regiments advanced up Big Round Top, they had to "climb up, catching to the rocks and bushes and crawling over the immense boulders, in the face of an incessant fire of the enemy."[69] The sharpshooters kept falling back, taking shelter and "firing down on them from behind the rocks and crags that covered the mountain side thicker than grave stones in a city cemetery."[70] Oates observed, "My men could not see their foe, and did not fire, except as one was seen here and there, running back from one boulder to another.[71] The forty-seventh Alabama regiment was on my immediate left, had kept in line with me during the ascent and halted in line with my regiment on Round Top."[72]

Oates continued, "As we advanced up the mountain, the sharpshooters ceased firing about halfway up, divided, and disappeared from my sight as though commanded by a magician."[73] Interestingly, Colonel James Jackson of the 47th Alabama wrote something similar

---

67. Oates, *The War*, 211; Oates, "Letter to Stoughton," 327.
68. White, *Civil War Diary*, 164–165.
69. Oates, "Battle of the Right," 174; Oates, *The War*, 211.
70. Ibid.
71. Oates, "Battle of the Right," 174–175.
72. Ibid., 175.
73. Ibid.

in a letter to the *Montgomery Daily Mail* newspaper, stating, "the Yankees posted at the foot of the mountain, disappeared before their [Jackson's regiment] fire, like the mist of morn before the sun."[74] The sharpshooters had separated into two groups and retreated around Big Round Top in different directions.[75] The greater number of them, Company F, and about half of Company B, hereafter denoted as B_1, went to the left. Major Stoughton and the remainder of Company B, denoted as B_2, went to the right.[76] The men in B_2 fired a few shots at Oates's flank forcing him to dispatch Company A from the 15th Alabama in pursuit, driving the Stoughton and the B_2 sharpshooters down the eastern side of Big Round Top.[77] Oates said when Company A left in pursuit of the sharpshooters, he did not see the company again until after the battle. Oates, with the 47th Alabama, continued his advance to the top of the mountain, not seeing any Union forces on the way to the summit.[78]

In Plum Run Valley, General Ward placed only the 4th Maine, Colonel Elijah Walker commanding, before Little Round Top. The 4th Maine, to the left of Smith's battery, had one company on Houck's Ridge, while the rest of the regiment extended across Plum Run Valley to the side of Big Round Top.[79] Lieutenant Charles F. Sawyer, 4th Maine adjutant, reported that "some of the Second U.S. Sharpshooters fell back through our line, and reported the enemy advancing a column on the hill to flank us, at the same time a few shots of the enemy were fired on our flank."[80] These retreating sharpshooters were "most of Company H" that had fallen back along the east side of Plum Run. After abandoning their position on Big Round Top, Company H retreated northward, passing through the 4th Maine line just before the "enemy advancing in column," that is, the 48th Alabama, shot at the 4th Maine line.

It was not long before the 48th Alabama emerged from thin growth that fringed Plum Run in the front of Walker's regiment.[81] Lieutenant Sawyer wrote, "A column of the enemy was then seen moving rapidly to our left, not over 50 yards distant, in the woods. The position of the regiment was then changed to engage the enemy on our left when we

---

74. Jackson, "Letter to Montgomery Daily Mail," 1.
75. Purifoy, "Lost Opportunity," 217; Oates, *The War*, 211; Oates, *Letter to J.L. Chamberlain*, 6.
76. Norton, *Attack and Defense*, 257.
77. Ibid.
78. Oates, *The War*, 211; Oates, "Letter to Stoughton," 327.
79. *OR*, 27, pt. 1, 509.
80. *Ibid.*
81. *Maine at Gettysburg*, 163–164; *OR*, 27, pt. 1, 509.

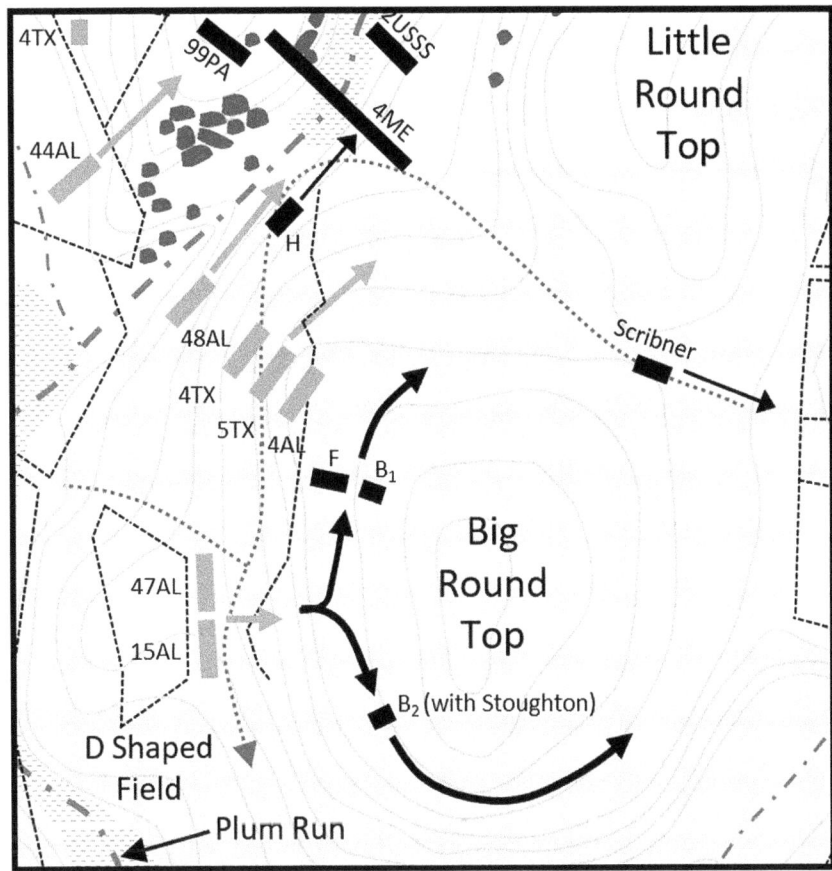

The 2nd Sharpshooters divides about halfway up the west side of Big Round Top, with companies F and B_1 going left and Stoughton with B_2 going right.

engaged them, they paying no attention to our firing, 5 to 8 rounds being expended before they returned the fire, which came on our front and left flank."[82]

General Evander Law had earlier informed Colonel William Perry that he expected the 44th Alabama to take Smith's battery, which had been playing on Law's line from the moment the advance began. This battery was situated not on Little Round Top but on Houck's Ridge, with a valley between them, the valley being destitute of trees and filled with immense boulders. The valley also contained Union infantry. Perry ordered the 44th Alabama forward and then wheeled to the left,

---

82. *OR*, 27, pt. 1, 509–510.

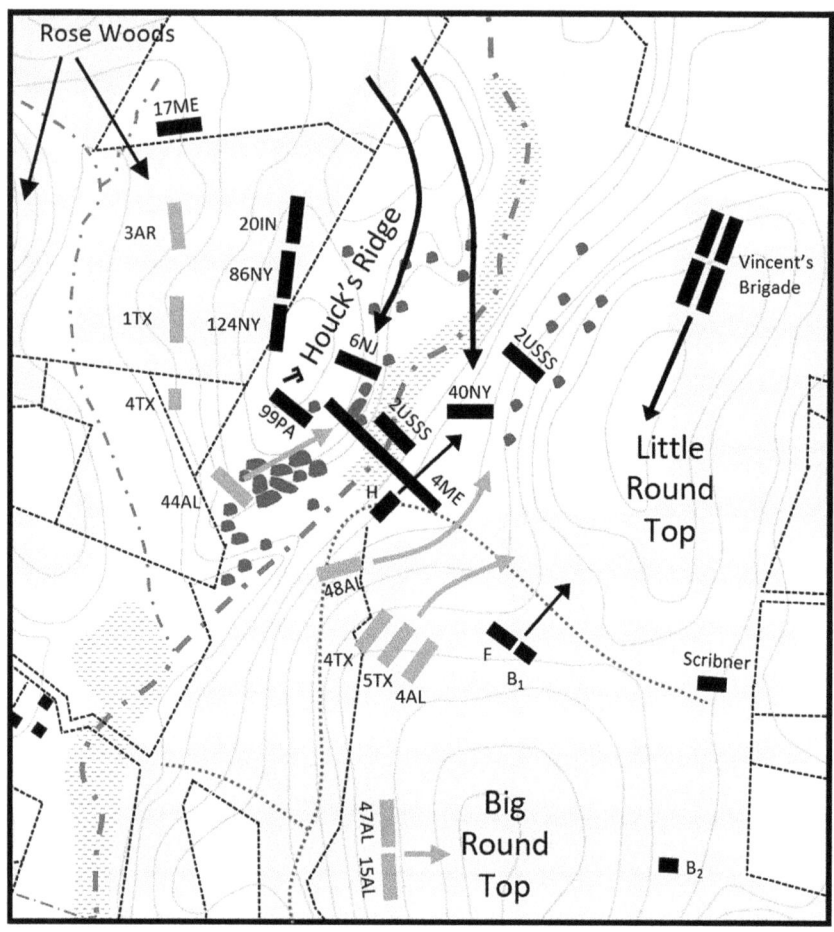

Action in Plum Run Valley. The 2nd Sharpshooters engages the two Alabama regiments. Company H passes through the 4th Maine line, falling back to the base of Little Round Top. Vincent's brigade rushes to the south side of Little Round Top.

its left opposite the battery, and its right extending toward the base of Big Round Top.[83] The 4th Maine immediately opened a destructive fire upon the 44th Alabama while Colonel William F. Perry was forming his lines, and at the same time, Walker arranged the 4th Maine as well as possible to confront the advancing enemy line.[84] Perry's regiment executed their left wheel under fire and within 200 yards of the enemy. As the men approached the valley, they received a deadly volley at short

---

83. *OR*, 27, pt. 2, 393–394.
84. *Maine at Gettysburg*, 163–164.

range. Halting without an order from Perry and availing themselves of the shelter that the rocks afforded, they returned the fire.[85] The 44th Alabama came on in a truly heroic manner; however, the 4th Maine checked the advance and Perry's regiment soon retired into the woods, where the trees and rocks completely concealed them. From behind these natural protections, Perry's men kept up a biting musketry fire upon the 4th Maine, who in the open valley were at a disadvantage and suffered large losses.[86]

The 40th New York and 6th New Jersey advanced into Plum Run Valley to support the 4th Maine and Smith's battery. The 6th New Jersey, Lieutenant Colonel Stephen R. Gilkyson commanding, moved forward, formed a line, and opened fire on the 44th Alabama.[87] The 48th Alabama bypassed the 4th Maine and met the 40th New York, Colonel Thomas W. Egan commanding, farther up the valley. Egan ordered his regiment to charge across the marsh, causing the 48th Alabama to fall back.[88] Colonel Sheffield ordered the 48th Alabama forward again. The regiment gallantly responded until within about 20 paces of the 40th New York line, where Union fire became severe. The 48th Alabama returned fire for some time, but the loss of men and their exposed position forced the regiment to fall back.[89]

During the action in Plum Run Valley, Union Colonel Strong Vincent, supported by First Lieutenant Charles E. Hazlett's Battery, moved to occupy Little Round Top. General Gouverneur K. Warren arrived ahead of Vincent and, upon reaching his observation post, witnessed the first attack of the 44th and 48th Alabama against the four regiments of Sickles's III Corps. The four regiments were the 4th Maine, 40th New York, 6th New Jersey, and 2nd Sharpshooters. As the Confederates advanced closer to Little Round Top, the five companies of sharpshooters, formerly of Stoughton's right wing, "blazed away from behind the rocks at the western base to resist their advance."[90] A moment later, while a party of sharpshooters [Company H] was trying to find shelter among the rocks scattered along the western flank of Little Round Top, the bulk of Ward's brigade began falling back upon the flank of Devil's Den.[91] The sharpshooters helped check the advance of the two Alabama regiments for a while, but the Confederate advance soon overwhelmed

---

85. *OR*, 27, pt. 2, 394.
86. *Maine at Gettysburg*, 164.
87. *OR*, 27, pt. 1, 509, 577; Smith, *A Famous Battery*, 104.
88. *Maine at Gettysburg*, 163; *OR*, 27, pt. 1, 526.
89. *OR*, 27, pt. 2, 395–396.
90. Goss, *Recollections of a Private*, 204.
91. The Comte De Paris, *History of the Civil War*, 615.

Ward's line and ended up losing ground.⁹²

Colonel Perry perceived that Union forces were giving way and ordered the 44th Alabama to advance. Perry's men sprang forward, sweeping the position, and took possession of Houck's Ridge, capturing 40 to 50 prisoners around Smith's battery.⁹³ As the Alabama regiments pushed forward, the 1st and 4th Texas and 3rd Arkansas joined the attack from the west across Houck's Ridge, and a domino effect occurred as the Union troops began to fall back.

Colonel Strong Vincent, commanding the Third Brigade, First Division, V Army Corps. Library of Congress.

Brigadier General Gouverneur K. Warren, Chief Engineer, Army of the Potomac. Library of Congress.

Around 5:53 p.m., Captain James Smith noted that Hazlett's guns from the summit of Little Round Top were firing into the valley, but assistance arrived too late. Smith wrote, "The 4th Maine on the left, with a line across the mouth of the gorge, have been forced back; the situation is most critical."⁹⁴ First to retreat were the troops on Houck's Ridge. As senior officer casualties mounted, the 86th

---

92. The Comte De Paris, *History of the Civil War*, 610–613; Toombs, *New Jersey Troops*, 210–214; William J. Wray, *History of the Twenty Third Pennsylvania Volunteer Infantry, Birney's Zouaves* (Philadelphia, PA, 1904), 395–396.
93. *OR*, 27, pt. 2, 394.
94. Smith, *A Famous Battery*, 103.

FIVE—Fall Back or Be Killed

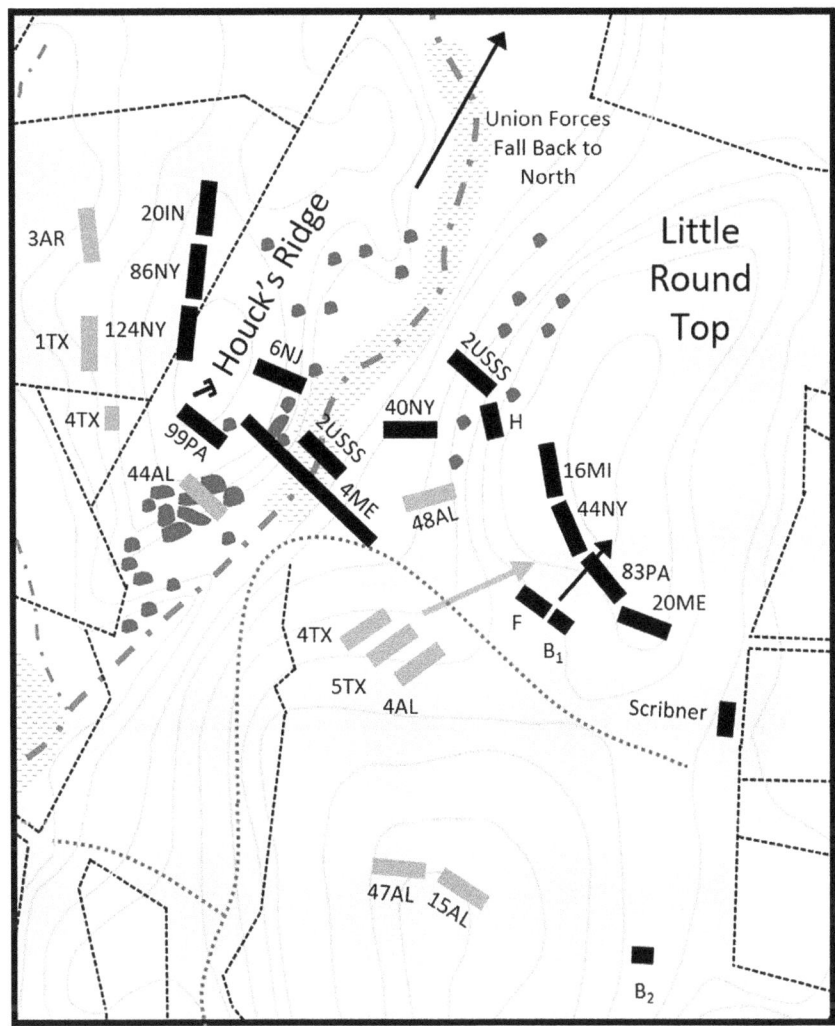

Vincent's brigade deploys on the south end of Little Round Top. Scribner is near a stone fence east of the gap between the Round Tops. Companies B₁ and F cross the Union line as the three Confederate regiments approach. Union forces in the valley eventually retreat to the north.

and 124th New York were likely the first to fall back. Lieutenant Colonel Benjamin Higgins with the 86th New York wrote, "In this position my regiment remained actively engaging the enemy for about half an hour, when, being wounded, I was obliged to leave the line, the major succeeding me in command. The regiment was then ordered [by Assistant

Adjutant Cooney] to about-face and march to the rear."⁹⁵ Lieutenant Colonel Francis M. Cummins with the 124th New York added, "We held this position for over two hours, when, after having lost, in killed and wounded, our colonel, Lieutenant-colonel, and major, 4 line officers and 82 enlisted men, you [Ward] ordered us to fall back."⁹⁶

The 99th Pennsylvania and 20th Indiana fell back upon seeing the brigade beginning to retire. Major John Moore of the 99th Pennsylvania wrote, "I held this position for over thirty minutes, until the brigade began to retire on the right, when I ordered the regiment to fall back slowly, covering the rear." Similarly, Lieutenant Colonel William Taylor of the 20th Indiana stated, "The regiment held the position assigned it until the brigade commenced to retire."⁹⁷

Next, the 6th New Jersey fell back. Lieutenant Colonel Stephen Gilkyson, seeing the troops to his right retiring (those just mentioned fighting on Houck's Ridge), ordered his regiment to retire, which it did in good order, halting with the rest of the troops. The 4th Maine and 40th New York were the last to retreat. Colonel Thomas Egan wrote, "All attempts to dislodge them [48th Alabama] from the second line proving unsuccessful, and discovering that they had gained ground upon my right, which threatened a flank movement, the regiments on my right having fallen to the rear and exposed us to a cross-fire, I was compelled to fall back." The sharpshooters at the base of Little Round Top, Stoughton's right-wing along Company H, fell back with the other regiments and remained with them until night, when the brigade was relieved, at which point the sharpshooters rejoined their regiment.⁹⁸

As the retreat was happening in the valley below, Colonel Oates and his two Alabama regiments rested on the summit of Big Round Top. About five minutes after Oates halted, Captain Leigh R. Terrell, assistant adjutant-general to General Law, rode up along the only pathway on the southeast side of the mountain and inquired why Oates had halted. Oates responded that in his opinion he should hold his current position as it was an especially important one. The position has a precipice on the east and north and a very steep, stony, and wooded mountainside on the west. The only potential enemy approach was a long wooded slope on the northwest. Oates said that given half an hour, he could convert it into a Gibraltar that could hold against 10 times the number of men that he had. Terrell informed Oates that General Law now commanded the division, replacing the wounded General Hood. Law sent

---

95. *OR*, 27, pt. 1, 511.
96. *Ibid.*, 512–513.
97. *Ibid.*, 506, 513.
98. *Ibid.*, 519, 526–527, 577–578.

Oates his compliments and instructions to press on, turn the Union left, capture Little Round Top if possible, and to lose no time in doing so. With the battle raging below, Oates advanced his two regiments down the north side of Big Round Top without encountering any opposition whatsoever.[99]

At this point in the battle, the 2nd Sharpshooters was a scattered regiment.[100] Initially, the regiment had fallen back from Slyder Farm, splitting into two groups, heading in different directions, with the right wing going north and the left wing heading east. Stoughton's right wing further scattered when some of the men stayed in line with the 4th Maine while others fell through the line, heading for cover among the boulders at the base of Little Round Top. The left wing, including Scribner's scouting party, most of Company H, and Major Stoughton, fell back to a defensible position behind a stone fence on the western slope of Big Round Top. The advance of the Alabama and Texas regiments scattered Stoughton's left wing as Scribner retreated to the east and north, Company H retreated northward, and companies F and B retreated eastward up Big Round Top. Scribner and Company H separated again as Company H headed to the base of Little Round Top while Scribner went into the gap between the Round Tops. Retreating up Big Round Top, companies F and B split into two groups, going in opposite directions around the hill. The task of delaying the advancing Confederate line had succeeded; however, the sharpshooters' cohesiveness as an organized regiment that day had passed. The fighting over the last hour and a half had indeed scattered the regiment, but Colonel Berdan had trained the men for just such emergencies, and every man could fight his own battle.[101] Even scattered as they were, the sharpshooters were still in the fight.

---

99. Oates, *The War*, 212–213; Oates, "Battle on the Right," 175.
100. Hamlin, "The Battle of Gettysburg," 350–351.
101. *Ibid.*

Six

Among the Boulders
Defending Little Round Top

(5:00 p.m. to 8:00 p.m.)

In war, you win or lose, live or die—and the difference is just an eyelash.[1]

Colonel Strong Vincent's command (Third Brigade, First Division, V Corps), with Colonel Joshua L. Chamberlain's 20th Maine in the lead, clambered up the eastern slopes of Little Round Top. The men continued to the southern slope, descending into the area between the two Round Tops, and formed their line.[2] As Vincent moved his brigade into position, the retreating sharpshooters, companies B, F, and H, and Sergeant Scribner's scouts were all going in different directions on and around Big Round Top.

As discussed at the end of the last chapter, companies F and B_1 went to the left halfway up Big Round Top, continuing in that direction across the gap between the Round Tops, ending up near the summit of Little Round Top.[3] Wyman White wrote, "We fell back so far before we came to the line of battle. Our company first came upon the 83rd Pennsylvania Regiment laying down among the rocks and trees near the top of the mountain which lay in line not more than a hundred feet from the summit of Little Round Top Mountain."[4] Company B_1 most likely followed Company F through the 83rd Pennsylvania line on Little Round Top and both companies took positions close behind the 83rd Pennsylvania. The two companies remained in this position until the brigade

---

1. Douglas MacArthur, https://www.brainyquote.com/authors/douglas-macarthur-quotes (accessed May 24, 2022).
2. Young, *The Battle of Gettysburg*, 237.
3. White, *Civil War Diary*, 164–165.
4. Ibid., 165.

commander moved Company B_1 about an hour later. Likewise, Major Stoughton and a dozen or so men from Company B_2 veered to the right and circled to the eastern side of Big Round Top. While evading the pursuing men from Oates's Company A, Stoughton and B_2 ended up lost in the woods.[5]

Company H, heading in the general direction of Little Round Top, left the woods east of Plum Run and skirted around the right of the advancing 48th Alabama. Passing through the 4th Maine line, the men from Company H fell in with other sharpshooters from their regiment scattered among the boulders at the western base of Little Round Top. These sharpshooters were within easy range of advancing Confederate troops and "sprinkled the guns with the blood of the men who crowded around them."[6] Additionally, Scribner and his scouts, with Adjutant Norton in tow, continued eastward somewhere between the two Round Tops, winding up near a stone fence.[7]

At about 4:45 p.m., Vincent had his brigade in position, placing each regiment in line down the slope of Little Round Top.[8] The line was a quarter circle, along the base of the hill and the north side of the depression opposite Big Round Top. The 20th Maine was on the left, then the 83rd Pennsylvania, the 44th New York, with the 16th Michigan on the right.[9] Initially, the 16th Michigan went into position on the extreme left of the brigade and deployed skirmishers. However, Vincent ordered Colonel Norval E. Welch to move his regiment to the right of the 44th New York. Welch wrote, "About 4 p.m. we moved rapidly to the extreme left of our line of battle, and went into position on the left of the

Colonel Joshua L. Chamberlain, commanding the 20th Maine Infantry. Library of Congress.

---

5. LaFantasie, "Oates Remembers," 61; Norton, *Attack and Defense*, 112–113.
6. Benedict, *Vermont in the Civil War*, 767.
7. Ladd and Ladd, "Letter of Capt. Walter G. Morrill," 1029.
8. Woods, *The Ebb and Flow of Battle*, 225.
9. Judson, *History of the Eighty-Third*, 67; Toombs, *New Jersey Troops*, 210; Nash, *A History of the Forty-Fourth Regiment*, 143.

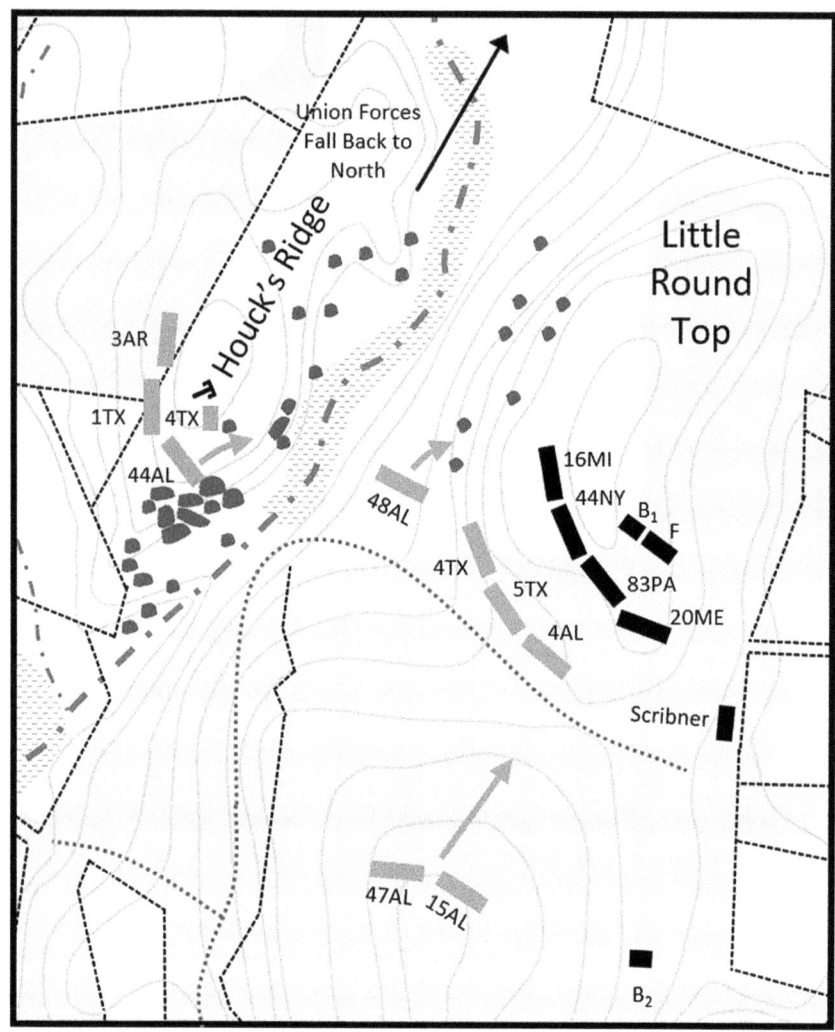

Union forces, including the right-wing sharpshooters and Company H, retreated out of Plum Run Valley as the Texas and Alabama regiments approached Little Round Top. On Big Round Top, Colonel Oates begins his descent into the gap between the Round Tops.

brigade. After deploying two of my largest companies as skirmishers—Brady's Sharpshooters from the left, and Company A from the right—I was ordered at double-quick to the right of the brigade, and to take my position on the right of the Forty-fourth New York."[10] There is no indica-

---

10. *OR*, 27, pt. 1, 628.

tion that the two skirmish companies returned to their regiment before the advancing Confederate line attacked.

Colonel Chamberlain positioned the 20th Maine to take advantage of the rough, rocky, and irregular wooded ground that sloped to their front toward Big Round Top. Around 4:45 p.m., Chamberlain detached Captain Walter G. Morrill's Company B, extending the 20th Maine's left flank across the hollow between the Round Tops. It was Morrill's job to prevent a surprise attack on the regiment's exposed flank and rear.[11] Chamberlain wrote, "Knowing that we had no supports on the left, I dispatched a stalwart company under the level-headed Captain Morrill with orders to move along up the valley to our front and left, between us and the eastern base of the Great Round Top, to keep within supporting distance of us, and to act as exigencies of the battle should require."[12] Corporal Nathan S. Clark of Company H wrote in his diary, "Orders were given to Lieut. Morrell commanding Co. B. to advance and deploy as skirmishers. No sooner said than done and out went Co. B to the front and left to protect our flank and was soon out of sight in the woods." Morrill moved immediately into the wooded area between the Round Tops and deployed his company as skirmishers, ordering his men to connect on the right with the 16th Michigan skirmishers.[13] However, Morrill's company would never connect with them.

About 4:55 p.m., almost 10 minutes after Vincent had formed his line, skirmishers from the 83rd Pennsylvania, 44th New York, and 16th Michigan had advanced

Captain Walter G. Morrill, commanding Company B, 20th Maine Infantry. Maine State Archives Collection.

---

11. OR, 27, pt. 1, 623; Theodore Gerrish, *Army Life: A Private's Reminiscences of the Civil War* (Portland, ME, 1882), 106–107.

12. OR, 27, pt. 1, 622–623; Joshua L. Chamberlain, Through Blood & Fire at Gettysburg (Gettysburg, PA, 1994), 10.

13. Nathan S. Clark, "Nathan S. Clark Diary, 20th Maine," *Historical Documents, Digital Maine Repository*, https://digitalmaine.com/hist_docs/2 (accessed December 27, 2021), 28; Ladd and Ladd, *The Batchelder Papers: Volume 2*, 1029.

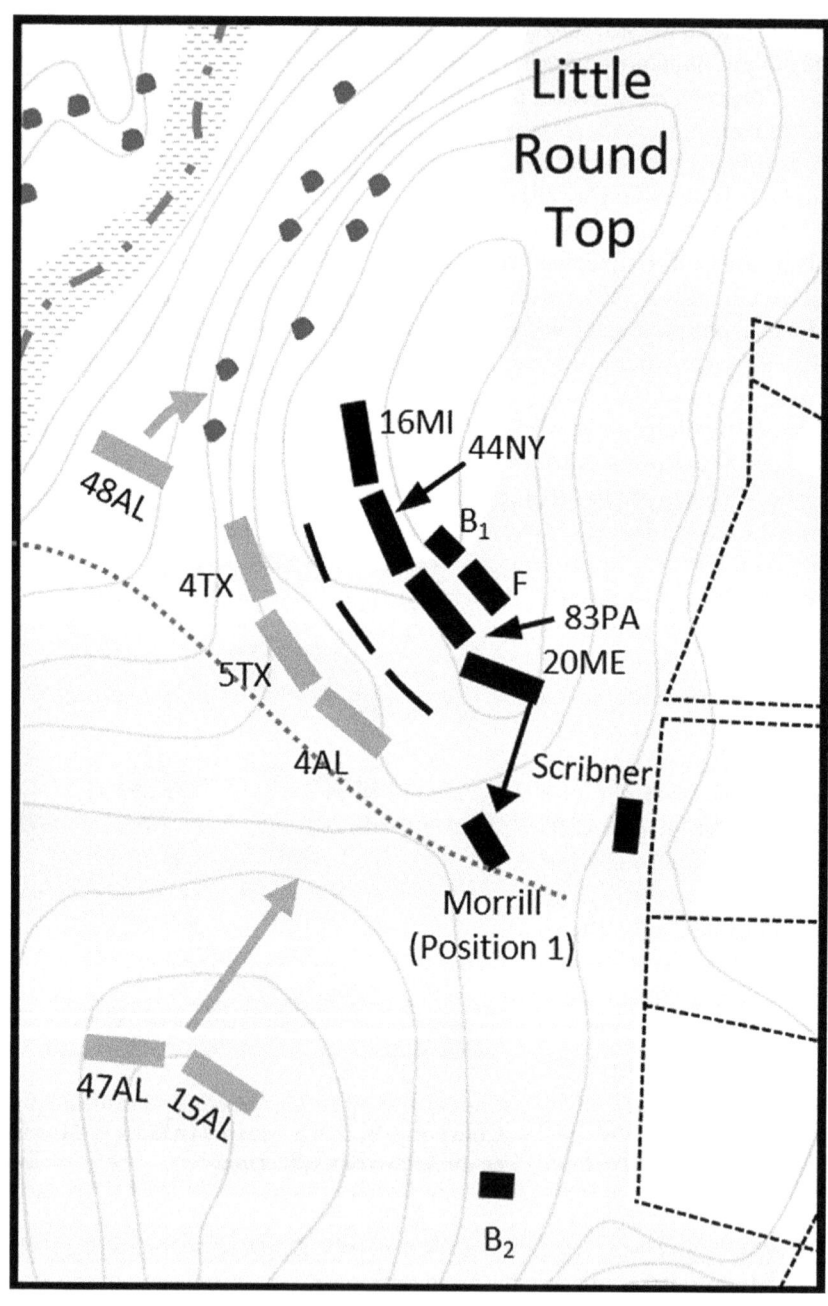

Chamberlain sends out Captain Morrill's Company B to protect the 20th Maine's left flank. A Union skirmish line moves forward and soon encounters the advancing Confederate line.

approximately 190 yards through the rocks and trees without seeing any indications of Confederate troops.[14] During the advance, the Michigan skirmishers separated from the Pennsylvania and New York skirmishers and inadvertently moved southward onto Big Round Top's northern side.[15] The Pennsylvania and New York skirmishers proceeded westward down the valley between the Round Tops, and before long met three Confederate regiments, advancing over the western side of Big Round Top. These regiments, from Law's brigade, were the 4th Alabama and the 4th and 5th Texas. At this point, both sides began firing at one another.[16] Now only a quarter mile away, the Confederates troops had bayonets fixed and were running and yelling like fiends as they approached the Union position. The enemy's approach drove the Pennsylvania and New York skirmishers back to the Union line, with the Confederates soldiers following close behind.[17]

Morrill and his men had scarcely deployed on the side of Big Round Top (Position 1) when the roar of battle indicated the enemy had come between his company and the regiment. Morrill wrote, "The enemy came in on our right and attacked the 20th Maine. I at once ordered my company to march by the left flank to uncover the enemy, and at the same time to guard against flank movement on the left. Having arrived on the open field at the left of the woods, I found some twelve or fifteen U.S. Sharpshooters under the command of a non-commissioned officer, who had been driven in by Hood's advance over Round Top, and he asked leave to remain under my command during the battle."[18] The non-commissioned officer was Sergeant Grove Scribner of Company H. Curtis Abbott wrote of Scribner, stating, "Sergt. Scribner's retreat with part of his squad not captured was over Roundtop and then a little past the open he met and joined the union regiment which had come over the Slopes."[19]

Adjutant Seymour Norton wrote, "We came upon the 20th Maine Regiment when I notified of the enemy's approach. Immediately after, the enemy's line of battle appeared!" He continued, "The enemy came up

---

14. Norton, *Attack and Defense*, 266; Gerrish, *Army Life*, 106–107. The distance in the original was 30 to 40 rods, which equals 165 to 220 yards. Here I used the average distance of 35 rods or 190 yards.
15. Kim Crawford, *The 16th Michigan Infantry in the Civil War* (East Lansing, MI, 2019), 182.
16. Norton, *Attack and Defense*, 258.
17. Judson, *History of the Eight-Third*, 67.
18. Ladd and Ladd, "Letter of Capt. Walter G. Morrill," 1029. This is the event mentioned in Chapter Three indicating Scribner, not Norton, was in command of the squad of scouts.
19. Kellogg and Kellogg, *The Curtis Abbott Papers*, 214.

in the ravine between Big Round Top and Little Round Top."[20] Scribner and Norton came upon Company B of the 20th Maine, not the regiment itself. Realistically, Scribner and his men were probably already at the stone wall when Morrill found them. Norton makes no mention of other skirmishers from the Michigan, Pennsylvania, or New York regiments, which means he had already moved beyond the left of the 16th Michigan and later the 20th Maine lines before skirmishers from either regiment advanced into the area between the Round Tops.

After forcing Scribner and Company H to retreat, the 4th Alabama and the 4th and 5th Texas cleared the stone fence, reformed lines, and pushed over the northwestern edge of Big Round Top in columns and deployed against the 44th New York and 83rd Pennsylvania. Morrill and the sharpshooters now took position behind a stone wall (Position 2), at the edge of a field, and maintained this position during the battle, undiscovered by Confederate forces. Morrill did not disclose his position until the enemy made its appearance to his right.[21]

Scarcely had the Union skirmishers deployed before the enemy's advancing lines of battle struck them. The 83rd Pennsylvania and 44th New York had no time to correct alignments or to protect themselves with temporary breastworks when the enemy assaulted the Union position.[22] The Confederates quickly formed a line of battle, with the 4th Alabama on the right, the 5th Texas in the middle, and the 4th Texas on the left. They attacked the whole Union line but threw the weight of their attack against the 83rd Pennsylvania and 44th New York. As the 4th Alabama swung around to attack the 83rd Pennsylvania from the south, the Texas regiments engaged the 83rd Pennsylvania's right, the 44th New York, and the 16th Michigan's left. Sheltered behind rocks and boulders, Vincent's men were well protected.[23] Wyman White wrote that the enemy charged up close to the Union line. "Some of them rushed up so we could have seen the whites of their eyes only for the smoke. Our men worked like beavers keeping up an awfully strong fire on the Rebels at short range and the rebels began to hesitate and their advance had broken down."[24]

During the assault on Vincent's center and right, the 15th and 47th Alabama moved in column along the foot of Big Round Top, passing to

---

20. Norton, *War Papers*, 14–15.
21. Ladd and Ladd, "Letter of Capt. Walter G. Morrill," 1029; Howard L. Prince, "Capt. Howard L. Prince's Address," *Dedication of the Twentieth Maine Monuments at Gettysburg, October 3, 1889*, http://www.gdg.org/Research/People/Chamberlain/20ded.html (accessed May 27, 2022).
22. Nash, *History of the Forty-Fourth Regiment*, 365–366, 370.
23. Norton, *Attack and Defense*, 174, 258; Judson, *History of the Eighty-Third*, 67.
24. White, *Civil War Diary*, 166.

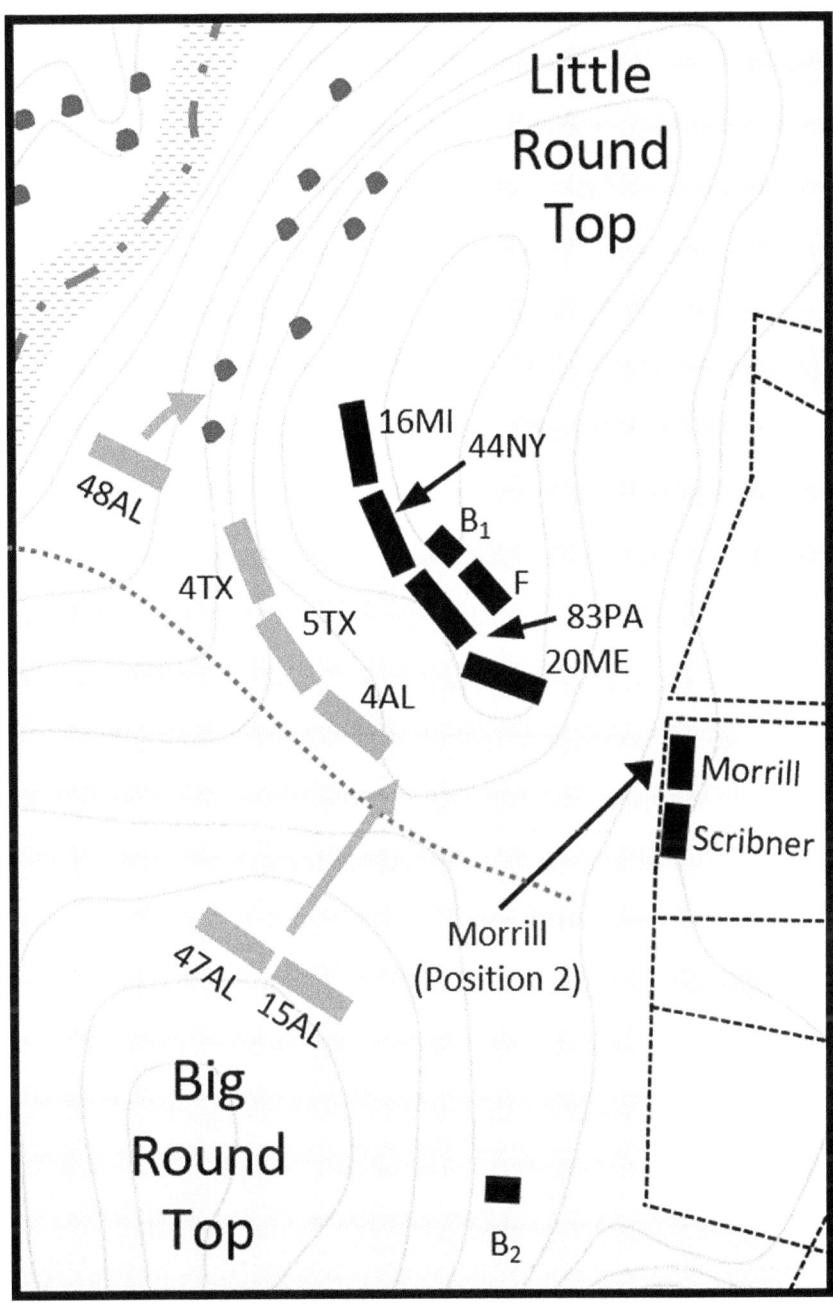

Captain Morrill moves Company B to their second position behind a stone fence and finds Scribner and his scouts.

the right of the 4th Alabama, and advanced against the 20th Maine.[25] Oates advanced rapidly and saw no enemy until he was within 40 or 50 paces of an irregular ledge of rocks. He called it "a splendid line of breastworks formed by nature, running about parallel with the front of the Forty-seventh Alabama and my two left companies, and then sloping back in front of my center and right at an angle of about thirty-five degrees."[26]

A sheet of smoke and flame burst from the Union line. Wyman White wrote that "no orders were necessary; every man was doing his level best shooting lead into the advancing Rebels."[27] As noted earlier, Wyman White stated that his Company F passed through the 83rd Pennsylvania's battle line.[28] It was also likely that Company B_1 passed through the same line, with both companies taking a position near the 83rd Pennsylvania. Oates recognized the sharpshooters, writing, "Our foes, who had so suddenly and mysteriously disappeared from Round Top, had evidently fallen back to a second line behind this ledge, and now, unexpectedly to us, the double line poured into us the most destructive fire I ever saw."[29] Oates identified the sharpshooters in a second line, likely based on uniform color. He distinguished the sharpshooters in their green uniforms from the 83rd Pennsylvania in blue. Ultimately, this means that companies F and B_1 were behind the 83rd Pennsylvania in a second line and not interspersed with the regiment.[30]

The Union fire staggered the attacking Confederate line causing them to fall back, but they soon rallied and advanced again.[31] Oates said, "I ordered my regiment to drive the Federals from the ledge of rocks, partly for the purpose of enfilading their line and relieving the 47th

---

25. Norton, *Attack and Defense*, 261.
26. Oates, "Battle on the Right," 176; Oates, *The War*, 214; *OR*, 27, pt. 2, 392.
27. White, *Civil War Diary*, 165; Judson, *History of the Eighty-Third*, 67.
28. White, *Civil War Diary*, 165.
29. Oates, "Battle on the Right," 176.
30. Interestingly, not all the sharpshooters may have been wearing green. Sergeant James M. Matthews of Company D wrote on June 7, 1863, that their green coats were to be turned in and they were to draw blouses in their place. He did not state the color of the blouses, but Matthews wrote that his green jacket was turned in to the Quartermaster Sergeant the next day. Corporal Curtis Abbott of Company H wrote four days later, on June 11, 1863, that "the uniform is dark green trimmed with green, with U.S. gutta percha buttons, which with high leather leggings makes a uniform unlike that in any other organization in the U.S. service." This suggests Company H was still wearing green jackets. Gettysburg licensed battlefield guide Gar Phillips said he read something about the uniforms stating the Sharpshooters still had green jackets but blue pants at Gettysburg (Pullen, *Soldiers in Green*, 145–146; Kellogg and Kellogg, *The Curtis Abbott Papers*, 211; Gar Phillips, personal communication, March 27, 2022). Oates's statement that his foes from Round Top were now in his front can only be explained by visual identification of the green uniforms.
31. Judson, *History of the Eighty-Third*, 67.

Six—Among the Boulders

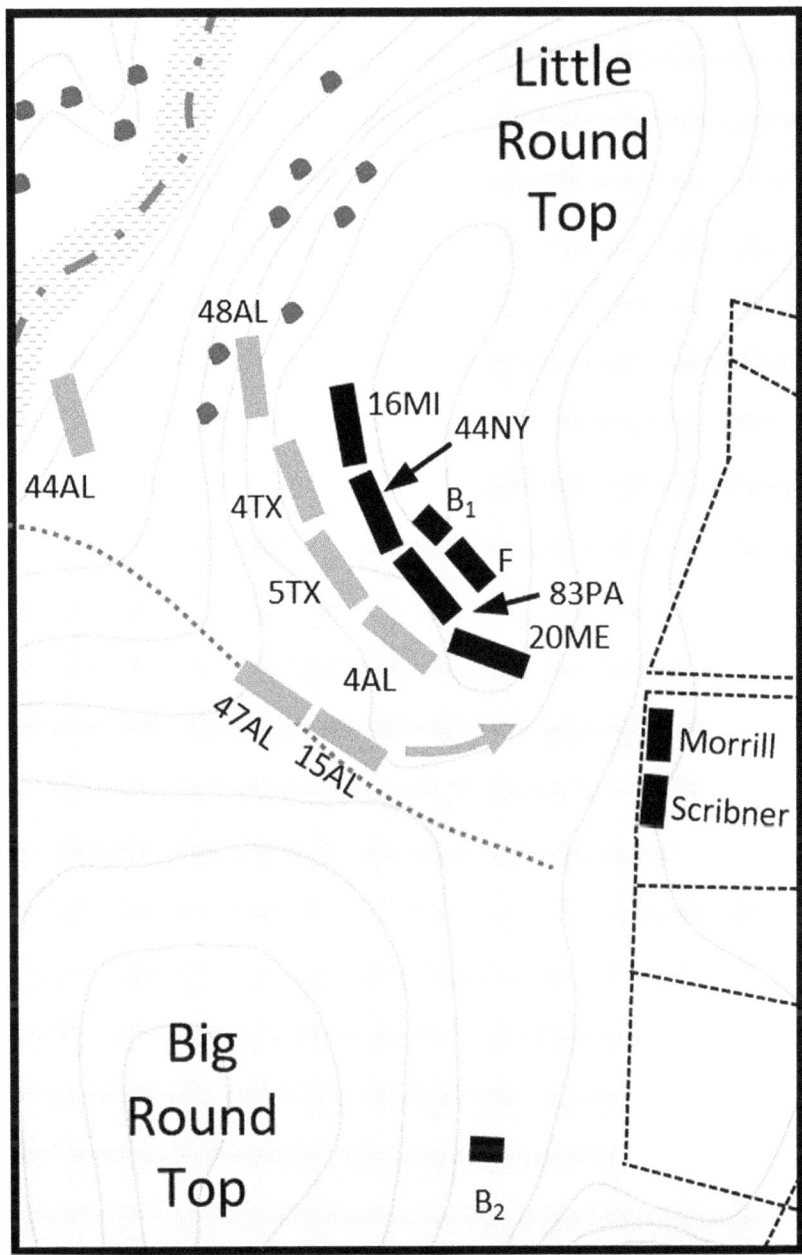

The 4th and 5th Texas and 4th Alabama attack the Union line as the 47th and 15th Alabama move into the gap between the Round Tops and then move to the right, extending the Confederate line to engage the 20th Maine.

Alabama. My men obeyed, and advanced about half way to the enemy's position, but the fire was so destructive that my line wavered like a man trying to walk against a strong wind, and then, slowly, doggedly, gave back a little."[32] Oates extended the 15th Alabama line farther to the right, passing the 20th Maine. He then advanced the 15th Alabama's right to a position that they could enfilade the 20th Maine and the 83rd Pennsylvania's left. To meet this attack, Chamberlain refused his left wing to a position nearly at right angles with the rest of his regiment.[33] The right of the 15th Alabama was now between the 20th Maine and Morrill's Company B and sharpshooters.

Finding they could not drive the Union men from their position, Confederate forces fell back a short distance and took cover behind the numerous nearby rocks.[34] Wyman White said, "I do not think they fell back very far as the trees and rocks and underbrush covered them from our sight. It was not long before they came up again yelling more furiously than they did the first time but that single line of Union troops and the two pieces of artillery was too much for their thousands. I think the breech loaders of the Sharpshooters was quite an item in the balance. In this charge they fell back more reluctantly than before but, with all their stubbornness, they were obliged to give way before the lively, well directed fire of the Union troops."[35] Oates's perspective was that "we drove the Federals from their strong defensive position; five times they rallied and charged us—twice coming so near that some of my men had to use the bayonet—but vain was their effort."[36]

After another Confederate retreat, the firing nearly stopped for a short time; but it was just the lull before the storm. Wyman White said, "Our men braced themselves and made themselves ready, as they were sure that the enemy was reforming for still another effort to possess the summit of Little Round Top. A third time these desperate men came up with their Rebel yell. First the fire was by volleys which soon turned to a continuous fusillade of rifle fire. The bullets hummed and spatted the rocks and trees, glancing off with a hideous screech and hum. But, as the men in our line were down behind the rocks and trees, comparatively few were hit by this shower of bullets. But by this time a new factor came in. A brigade of the Fifth Army Corps had just come over the

---

32. Oates, "Battle on the Right," 176.
33. Norton, *Attack and Defense*, 261. Refusing a line is a movement used to prevent an enemy from flanking your line. Part of your line reforms at an angle, and the entire line is facing the enemy even when extending their line in a flank movement. Enfilade is to direct a volley of gunfire along the length of a target.
34. *Ibid.*, 258.
35. White, *Civil War Diary*, 166.
36. Oates, "Battle on the Right," 177.

summit, having just arrived after a terrible forced march. They came up just in the nick of time."[37] Included with the V Corps Third Brigade was the 140th New York, Colonel Patrick O'Rorke commanding, who saved the 16th Michigan's right flank.

As General Law extended his line to the right, and while the back-and-forth struggle existed in the middle of the Union line, the Confederate left was attempting to flank the Union right. The 4th and 5th Texas and the 48th Alabama moved unseen along the western slope of Little Round Top until they passed beyond Vincent's right flank, held by the 16th Michigan.[38] The Confederate line courageously proceeded up Little Round Top, but the steepness of a slope covered with loose stones made it impossible to maintain an orderly advance. J.W. Stevens with the 5th Texas said, "The ground is covered with large boulders, from the size of a wash pot to that of a wagon bed, so to preserve anything like line of battle is impossible. As we start up the mountain, we got a plunging volley from the enemy, who are posted behind the rocks on the crest. They are not more than 25 or 30 steps away and well protected behind the rocks, while we are exposed to their fire."[39] Colonel Bryan also with the 5th Texas wrote, "From this position we failed to drive them. Our failure was owing to the rocky nature of the ground over which we had to pass, the huge rocks forming defiles through which not more than three or four men could pass abreast, thus breaking up our alignment and rendering its reformation impossible."[40]

The Confederate regiments pushed on, not even stopping to fire. When they reached the Union line, they engaged the 16th Michigan in hand-to-hand combat, firing and using the bayonet. The 16th Michigan refused the right of their line so that the men faced in a northerly direction, their right resting at the foot of large rocks that formed the crest of the Little Round Top.[41] The Confederate assault caused the 16th Michigan's right to fall back in disorder. The time was about 5:48 p.m. Approximately two minutes later, Colonel Patrick O'Rorke led the 140th New York at a full run over the crest of Little Round Top, arriving on the 16th Michigan's right. With no time to form a line of battle, load their guns, or fix bayonets, the 140th New York rushed upon the advancing Confederate line and checked their movement. O'Rorke's men charged down the hill and drove the Rebel infantry back into the valley. John West with the 4th Texas wrote, "We renewed the charge several times,

---

37. White, *Civil War Diary*, 166–167.
38. Norton, *Attack and Defense*, 259.
39. Stevens, *Reminiscences of the Civil War*, 114.
40. *OR*, 27, pt. 2, 411.
41. Crawford, *The 16th Michigan Infantry*, 194.

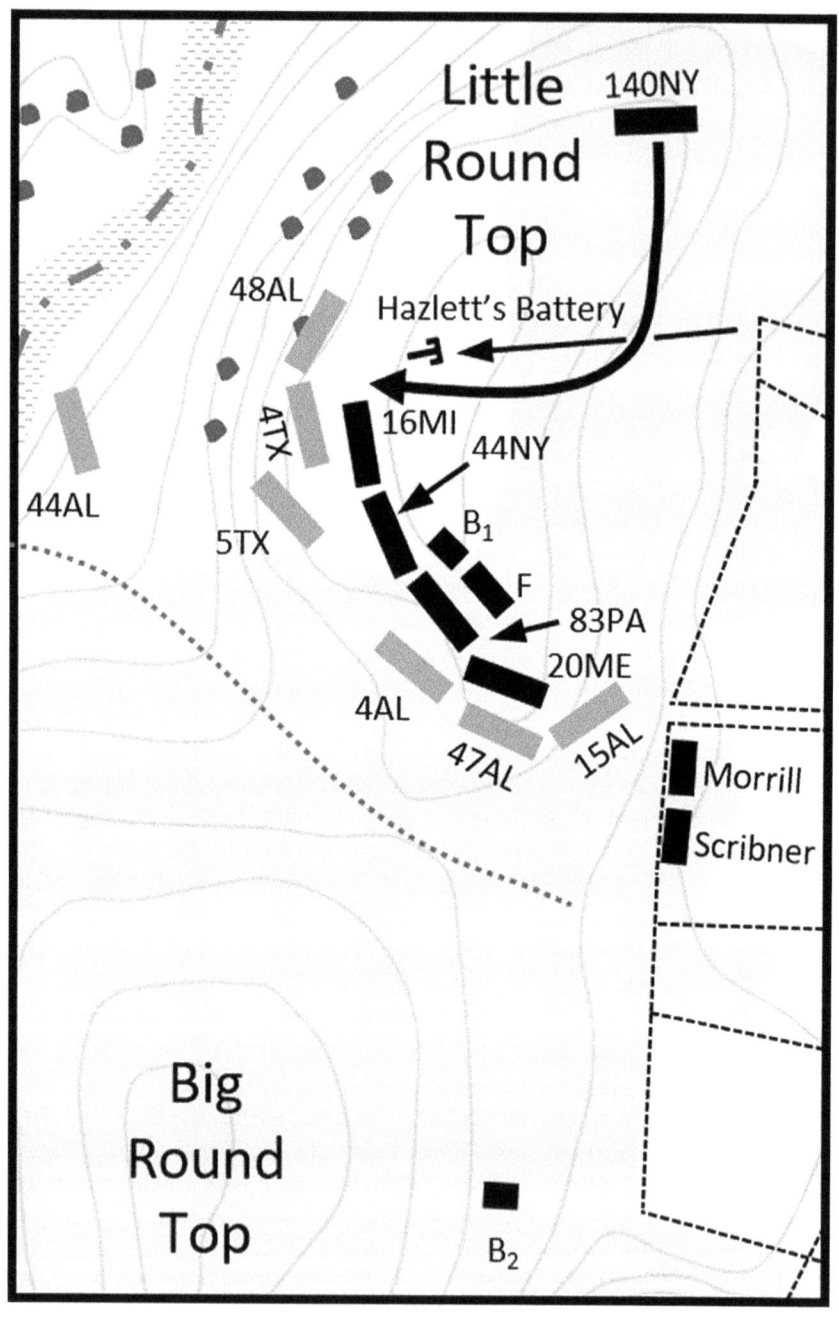

Oates tries to outflank the 20th Maine, while the left of the Confederate line moves farther left to flank the right of the 16th Michigan.

Six—Among the Boulders 157

but the slaughter of our men was so great that after four or five efforts to advance we retired about sunset and slept behind the rocks."[42]

At approximately 5:53 p.m., First Lieutenant Charles E. Hazlett's Battery D, 5th U.S. Artillery, came rushing up to the top of Little Round Top and opened fire.[43] A squad from the 155th Pennsylvania assisted in hauling up the four pieces of Hazlett's battery to the summit.[44] Although the location was extremely dangerous, Hazlett took his position, directing his fire against the Confederate reserve in the valley.[45] The dangerous nature of the position was due to Confederate sharpshooters posted among the rocks of Devil's Den on the opposite side of Plum Run Valley. The exposed Union men and artillery on the summit and western slope of Little Round Top were easy targets for the rebel sharpshooters. Brigadier General Stephen H. Weed barely completed the disposition of his troops when, shortly after 6:00 p.m., a Confederate sharpshooter from the 3rd Arkansas mortally wounded Weed as he stood on the summit near Hazlett's battery.[46] Lieutenant Hazlett, while bending over the fallen general to render assistance, fell dead beside Weed soon thereafter, both apparent victims of Confederate sharpshooters. The Confederates' effective fire drove the Union troops on Little Round Top to seek cover behind the large rocks, effectively abandoning the Union artillery for a time.[47]

The Bucktails of the Pennsylvania Reserves (Third Division, V Corps), skilled as sharpshooters themselves, had previously moved forward before General Weed received his mortal wound. The Bucktails advanced over the rocks as skirmishers, answering the strong force of Confederate sharpshooters in the rocks around Devil's Den.[48] Additionally, to help address the Confederate sharpshooters across the valley, "a company or two of Berdan's sharpshooters from the III Corps was brought up on Little Round Top and were hastily distributed among the

---

42. Norton, *Attack and Defense*, 26–27; West, *A Texan in Search of a Fight*, 85–86.
43. R.K. Beecham, *Gettysburg: The Pivotal Battle of the Civil War* (Chicago, IL, 1911), 189–191; Nash, "Dedication of Monument," 365–366; Norton, *Attack and Defense*, 260; White, *Civil War Diary*, 166; Matt Spruill, *Summer Thunder: A Battlefield Guide to the Artillery at Gettysburg* (Knoxville, TN, 2010), 130.
44. The 155th Regimental Association, *Under the Maltese Cross, Antietam to Appomattox: Campaigns 155th Pennsylvania Regiment* (Pittsburg, PA, 1910), 170.
45. The Comte De Paris, *History of the Civil War*, 618; Toombs, *New Jersey Troops*, 210–213.
46. Calvin L. Collier, *They'll Do to Tie To! The Story of Hood's Arkansas Toothpicks, Third Arkansas Infantry Regiment, C.S.A.* (Little Rock, AR, 2015), 141.
47. Fox, "New York at Gettysburg," 49; Norton, *Attack and Defense*, 299–300; Beecham, *Gettysburg: The Pivotal Battle*, 189.
48. The 155th Regimental Association, *Under the Maltese Cross*, 170; Ladd and Ladd, *The Batchelder Papers*, 512.

rocks and crevices."⁴⁹ There is no record of who ordered the sharpshooters to this position. However, it may have been Colonel Kenner Garrard of the 146th New York, who succeeded to command of the brigade when Confederate sharpshooters wounded General Weed.⁵⁰

The Bucktails on the right, and a company of Berdan's sharpshooters on the left, took positions on Little Round Top in advance of the main Union line and of the skirmishers.⁵¹ The Union sharpshooters returned the Confederate fire with satisfactory effect and forced the Confederate sharpshooters to seek shelter, effectually checking their activity.⁵² Berdan's sharpshooters were in position near Hazlett's battery, and it was only after their arrival that Hazlett's gunners were permitted to load, and that their fire became effective, as the Union artillery was brought into play upon the Confederate rocky stronghold.⁵³

As the Confederates sought shelter behind the rocks, one of the most murderous sharpshooting duels of the Civil War opened. Bullets whistled, ricocheted, and whined among the crevasses. Flying clouds of rock dust added thickening to the drifting wisps of smoke.⁵⁴ This fire of the Union sharpshooters was very effective, as observed the next day when the V Corps lines advanced beyond Devil's Den and discovered scores of dead Confederate sharpshooters in the rocks, crevices, and recesses of the Den.⁵⁵

The authors of the statements just described do not provide the identity of the Berdan sharpshooters in position in front of Hazlett's battery. However, Lieutenant Colonel William F. Fox with the 107th New York, writing in his book *New York at Gettysburg, Vol. 3*, gives a clue. Fox wrote, "This detachment belonged to the Second U.S. Sharpshooters (Birney's Division), which in skirmishing with Law's Brigade had fallen back, passed over Big Round Top, only to appear again on Law's right flank, and subsequently, on the front slope of Little Round Top."⁵⁶

This detachment of sharpshooters was Company B_1 that, with Company F, had earlier passed through the 83rd Pennsylvania line. Several pieces of evidence indicate B_1 was the detachment. First, only two companies *passed over* Big Round Top: F and B_1. Wyman White writes that his company fell back and then "up over the western slope of the Big Round

---

49. Beecham, *Gettysburg: The Pivotal Battle*, 190; Fox, "New York at Gettysburg," 49.
50. Fox, "New York at Gettysburg," 49.
51. The 155th Regimental Association, *Under the Maltese Cross*, 174.
52. Beecham, *Gettysburg: The Pivotal Battle*. 191.
53. Luther W. Minnigh, *Gettysburg: What They Did Here* (Baltimore, MD, 1892), 46; Beecham, *Gettysburg: The Pivotal Battle*, 191.
54. Collier, *They'll Do to Tie To*, 142.
55. The 155th Regimental Association. *Under the Maltese Cross*, 172.
56. Fox, "New York at Gettysburg," 49.

Top." White makes no mention of Company F moving from behind the 83rd Pennsylvania line.⁵⁷ Additionally, only one company appeared on Law's right flank and then again on the front slope of Little Round Top. Second, we can rule out companies D, A, E, G, C, and H, as all six companies were in Plum Run Valley and had retreated northward with the other regiments by the time of this event. Third, it was not Scribner and his scouts, as they were currently with Captain Morrill's Company B, 20th Maine, southeast of this location. Fourth, Major Stoughton and Company B_2 were, at this time, lost in the woods on the eastern side of Big Round Top. Furthermore, Stoughton led B_2 to the right, around Big Round Top, and not over it. Finally, the monument to the Michigan Sharpshooters on Little Round Top states that "Company B, 2d Regiment U.S. Sharpshooters, fought upon this field July 2d near the Slyder house on extreme left, afterwards at this point," with "this point" being the position of the monument on Little Round Top, near the right of the 16th Michigan and in front of Hazlett's battery (see map in Appendix C).

The Union left and center prepared for the desperate final Confederate charge.⁵⁸ Oates claimed, "It was our time now to deal death and destruction to a gallant foe, and the account was speedily settled with a large balance in our favor; but this state of things was not long to continue. The long blue lines of Federal infantry were coming down on my right and closing in on my rear. My position rapidly became untenable."⁵⁹ Reports from his captains informed Oates that two regiments of the Union infantry were closing in on his rear. Most likely, these were Morrill and Stoughton. Oates paints a vivid picture, writing, "Just then I saw them [Stoughton and B_2] halt behind a fence, 200 yards distant, from which they opened fire on us. At this moment, the Fifteenth Alabama had infantry to the right of them, dismounted cavalry to the left of them, infantry in front of them, and infantry in the rear. With a withering and deadly fire poured in upon us from every direction, it seemed that the entire command was doomed to destruction. While one man was shot in the face, his right hand or left hand comrade was shot in the side or back. Some were struck simultaneously with two or three balls from different directions."⁶⁰

Oates continues, "Stoughton's sharp-shooters which had been lost

---

57. White, *Civil War Diary*, 166.
58. Nash, "Dedication of Monument," 365–366.
59. Oates, "Battle on the Right," 177; William C. Oates, *Account of Colonel William C. Oates, 15th Alabama Infantry; Re: Battle of Gettysburg*, Library & Research Center (Gettysburg NMP, Gettysburg, PA), 13.
60. Oates, *The War*, 219; Oates, *Account of Colonel William C. Oates*, 14–15; Oates, "Battle on the Right," 177–178.

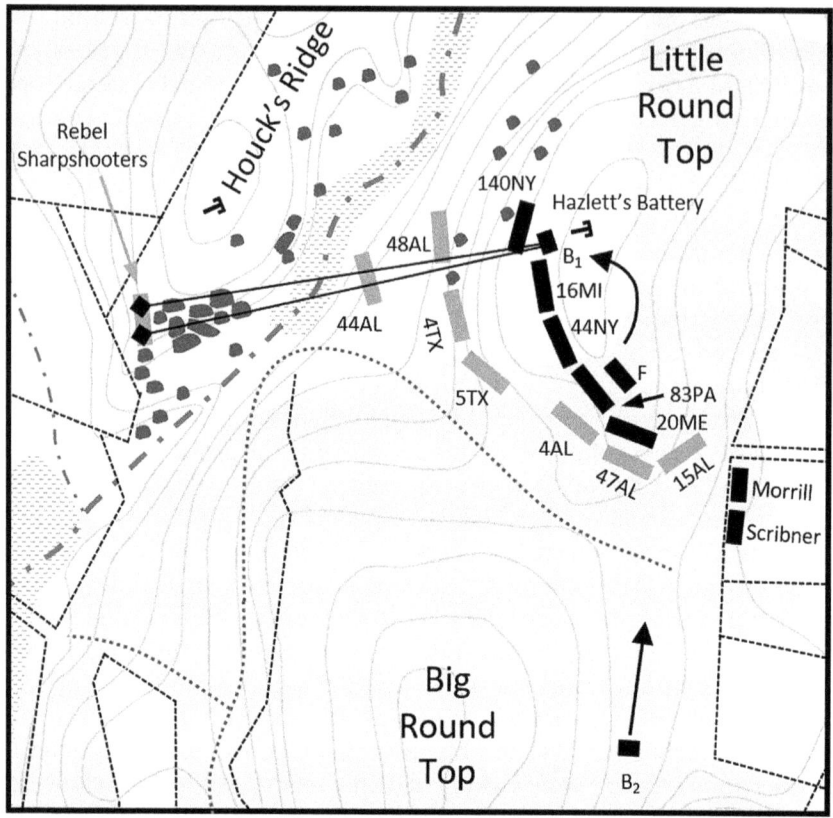

The Confederate line wavers. Company B_1 changes position to engage Confederate sharpshooters in Devil's Den. Company B_2 moves toward the sound of battle.

in the woods guided by the firing came up in my rear to within about 150 yards and opened on me shooting my men in the back. As we ran out receiving Stoughton's fire from our left, you [Chamberlain] charged me again." Stoughton verifies this encounter, stating, "They [sharpshooters] poured a destructive fire into his flank and rear."[61] Oates repeats this account in the letter to Dr. F.A. Dearborn, stating, "But guided by the firing he [Stoughton] came to that stone fense, halted his battalion behind it & fired into my rear steadily until I retreated."[62] This was Stoughton's second attack on Oates, with the first being at the stone fence described in Chapter Five.

Oates continues: "With a New York regiment assailing me in front

---

61. Oates, *Letter to J.L. Chamberlain*, 3; Oates, *The War*, 219; *OR*, 27, pt. 1, 519.
62. LaFantasie, "Oates Remembers," 61.

Six—Among the Boulders

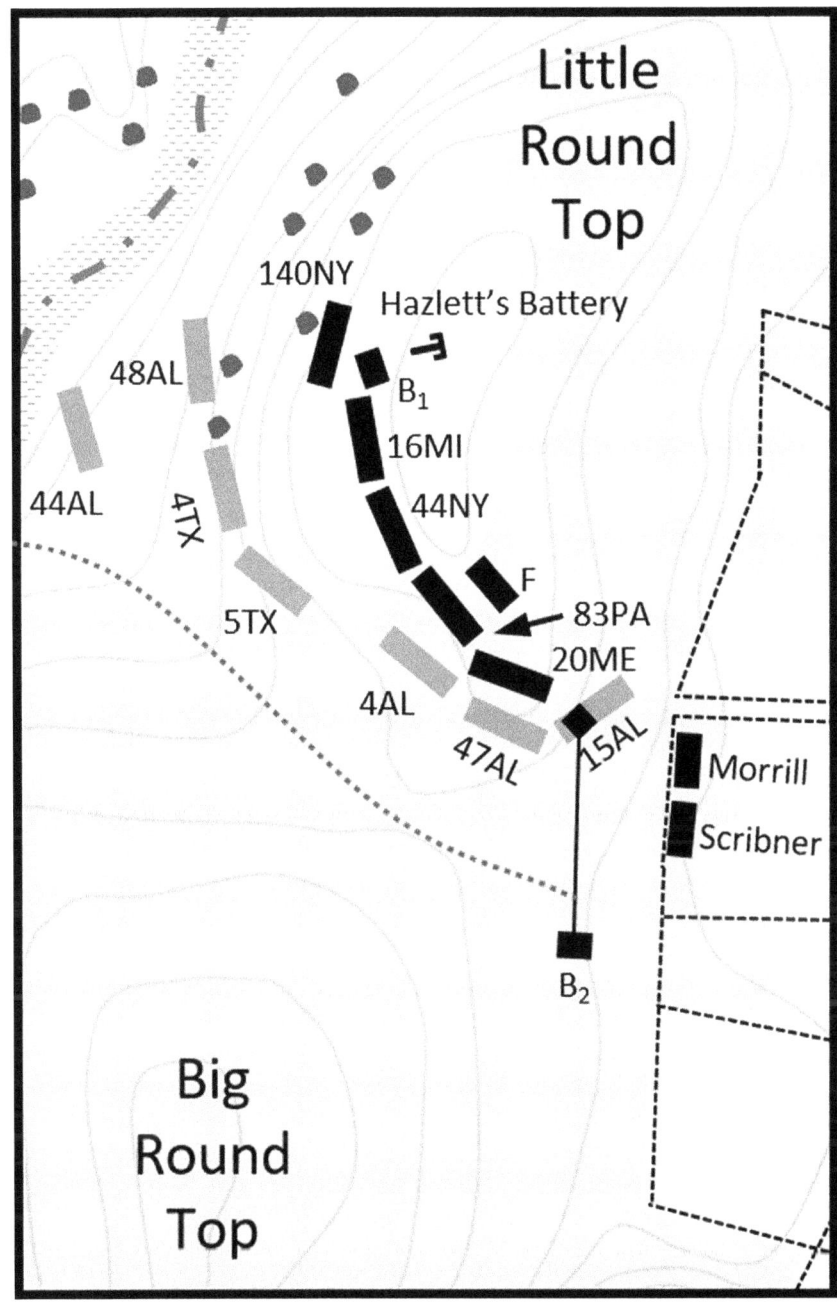

Oates is taking fire from all sides as Stoughton and Company B_2 move forward toward the fighting and attack. Oates then orders a retreat.

and you [Stoughton] in the rear, it forced my thinned ranks to face and fire in both directions, which we could not long endure. Half my men still able for duty were without ammunition. Finally, I discovered that the enemy had flanked me on the right, and two regiments were moving rapidly upon my rear and not 200 yards distant, when, to save my regiment from capture or destruction, I ordered a retreat."[63]

Oates claimed that after the war he "learned these were the *battalions* of Stoughton's sharp-shooters, each of which carried a *flag*, hence the impression that there were two regiments" (emphasis added).[64] These are questionable statements. The number of men that constitutes a regulation-size battalion (three companies minimum) or regiment (ten companies) would far exceed the number of sharpshooters with Norton (12–15) or Stoughton (10–15). Furthermore, Oates references Captain Howard L. Prince's speech, which claimed that only Morrill's Company B, which was small with about 50 men, and a few of the sharpshooters were all the soldiers behind the stone fence in the woods.[65] Prince said,

> A word may be said as to the belief of Col. Oates that his right was menaced by "long lines of Union infantry." He states that two of his Captains of the 15th reported a command with flags moving from the right. Unless this was purely imaginary, it must have been a distant view of the advance of the reserves, who were so far away that they did not reach the ground till the action was fully over. It is not impossible that a sentinel on the extreme edge of the wood might have described them, but no one on the battle line knew of them; Capt. Morrill did not see them.[66]

This statement in the speech supports the claim that Morrill and Scribner were at an unknown distance to the right of Stoughton and Company B_2 and that each one was probably unaware of the other. Also, no other account, sharpshooters or otherwise, indicates the sharpshooters were carrying flags that day.

Most Union troops, their numbers depleted, had expended the allotted 60 rounds of ammunition issued to them.[67] Chamberlain wrote, "It was imperative to strike before we were struck by this overwhelming force in a hand-to-hand fight, which we could not probably have withstood or survived. At about 7:15 p.m., I ordered the bayonet. Holding fast by our right, and swinging forward our left, we made an extended 'right wheel,' before which the enemy's second line, now not 30 yards away, broke and fell back, fighting from tree to tree, many being captured, until we had

---

63. OR, 27, pt. 2, 392; Oates, "Letter to Col. H.R. Stoughton," 327–328.
64. Oates, *The War*, 219.
65. LaFantasie, "Oates Remembers," 61.
66. Prince, "Capt. Howard L. Prince's Address."
67. Nash, *History of the Forty-Fourth Regiment*, 146.

Six—Among the Boulders

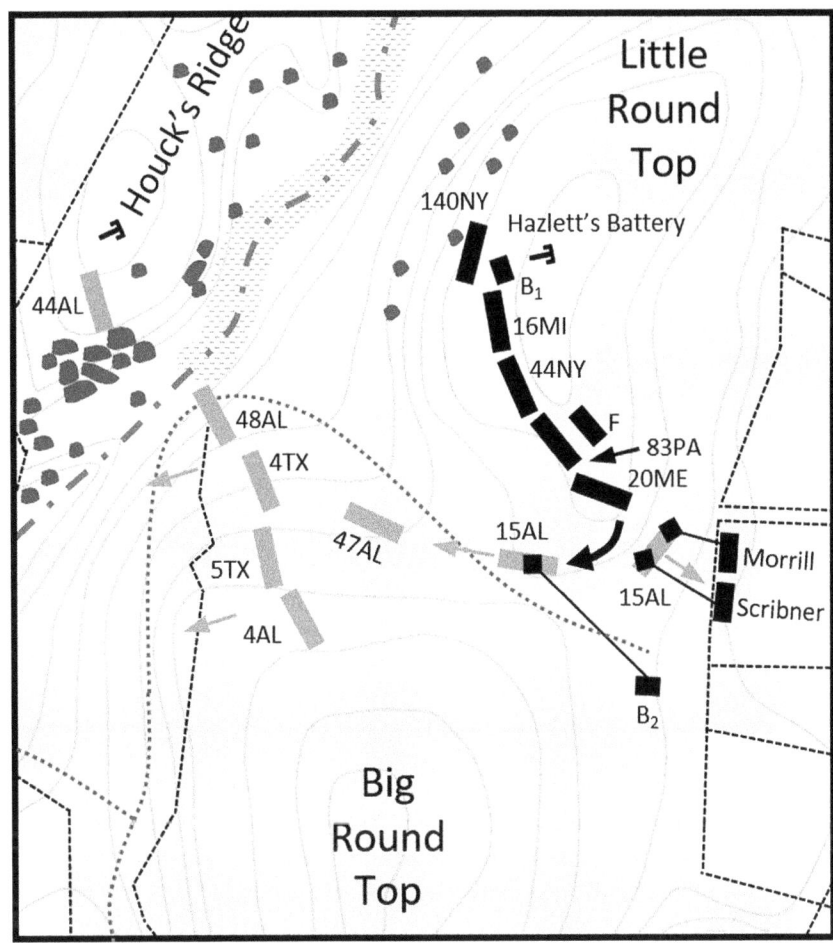

Chamberlain orders bayonets and the 20th Maine charges down the hill. Confederate forces retreat from the immediate area.

swept the valley and cleared the front of nearly our entire brigade. The effect was surprising; many of the enemy's first line threw down their arms and surrendered."[68] Chamberlain ordered a charge and the 20th Maine rushed upon the 15th Alabama, driving the Confederates back. Some of the retreating Alabama men found themselves between the Maine regiment and Morrill's Company B with Scribner's sharpshooters.[69]

---

68. *OR*, 27, pt. 1, 624.
69. Benjamin F. Rittenhouse, "The Battle of Gettysburg as Seen from Little Round Top," A Paper Read Before the District of Columbia Commandery MOLLUS (Washington, D.C., 1887), 7.

At this time, Captain Morrill's Company B acted against the retreating Alabama men. By his demonstrations, as well as his well-directed fire, Morrill added much to the effect of the charge.[70] In his letter to Chamberlain, Morrill commented, "About that time your regiment charged them, at which time we opened fire on them, at the same time giving loud commands to charge, in order to have them think I had a large body of troops there. At which time they broke and run going in the direction of Big Round Top."[71] From this and previous accounts, it seems that Stoughton and B_2 were behind Oates and fired their first volley before Chamberlain's bayonet charge. Morrill says he did not order his attack until after Chamberlain started his charge. As Oates and his men turn and retreat, Stoughton and B_2 are now firing into Oates's left. Oates received fire from two separate groups (Stoughton/B_2 and Morrill/Scribner), in two different locations (flank and rear), and at two different times (before and after Chamberlain's charge).

The bayonet charge confounded the rebels. Private Theodore Gerrish of the 20th Maine wrote, "We struck them with a fearful shock. They recoil, stagger, break and run, and like avenging demons our men pursue. The rebels rush toward a stone wall, but, to our mutual surprise, two scores of rifle barrels gleam over the rocks, and a murderous volley was poured in upon them at close quarters. A band of men leap over the wall and captured at least a hundred prisoners. This unlooked-for reinforcement was Company B, which we supposed were all captured."[72] It seems not all the 15th Alabama headed west toward Big Round Top as Oates states. As we will see, the order was to "run in the direction from where they came." As Gerrish states, some headed directly toward the stone wall, where Morrill's Company B and Scribner's sharpshooters were waiting.

According to both Major Stoughton and Adjutant Norton, it was here that the sharpshooters "took in and sent back quite a number of prisoners. I do not remember the number."[73] Stoughton claimed it was 22 prisoners and recognized Norton for "his coolness and bravery during this day's engagement."[74] Even though the number of men captured (i.e., 22) is the same as the lost water detail Oates mentions, it is unclear whether these are the same 22 men. The 20th Maine ended up capturing nearly as many prisoners as they had men in their regiment.

---

70. OR, 27, pt. 1, 624; Norton, *Attack and Defend*, 112.
71. Ladd and Ladd, "Letter of Capt. Walter G. Morrill," 1029.
72. Gerrish, *A Private's Reminiscences*, 106–107.
73. Norton, *War Papers*, 15.
74. OR, 27, pt. 1, 519.

The fighting in the Valley of Death was over and Little Round Top was still in Union hands.[75]

On reflection, Oates did order a retreat but did not retire in order. He advised the officers and men that when he gave the signal, everyone should run in the direction from where they came, and halt on the top of the mountain. When Oates gave the signal, they all "ran like a herd of wild cattle." Oates and his regiment ran to the summit of Big Round Top and halted. At dusk Oates had the regiment move back to an old house near the line of advance, where they camped for the night.[76]

Holding fast by their right and executing an extended right wheel, the 20th Maine, with the help of a handful of sharpshooters, swept everything before them and cleared the enemy from the entire level lands between the Round Tops. The Confederates' plan of battle, to envelop and turn the Union left, had failed. A much smaller force had defeated their choicest troops, commanded by their ablest lieutenant, and was then driven ingloriously from the field.[77]

By 8:00 p.m., the fighting for the day had ceased and the battle was won on this part of the field as the enemy fell back to Big Round Top and the farmlands beyond. Lee's drive to occupy Little Round Top had failed after three gallant attempts, and as Wyman White stated, "Southern troops had the chance to see the difference between attacking and being attacked." In the contest for the Round Tops, the critical importance of which all historians of the battle should recognize, the 2nd U.S. Sharpshooters took an important role, as many Confederates fell by their rifles. After dark, and after securing the Union left, the scattered companies of the 2nd Sharpshooters gathered together near the Taneytown Road behind the Round Tops.[78]

---

75. Rittenhouse, "The Battle of Gettysburg as Seen from Little Round Top," 7.
76. Oates, "Battle on the Right," 178; Oates, "Letter to Col. H.R. Stoughton," 327–328.
77. Nash, *History of the Forty-Fourth Regiment*, 146.
78. Beecham, *Gettysburg: The Pivotal Battle*, 189–191; White, *Civil War Diary*, 167; Benedict, *Vermont in the Civil War*, 768.

Seven

The Days After
Pickett's Charge, Picket Lines, and Conclusions

> *The fields are completely strewn with dead—also with muskets, knapsacks, blankets, & caps. It was the most horrible sight I ever saw. The stench was so great that I thought I would faint away.*[1]

For the 2nd Sharpshooters, the next few days involved skirmishing and mop-up duty until they marched from the Gettysburg area on July 7. The regiment was active on July 3 and 4, 1863, just not to the level of July 2. Captain Abraham Wright, in command of Company A, 2nd Sharpshooters, describes an event on July 3. In a letter to *The National Tribune*, Wright wrote,

> Our regiment, the 2d Berdan Sharpshooters, was taken from the left not on a double-quick but a run, passed behind the line, marching by fours until a certain point was reached, when the order was given: "By the left flank—March." This brought us into line of battle. We moved to the front. My company (A) being the right of the line came directly behind what I have always understood to be the 14th Conn. Our men came to an involuntary halt a few rods behind the line and commenced firing over the heads of those in line for they were on their knees or otherwise low. We fired only a few shots when the rebels began to throw down their arms and hold up their hands and at this the line in front of us jumped to their feet and rushed over the stone wall to capture those who were then coming in. The field between us and the Emmitsburg Road was covered with rebels running to the rear. We could have picked off many of them, but our bullets

---

1. Anthony Gardner Graves, Jr., "Letter to John, July 9, 1863," *1862–65: Anthony Gardner Graves, Jr. Letters*, https://sparedshared22.wordpress.com/2021/07/09/1862-65-anthony-graves-letters (accessed December 7, 2021). Anthony Graves was with the 44th New York on Little Round Top.

would have gone very close to the heads of our own men, and, somehow, we did not have much desire just to kill some one.[2]

Wright continued, "Some time later we went out after a battery. We passed Gen. Stannard who expressed surprise that we should try such an experiment." Captain William H. Nash of the 1st Sharpshooters asked for volunteers to go out and silence a couple of guns that from a position right and rear of the Codori house were keeping up a troublesome fire on Major General Abner Doubleday's Third Division. A dozen or so Vermonters, under command of Adjutant Seymour Norton, advanced out to the front of the breastworks of the I Corps. In a matter of moments, Norton and his Vermonters accomplished the objective with the loss of one man killed and one wounded, driving the enemy artillery back with a serious loss of cannoneers.[3] The party returned through the line of the 2nd Vermont Brigade (I Corps, Third Division, Third Brigade), and Brigadier General George J. Stannard praised them for their achievement.[4]

On July 4, Major Stoughton, with the regiment located a few hundred yards to the left of the cemetery, moved forward to Emmitsburg Road and deployed four companies (E, H, D, F) as skirmishers. Stoughton's four companies moved through a field opposite the road and to the woods in front, pushing the enemy back to his earthworks, about 150 or 200 yards from his first position. Stoughton's men, under sharp fire from enemy sharpshooters, held this position through the day, until relieved at 7:30 p.m. by a New Jersey regiment.[5]

On the morning of July 5, the Confederate Army had retreated, hurrying toward the Potomac River. The 2nd Sharpshooters was immediately sent forward to reconnoiter and report Confederate movements, which the sharpshooters completed after going three miles. They returned to their brigade, having discovered unmistakable evidence of the Confederate's hasty retreat, with many of their wounded left behind in farmhouses and sheds along the now deserted road.[6] For the next several days the men wandered the field, examining the aftermath of the battle and retrieving their fallen comrades. The bodies of men and animals were everywhere, and Wyman White called it "a gruesome sight

---

2. A. Wright, "The 2D U.S. Sharpshooters," *The National Tribune* (Washington, D.C., 1909), 2.
3. *OR*, 27, pt. 1, 519; Benedict, *Vermont in the Civil War*, 768; Norton, *War Papers*, 1–2.
4. Benedict, *Vermont in the Civil War*, 768; Norton, *War Papers*, 1–2.
5. *OR*, 27, pt. 1, 519; White, *Civil War Diary*, 173; Benedict, *Vermont in the Civil War*, 769.
6. Stevens, *Berdan's United States Sharpshooters*, 341–342; Pullen, *Soldiers in Green*, 164.

and a sight not to be forgotten."[7] Finally, on July 7, the fourth day after the battle, the 2nd Sharpshooters left the field and marched about 17 miles to "Mechanicsville."[8]

Most Confederates who wrote about the battle had an opinion on what went wrong. Based on their own words, they seemed to think they lost the battle rather than that the Union won it, or, if you will, that Lee's army snatched defeat from the jaws of victory. Coddington states, "The occupation of Little Round Top at the right time and right place by Vincent's Brigade was the result of a combination of circumstances and a stroke of rare good luck for which no one person in the Union high command could claim the credit, and in fact none tried to."[9] The key phrase is "combination of circumstances." What circumstances, as they pertain to the southern end of the battlefield, hindered the Confederates, or favored the Union?

The first and foremost is the battlefield terrain. As mentioned in Chapter One, on July 2, 1863, the Union Army at Gettysburg held one of the best examples of a defensive position occupied by either army during the war. The Union position was tactically strong with well-wooded hilltops. Meanwhile, Confederates troops advanced over a mostly open plain.[10] Maybe the very obviousness of terrain may explain why it sometimes gets disregarded as a primary reason for defeat. Charles Erdmann wrote, "When all other things are equal, when the die is cast upon some fire-swept field, victory will come to him who makes best use of the ground."[11] Sun Tzu says, "Fight downhill; do not ascend to attack."[12] And yet, the Confederate army time after time "ascended to attack" at places like Houck's Ridge, Big Round Top, Little Round Top, and Culp's Hill to the north. Even the Peach Orchard was on elevated ground. Many of the Confederate leadership commented on the strong nature of the Union position, but still, they attacked. Frederick the Great wrote, "Knowledge of the country is to a

---

7. White, *Civil War Diary*, 172, 174–175.

8. Pullen, *Soldiers in Green*, 165; White, *Civil War Diary*, 175. Originally incorporated as the Town of Mechanicstown in 1751, an act of the Maryland General Assembly changed the name to Thurmont on January 18, 1894. This name change was due to several other nearby towns having similar names, such as Mechanicsburg, Pennsylvania, and Mechanicsville, Maryland. Source: Anne Cissel, "From Mechanicstown to Thurmont," https://www.emmitsburg.net/history_t/archives/places/mechanicstown_to_thurmont.htm (accessed May 28, 2022).

9. Edwin B. Coddington, *The Gettysburg Campaign: A Study in Command* (New York, 1968), 390.

10. Tolles, "Army Movements," 542–543.

11. Charles E. Erdmann, "Application of Geology to the Principles of War," *Bulletin of the Geological Society of America* 54 (August 1943), 1191.

12. Sun Tzu, *The Art of War*, trans. Samuel B. Griffith (Oxford, 1971), 116.

general what a rifle is to an infantryman. If he does not know the country, he will do nothing but make gross mistakes."[13]

Another circumstance, and a by-product of the terrain, would be the strategy each side utilized. The Prussian general and military theorist Carl Von Clausewitz wrote:

> It is easier to hold ground than take it. It follows that defense is easier than attack assuming both sides have equal means. Just what makes defense so much easier? It is the fact that time which is allowed to pass unused accumulates to the credit of the defender. Any omission of attack—whether from bad judgment, fear, or indolence—accrues to the defenders' benefit. Another benefit derives from the advantage of position, which tends to favor the defense. We must say that the *defensive form of warfare is intrinsically stronger than the offensive* [italics in original].[14]

If an army is acting on the defensive, the chief object of its commander is to establish himself in some position from which he can best repel an attack with as little loss to himself and as great a loss to his opponent as possible.[15] The tactical features that render a defensive position excellent are hills, woods, streams, and marshes.[16] George C. Marshall said, "The intelligent leader knows that the terrain is his staunchest ally, and that it virtually determines his formation and scheme of maneuver."[17] Meade, by remaining on the defensive and leading skillfully, won the battle at Gettysburg even though Lee's army escaped.[18]

Historians Grady McWhiney and Perry D. Jamieson wrote that offensive tactics that American forces used so successfully in the Mexican War, were much less effective in the 1860s because the rifle had vastly increased the defender's strength. The Confederates could have offset their numerical disadvantage by remaining on the defensive and forcing the Federals to attack. However, Lee was against remaining on the defensive and his army continued to fight, despite mounting casualties, with the same courageous dash and reckless abandon ... favoring offensive warfare.[19] In a June 8, 1863, letter to Secretary of War James A. Seddon in Richmond, Virginia, Lee wrote, "As far as I can judge, there

---

13. Frederick the Great, *Instructions for His Generals*, trans. Thomas R. Phillips (Mineola, NY, 2005), 47.
14. Carl Von Clausewitz, *On War*, ed. and trans. Michael Howard and Peter Paret (New York, 1993), 427–428.
15. Tolles, "Army Movements," 541–542.
16. *Ibid.*, 542.
17. Marshall, *Infantry in Battle*, 69.
18. Albert Castel, *Victors in Blue: How Union Generals Fought the Confederates, Battled Each Other, and Won the War* (Lawrence, KS, 2011), 190.
19. Grady McWhiney and Perry D. Jamieson, *Attack and Die: Civil War Military Tactics and the Southern Heritage* (Tuscaloosa, AL, 1982), xv.

is nothing to be gained by this army remaining on the defensive, which it must do unless it can be re-enforced. I am aware that there is difficulty and hazard in taking the aggressive with so large an army in its front, intrenched behind a river, where it cannot be advantageously attacked."[20]

The commander of an attacking army must first thoroughly learn the position of his enemy by all the means at his command, such as spies, scouts, deserters, prisoners, reconnaissance, and so on. He then verifies the point and mode of attack and then chooses his routes of approach.[21] Generals Hood and Law did these things when planning the attack against the Union left. Both men sent out scouts to reconnoiter the Round Tops, and Law interrogated the sharpshooters captured during the afternoon.

Offensive battles are always more difficult to control than defensive, and there were two special difficulties for the Confederate Army on this occasion. First was the great extent of the Confederate lines, about five miles long, and their awkward shape, making intercommunication slow and difficult. Lee deployed his army upon a more extended front than that of Meade, without anywhere concentrating the force necessary for breaking up the enemy's lines.[22] The second difficulty was the type or character of the attack ordered. Lee's attack was an *en echelon*, meaning the movement started with one command and was then taken up successively by others. This approach differs from the simultaneous attack where all elements move at the same time. Lee's *en echelon* plan slowed communications and produced awkward battle lines, and disruptive terrain hindered the attack.

A third circumstance would be the interactions between General Lee and his staff. As stated in the preface to this volume, there are four levels of warfare: political, strategic, operational, and tactical. During an engagement or battle, a commander and his officers necessarily use elements from all levels. Thus, a commander might pursue a clever strategy to place his foe at a disadvantage before the onset of fighting, and his infantry might employ effective tactics, but his subordinate officers fail to properly implement his plans, and because of this, the overall attack fails and the battle is lost. The elements on each level of warfare never operate in a vacuum but can influence, sometimes greatly, other

---

20. Henry Steele Commager, ed., *The Blue and the Gray: The Story of the Civil War as Told by Participants* (New York, 1982), 591.
21. Tolles, "Army Movements," 543.
22. Alexander, *Military Memoirs*, 393–394; The Comte De Paris, *History of the Civil War*, 642, 599–600.

levels of activity.²³ For example, battles and large engagements consist of numerous tactical operations, so a particular assault can succeed but the battle still be lost. Applying this more detailed type of analysis to Civil War battles shows that many more assaults are successful on a purely tactical level than is commonly recognized, and in many battles, the attacking side loses not because of a failure of tactics but because of errors made on an operational or even strategic level.²⁴

Lee gave general instructions to each corps commander, but he left much to their discretion in carrying them out.²⁵ The management of the battle's timing on the Confederate side during this afternoon was conspicuously bad. The fighting was superb, but there appears to have been little supervision, and there was entire failure everywhere to conform to the original plan of the battle as Lee had indicated it.²⁶ The Confederate regimental commanders, according to their reports, acted generally on their initiative.²⁷ Lee's plan of battle was simple. He wanted to turn the enemy's left flank with his First Corps, and after the work began there, to demonstrate against the Union lines with the other two corps to prevent the threatened flank from being reinforced. These demonstrations would then turn into a real attack as the flanking wave of battle rolled over the troops in their front.²⁸ The plan Lee adopted made success dependent upon the combined action of several corps, between which there was no connection. The consequences of this plan escalated during each phase of the battle, and the hesitations of Lee's lieutenants magnified the problems. This battle plan setup proves to be the principal cause of his defeat.²⁹

Furthermore, Lee instructed Longstreet to initiate a series of assaults, by brigades *en echelon*. The orders for the fight were explicit, namely, that each brigade commander should govern his advance by the movements of the brigade neighbor on his right. When that body had advanced and was engaged in the fight, then he was to follow, pressing forward against the troops in his front. Lee expected that somewhere along the course his troops would find a weak spot in the Union line and break through, and thus inflict a fatal blow upon Meade.³⁰ As we have seen, Longstreet's attack was too long delayed and many hours later than what Lee had envisioned. If Longstreet had

---

23. Nosworthy, *The Bloody Crucible of Courage*, 276–277.
24. Ibid., 277.
25. Alexander, *Military Memoirs*, 393–394.
26. Ibid.
27. Norton, *Attack and Defense*, 124.
28. Fitzhugh Lee, *General Lee* (New York, 1898), 276–277.
29. The Comte De Paris, *History of the Civil War*, 150.
30. Young, *The Battle of Gettysburg*, 262–264.

commenced sooner, Union commanders would not have had time to post troops or artillery on their left and probably would not have been able to receive the reinforcements from the VI Corps.[31] Longstreet's delay gave Sickles time to advance his line to the Peach Orchard, which was a questionable tactical move as it exchanged strong ground for weak. If the Confederate attack had been properly organized and conducted, Sickles's advance would have given the Confederates an opportunity not otherwise possible, as an organized and better manned Confederate line would have been quite sure to crush the isolated Union III Corps.[32]

Moreover, had Lee known the situation of Sickles's new line, "Hood would have been thrown more to his right."[33] General Lee wrote, "I still think if all things could have worked together it would have been accomplished. But with the knowledge I then had, & in the circumstances I was then placed, I do not know what better course I could have pursued."[34] It sounds as if Lee never received the information about Sickles changing his line. General Hood was adamant that he could have taken Big Round Top, writing, "I shall ever believe that had I been permitted to turn Round Top Mountain, we would not only have gained that position, but have been able finally to rout the enemy."[35] Hood was referring to the flanking movement around the rear of Big Round Top that Lee and Longstreet refused to authorize. A flanking movement designed to bypass a strongly defended position was risky. If coordinating the movements of units that were within sight and sound of each other was difficult, one can only imagine how hard it was to coordinate the movements of units that were marching thousands of yards from each other.[36]

General Law summed up the loss by writing, "The whole matter then resolves itself into this: General Lee failed at Gettysburg on the 2d and 3d of July because he made his attack precisely where his enemy wanted him to make it and was most fully prepared to receive it."[37] Lee took responsibility regardless of what his generals said. Lee wrote, "No blame can be attached to the army for its failure to accomplish what was projected by me, nor should it be censured for the unreasonable

---

31. The Comte De Paris, *History of the Civil War*, 642.
32. Alexander, *Military Memoirs*, 392–393.
33. Lee, *General Lee*, 282.
34. Douglas Southall Freeman, ed., *Lee's Dispatches* (New York, 1915), 110. Dispatch 60 on July 13, 1863.
35. Hood, *Advance and Retreat*, 58–59.
36. Earl Hess, *The Union Soldier in Battle: Enduring the Ordeal of Combat* (Lawrence, KS, 1997), 58.
37. Law, "Round Top," 301.

SEVEN—The Days After   173

expectations of the public—I am alone to blame, in perhaps expecting too much of its prowess & valour."[38]

Tactical circumstances come from the viewpoint of Confederate Colonel William C. Oates, as his conclusions are more centered on how command decisions of Longstreet and Law affected his 15th Alabama regiment. The following is a summation of several key issues that Oates believed prevented him from occupying Little Round Top. The first issue involves missing men. Oates said, "The absence of Company A from the assault on Little Round Top and the number overcome by heat who had fallen out on scaling the rugged mountain, reduced my regiment to less than four hundred officers and men who made that assault."[39] He also referred to the water detail, writing, "The loss of the 22-man water detail and lack of the water contributed largely to our failure to take Little Round Top a few minutes later."[40] Finally, he refers to the lost skirmishers. Oates wrote, "With the five companies of skirmishers which had gone to the east of the mountain they might have made my assault successful. Another lost opportunity."[41]

Oates next questions Law's decision to move the 48th Alabama from his rear/flank, writing, "If the Forty-eighth Alabama had not been transferred to the left, but had remained to protect the rear, it would have taken care of the sharp-shooters, my flanking column would have captured Little Round Top before Vincent's brigade arrived and it would have won the battle for the Confederates."[42] Oates also wonders if Longstreet was even aware of actions on the Confederate right. Oates made two statements on this topic, the first being, "Had General Longstreet been where the attack began, he would have seen the necessity of protecting my flank from the assault of the United States sharp-shooters. Had that been done, I would, with the six hundred veterans I had, have reached Little Round Top before Vincent's Brigade did and would easily have captured that place, which would have won the battle." Oates's second comment was, "Or had he [Longstreet] seen the Fifteenth and Forty-seventh regiments when they reached the top of Great Round Top and ordered a battery and another regiment to aid me in holding that mountain, it would have been held."[43]

Oates seemed to be questioning the whole command structure when he wrote, "The change made in his line by General Sickles, which

---

38. Freeman, *Lee's Dispatches*, 110.
39. Oates, *The War*, 222.
40. *Ibid.*, 212.
41. *Ibid.*, 216.
42. *Ibid.*, 245.
43. *Ibid.*, 222.

was unknown to General Lee, greatly impaired his plan. When Longstreet found the change in Sickles' lines, of which he knew that General Lee was not aware, he should have adopted General Hood's suggestion to turn the flank and attack in the rear. Longstreet obeyed Lee's order literally, although Hood showed him the necessity of a change. General Law fully concurred with Hood's views."[44] Interestingly, Colonel Oates wrote that General Longstreet disapproved of the plan of attack because Lee was departing from the policy, declared by Lee before he moved from Virginia, of an aggressive defensive campaign, which Longstreet approved. Longstreet may have been right; it might have been best for Lee to have flanked Meade out of his strong position and have forced him to attack and thus to have acted on the defensive.[45]

Finally, on many battlefields, a regimental commander's control over his companies broke down, and the basic unit of Civil War field armies fragmented into tiny pieces while advancing on or defending a position.[46] As mentioned in Chapter Four, the Confederate advance was anything but orderly. When Hood ordered the advance, the whole division made a mad rush down through the wheat, firing and yelling like demons. The Confederate line advanced in quick time, with some running neck and neck, each striving to be first at the stone fences that protected the Union line of skirmishers, who were firing into the faces of the advancing Confederates. Under battle conditions, the structure of even a well-trained company or regiment perfectly formed up and pointed in the correct direction at a clear objective would begin to disintegrate the minute it began moving forward.[47] This type of advance is an example of a tactical or even operational error affecting Lee's strategic level of battle.

Other circumstances include Lee overextending his line and attacking when and where Meade expected him to attack, and Sickles advancing his line to the Peach Orchard, which, as it pertains to the 2nd Sharpshooters, caused Ward to push Stoughton's understrength regiment out onto the fields of Slyder Farm. Lee had bad execution by his subordinates, such as Longstreet's delay and regimental commanders acting generally on their initiative. The Union's stroke of luck was Colonel Strong Vincent's brigade winning the race to occupy Little Round Top just minutes ahead of the approaching Confederate line. Also, the 140th New York reached the crest of Little Round Top in the nick of time. If they had arrived "thirty or sixty seconds later," Hood's Texas

---

44. *Ibid.*, 223–224.
45. *Ibid.*, 224.
46. Hess, *The Union Soldier in Battle*, 58.
47. Rose, *Men of War*, 123.

SEVEN—The Days After

Brigade would have seized the hill.[48] Finally, Oates's decision to chase Stoughton's sharpshooters over Big Round Top delayed the 15th and 47th Alabama regiments for up to 40 minutes and allowed Vincent to win the aforementioned race to Little Round Top. This list is not exhaustive but goes to show that various incidents happened throughout the day that ended up putting the 2nd Sharpshooters in front of General Hood's Division and gave Major Stoughton's men the opportunity to defend the Union's left in and around Slyder Farm and the Round Tops.

Colonel Oates is one of the few Confederate authors to give credit to the 2nd Sharpshooters as the primary reason he did not take Little Round Top, which in Oates's mind would have won the battle. In a letter to Colonel Stoughton, Oates praises Stoughton's men, indicating two events that prevented him from attaining Little Round Top. Oates wrote:

> The great service which you and your command did was, *first, in changing my direction*, and in drawing my regiment and the 47th Alabama away from the point of attack. You drew off and delayed this force of over 1,000 men from falling on Vincent and the Union left at the same time of the attack of Law's other three regiments, the Texas and two Georgia brigades in front, and but for this service on your part I am confident we would have swept away the Union line and have captured Little Round Top, which would have won the battle for us. Again, when Vincent had fallen and I was within 150 yards of the top of Little Round Top, *you forced me to retire by appearing in my rear and opening fire on me*. The foregoing is substantially my recollection of you and your command at the great battle of Gettysburg[49] [emphasis added].

Oates credits Stoughton's sharpshooters with preventing him from capturing Little Round Top because Stoughton's men delayed and redirected Oates, and then when Stoughton appeared in the rear of Oates at the base of Little Round Top, Stoughton's fire forced Oates to retire. These comments are high praise, considering Oates was in the middle of attacking Colonel Chamberlain and the 20th Maine when Stoughton's men attacked.

As mentioned in the Introduction and shown throughout the text, the 2nd Sharpshooters executed a textbook example of a delaying action across Slyder Farm and the western slope of Big Round Top. A delaying action is a battle fought by a clearly outnumbered and outgunned force to try to slow down the advance of a superior force and buy enough time for other friendly forces to either escape or arrive. This action also trades

---

48. Porter Farley, "Bloody Round Top," *National Tribune* (Washington, D.C., 1883), 1.
49. Oates, "Letter to Col. H.R. Stoughton," 328.

space for time by slowing down the enemy's momentum and inflicting maximum damage on the enemy without becoming decisively engaged. The sharpshooters, using the terrain and obstacles to slow or hinder Hood's advance, inflicted heavy casualties on Hood's men. Stoughton used the rocky terrain at the stone fence as he fell back to an elevated and heavily wooded position on the side of Big Round Top. The advancing Confederate line traversed relatively open farmland before crossing the marshy ground of Plum Run. Finally, Stoughton had an avenue of retreat up Big Round Top, using the boulders as cover and the foliage as concealment. Stoughton seems to have had a sense of the battlefield terrain and knew how best to utilize it to his advantage. At Gettysburg, natural and manmade obstacles fragmented advancing Confederate regiments, depleting their strength, slowing momentum, and reducing their already limited manpower. Colonel Oates's decision to chase the 2nd Sharpshooters up Big Round Top consumed valuable time and further delayed the Confederates' mission of turning the Union's left flank and taking Little Round Top before the arrival of Union reinforcements.[50]

For the 2nd Sharpshooters, their involvement at Gettysburg arose from two key movements: Lee extending his line to the south, and Sickles's response by advancing his line to the Peach Orchard. These positional movements were the crucial events that moved Stoughton's men to the left and forward onto the John Slyder farm with Hood's division in their front. Stoughton's command rendered an important service by delaying the advance of Hood's division as their attack began, assisted in the defense of Plum Run Valley with the 4th Maine, and rerouted Oates's two regiments in their efforts to gain Little Round Top until it was too late for them to achieve that goal.[51] Additionally, the 2nd Sharpshooters helped defend Little Round Top after retreating through the 83rd Pennsylvania line. Sergeant Scribner and his scouts, along with some men from Company H, fell in with Company B of the 20th Maine and participated in Chamberlain's historic charge. Others from Company B_1 silenced Confederate sharpshooters in the Devil's Den area who were harassing Union soldiers and artillery. The superior training and equipment of the 2nd Sharpshooters made these actions possible. Wyman White summed it up well, stating, "I think the breech loaders of the Sharpshooters was quite an item in the balance."[52] There is a lot of truth in that statement. The incessant, accurate, and rapid firing of the sharpshooters markedly thinned the Confederate ranks.

---

50. Military Factory (accessed April 20, 2022); Tucker, *Storming Little Round Top*, 137.
51. Stevens, *Berdan's United States Sharpshooters*, 326.
52. White, *Civil War Diary*, 166.

When the Union Army dissolved the III Corps in 1864, the powers that be transferred the sharpshooter outfits to the II Corps, where they retained their regimental organizations until the end of their three-year enlistments. On the final disbandment, General DeTrobriand issued the following valedictory order, General Order No. 12, on February 16, 1865. He said:

> The United States Sharpshooters, including the first and second consolidated battalions, being about to be broken up as a distinct organization in compliance with orders from the War Department, the brigadier-general commanding the division will not take leave of them without acknowledging their good and efficient service during about three years in the field. The United States Sharpshooters leave behind them a glorious record in the Army of the Potomac since the first operations against Yorktown in 1862 up to Hatcher's Run, and few are the battles or engagements where they did not make their mark. The brigadier-general commanding, who had them under his command during most of the campaigns of 1863 and 1864, would be the last to forget their brave deeds during that period, and he feels assured that in the different organizations to which they may belong severally, officers and men will show themselves worthy of their old reputation; with them the past will answer for the future.[53]

Even though the Union army was besieging Petersburg, a campaign where sniping was a daily occurrence, the high command showed no interest in continuing the existence of these unique regiments beyond their original terms of service. The Army either transferred veterans and recruits to line regiments from their respective states or disbanded sharpshooter regiments, sending the men home, many of them carrying the rifles they had used so effectively during the conflict.[54] Why were such valuable units allowed to fade into history? Then, as now, commanders are often suspicious of, or openly hostile toward, elite organizations. Early on, Berdan's sharpshooters established a reputation for individuality and disregard for many military principles.[55]

By World War I, while there were many excellent riflemen within the U.S. ranks, there were still no regiments of sharpshooters or dedicated sharpshooting rifles. Despite the manuals leading military authorities wrote, the training given, and the experience gained, after the war much of the U.S. Army high command forgot what they had learned. Once again, the U.S. Army had to reinvent the wheel, but at least this

---

53. Stevens, *Berdan's United States Sharpshooters*, 499–500.
54. Joseph G. Bilby, *Civil War Firearms: Their Historical Background, Tactical Use and Modern Collecting and Shooting* (Conshohocken, PA, 1999), 112; Pegler, *Sharpshooting Rifles*, 76.
55. Bilby, *Civil War Firearms*, 112.

time there lingered a faint memory of what the sharpshooters achieved during the Civil War.[56]

The Berdan Sharpshooters had become the stuff of legend and the Army realized that the sharpshooter (now sniper) was a permanent feature of the modern battlefield. Although World War I ended before the Army could field significant numbers of American sniper units, the lessons learned in 1861–65, and the training that had evolved as a result, eventually led to the establishment of today's sniper training schools and the deployment of snipers as some of the most highly trained and efficient soldiers in today's armies.[57]

Reflecting on the 2nd Sharpshooters at Gettysburg, George Benedict stated, "Oates' advance upon Round Top was so slow was in large part due to the sharpshooters, who fell back slowly from rock to rock, while the enemy to his surprise found his numbers diminishing steadily before an almost invisible skirmish line." Were it not for their obstinate defense of the position at the D-shaped field, and the pass between the Round Tops, contesting the Confederate advance every inch of the way, Oates's boast to have been able to take Little Round Top might have been true.[58]

In the Introduction, the question was asked, "Do great battles sometimes turn on small events?" To refine this question with a focus on the battle at hand, it can be restated: Did the 2nd Sharpshooters, in redirecting and delaying the advance of Law's brigade, change the fate of the battle? The understrength 2nd Sharpshooters, with about 170 men, held off five regiments for up to an hour, long enough for Colonel Strong Vincent's brigade to occupy Little Round Top. The 2nd Sharpshooters delaying action across Slyder Farm and upon Big Round Top was a much larger and more important part of the overall victory than what most participants realized, and some historians understand.

Charles Stevens expressed it succinctly when he wrote, "With such stinging effect did the Second Regiment pepper the Confederates up and down the mountain sides, from behind bowlders and trees, and finally from across the ravine, that some of the rebel officers termed it a perfect hornet's nest of sharpshooters."[59] For the 2nd U.S. Sharpshooters, this statement was probably the most appropriate and significant description of their actions that day.

---

56. Pegler, *Sharpshooting Rifles*, 76; Bilby, *Civil War Firearms*, 112.
57. Pegler, *Sharpshooting Rifles*, 76.
58. Benedict, *Vermont in the Civil War*, 767; Stevens, *Berdan's United States Sharpshooters*, 329.
59. Stevens, *Berdan's United States Sharpshooters*, 329.

Appendix A
Abbreviated Order of Battle

Army of the Potomac
Major General George G. Meade

III Army Corps
Major General Daniel E. Sickles
Major General David B. Birney

First Division
Major General David B. Birney
Brigadier General J.H. Hobart Ward

First Brigade
Brigadier General Charles K. Graham
63rd Pennsylvania (Major John A. Danks)

Second Brigade
Brigadier General J.H. Hobart Ward
Colonel Hiram Berdan

20th Indiana Infantry (Colonel John Wheeler)
3rd Maine Infantry (Colonel Moses B. Lakeman)
4th Maine Infantry (Colonel Elijah Walker)
86th New York Infantry (Lieutenant Colonel Benjamin L. Higgins)
124th New York Infantry (Colonel Van Horne Ellis)
99th Pennsylvania Infantry (Major John W. Moore)
1st United States Sharpshooters (Lieutenant Colonel Caspar Trepp)
2nd United States Sharpshooters (Major Homer R. Stoughton)

- Company A (Captain Abraham Wright)
- Company B (Captain Adolphus A. Guest)
- Company C (Captain Ira J. Northrop)

- Company D (Captain Jacob McClure)
- Company E (Captain Frank D. Sweetser)
- Company F (Captain Edward T. Rowell)
- Company G (Captain Harvard F. Smith)
- Company H (Captain Albert Buxton)

Third Brigade

Colonel P. Regis De Trobriand

17th Maine Infantry (Lieutenant Colonel Charles B. Merrill)
3rd Michigan Infantry (Colonel Byron R. Pierce)
5th Michigan Infantry (Lieutenant Colonel John Pulford)
40th New York Infantry (Colonel Thomas W. Egan)
110th Pennsylvania Infantry (Lieutenant Colonel David M. Jones)

Second Division

Brigadier General Andrew A. Humphreys

Third Brigade

Colonel George C. Burling

6th New Jersey (Lieutenant Colonel Stephen R. Gilkyson)

Artillery Brigade

Captain George E. Randolph

4th New York Independent Battery (Captain James E. Smith)

V Army Corps

Major General George Sykes

First Division

Brigadier General James Barnes
Brigadier General Charles Griffin

Third Brigade

Colonel Strong Vincent
Colonel James C. Rice

20th Maine Infantry (Colonel Joshua L. Chamberlain)
16th Michigan Infantry (Lieutenant Colonel Norval E. Welch)
44th New York Infantry (Colonel James C. Rice)
83rd Pennsylvania Infantry (Captain Orpheus S. Woodward)

Second Division

Brigadier General Romeyn B. Ayres

Third Brigade
Brigadier General Stephen H. Weed
Colonel Kenner Garrard

140th New York Infantry (Colonel Patrick O'Rorke)
146th New York Infantry (Colonel Kenner Garrard)
91st Pennsylvania Infantry (Lieutenant Colonel Joseph H. Sinex)
155th Pennsylvania Infantry (Lieutenant Colonel John H. Cain)

Artillery Brigade
Captain Augustus P. Martin

Battery D, 5th United States Artillery (Lieutenant Charles E. Hazlett)

XII Army Corps
Major General Henry W. Slocum
Brigadier General Alpheus S. Williams

Second Division
Brigadier General John W. Geary

First Brigade
Colonel Charles Candy

5th Ohio Infantry (Colonel John H. Patrick)
7th Ohio Infantry (Colonel William R. Creighton)
29th Ohio Infantry (Captain Wilbur F. Stevens)
66th Ohio Infantry (Lieutenant Colonel Eugene Powell)
28th Pennsylvania Infantry (Captain John H. Flynn)
147th Pennsylvania Infantry (Lieutenant Colonel Ario Pardee, Jr.)

Army of Northern Virginia
General Robert E. Lee

First Corps
Lieutenant General James Longstreet

Hood's Division
Major General John B. Hood
Brigadier General Evander M. Law

Law's Brigade
Brigadier General Evander M. Law

4th Alabama Infantry (Colonel Lawrence H. Scruggs)
15th Alabama Infantry (Colonel William C. Oates)
44th Alabama Infantry (Colonel William F. Perry)
47th Alabama Infantry (Colonel James W. Jackson)
48th Alabama Infantry (Colonel James L. Sheffield)

Robertson's Brigade (Hood's Texas Brigade)

Brigadier General Jerome B. Robertson

3rd Arkansas Infantry (Colonel Van H. Manning)
1st Texas Infantry (Colonel Phillip A. Work)
4th Texas Infantry (Colonel John C.G. Key)
5th Texas Infantry (Colonel Robert M. Powell)

Third Corps

Lieutenant General Ambrose P. Hill

Anderson's Division

Major General Richard H. Anderson

Wilcox's Brigade

Brigadier Gen Cadmus M. Wilcox

8th Alabama Infantry (Lieutenant Colonel Hilary A. Herbert)
9th Alabama Infantry (Captain J. Horace King)
10th Alabama Infantry (Colonel William H. Forney)
11th Alabama Infantry (Colonel John C.C. Sanders)
14th Alabama Infantry (Colonel Lucius Pinckard)

Pender's Division

Major General William D. Pender

Third Corps Artillery Reserve

Colonel R. Lindsay Walker

Pegram's Artillery Battalion (Major William J. Pegram)
McIntosh's Artillery Battalion (Major David G. McIntosh)
Garnett's Artillery Battalion (Lieutenant Colonel John Garnett)
[from Heth's Division]

Lane's Brigade

Brigadier General James H. Lane

7th North Carolina Infantry (Major J. McCleod Turner)
18th North Carolina Infantry (Colonel John D. Barry)
28th North Carolina Infantry (Colonel Samuel D. Lowe)

33rd North Carolina Infantry (Colonel Clark M. Avery)
37th North Carolina Infantry (Colonel William M. Barbour)

Scale's Brigade

Brigadier General Alfred M. Scales
13th North Carolina Infantry (Colonel Joseph H. Hyman)
16th North Carolina Infantry (Captain Leroy W. Stowe)
22nd North Carolina Infantry (Colonel James Conner)
34th North Carolina Infantry (Colonel William L.J. Lowrance)
38th North Carolina Infantry (Colonel William J. Hoke)

Appendix B
Engaged Strengths on June 30, 1863, Muster Roll[1]

2nd Regiment Sharpshooters: Engaged = 169*
- Total Losses = 43 (5k, 23w, 15mc); 25.4% loss

Hood's Division: Engaged = 7373; Losses = 2407 (483k, 1396w, 528mc); 32.6% loss

Robertson's Brigade: Engaged = 1734; Losses = 603 (152k, 313w, 138mc); 34.8% loss
- 3rd Arkansas: Engaged = 479; Losses = 182 (41k, 101w, 40mc); 38.0% loss
- 1st Texas: Engaged = 426; Losses = 97 (29k, 46w, 22mc); 22.8% loss
- 4th Texas: Engaged = 415; Losses = 112 (28k, 53w, 31mc); 27.0% loss
- 5th Texas: Engaged = 409; Losses = 211 (54k, 112w, 45mc); 51.6% loss

Law's Brigade: Engaged = 1933; Losses = 535 (79k, 317w,139mc); 27.7% loss
- 4th Alabama: Engaged = 346; Losses = 92 (18k, 55w, 19mc); 26.6% loss
- 15th Alabama: Engaged = 499; Losses = 178 (18k, 77w, 83mc); 35.7% loss
- 44th Alabama: Engaged = 363; Losses = 88 (25k, 58w, 5mc); 24.2% loss
- 47th Alabama: Engaged = 347; Losses = 69 (10k, 46w, 13mc); 19.9% loss
- 48th Alabama: Engaged = 374; Losses = 106 (8k, 81w, 17mc); 28.3% loss

*Estimate. Total losses explanation: k = killed; w = wounded; mc = missing/captured.

---

1. Busey and Martin, *Regimental Strengths and Losses*, 50, 131, 260–262. Engaged strengths are present for duty equipped or battle strength of the units when they reached the immediate battle area. Losses are for the entire three-day battle, not just July 2, 1863.

Appendix C
Supplemental Figures

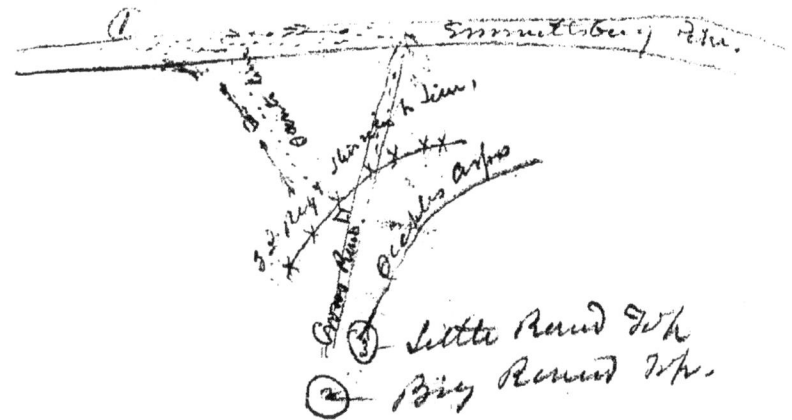

Adjutant Seymour Norton's sketch showing the route of the offensive patrol. From Norton, *War Papers.*

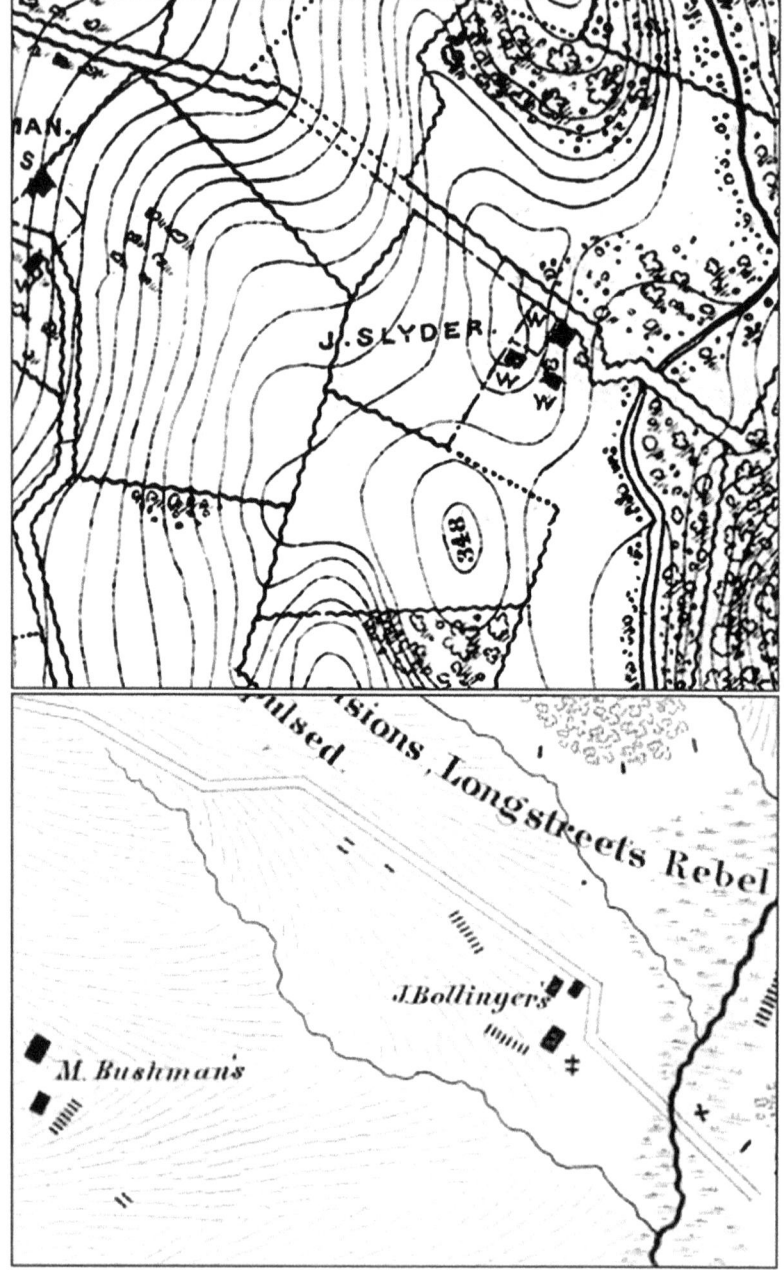

The brook when comparing G.K. Warren's *Battle field of Gettysburg* map (top) against S.G. Elliott & Company's *Elliott's Map of the Battlefield of Gettysburg, Pennsylvania* map (bottom).

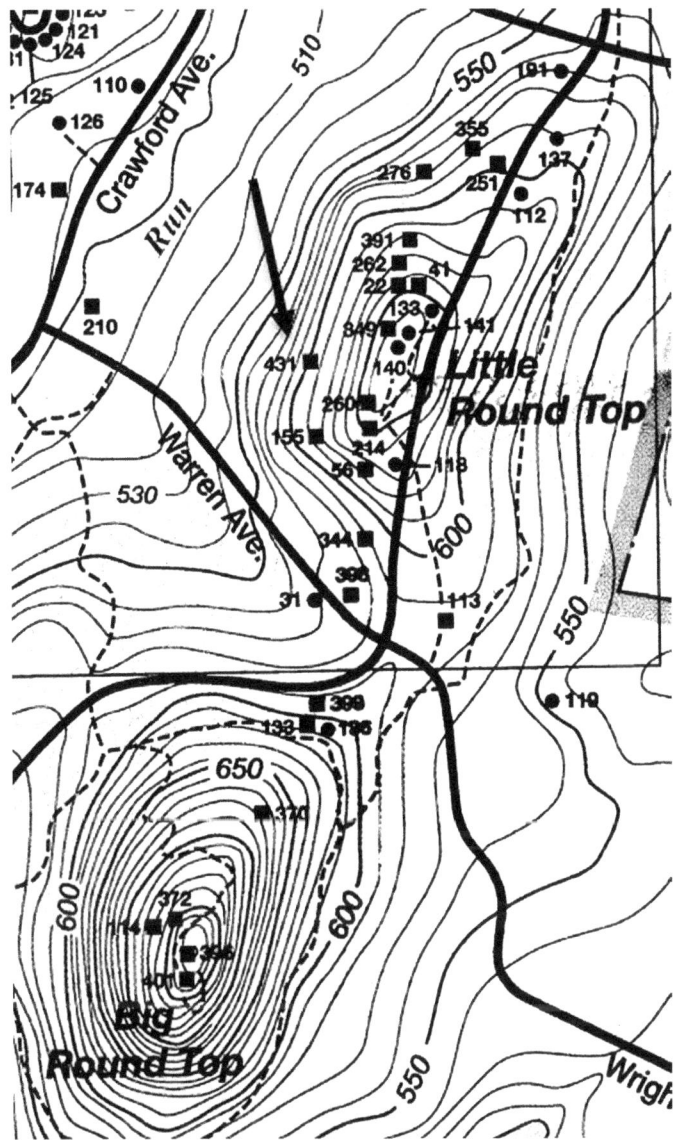

Above: Arrow points to the location of regimental marker 431, recognizing Michigan companies from the 1st and 2nd Sharpshooters. *Top of following page*: The plaque on the west side of the monument indicates Company B, 2nd Sharpshooters fought at this location on July 2, 1863. *Bottom of following page*: Modern-day photograph of Devil's Den from regimental marker 431 on Little Round Top. Credit: Tim Kissel, *Gettysburg National Military Park*, in Battlefield America: A Civil War Map Series, Map 104, Aurora, CO, 1 sheet. Author's collection.

Appendix C

Appendix D
2nd Sharpshooters Company Captains

Company A: Captain Abraham Wright

Abraham Wright lived in Red Wing, Minnesota, where he was a carpenter. At the time of his enlistment, he was 29 years old, six feet tall with a light complexion, hazel eyes, and auburn hair. He mustered into Company A on October 5, 1861. Wright was promoted to first sergeant (date unknown), then to first lieutenant on July 18, 1862, and finally to captain on May 8, 1863. Wright received wounds at Gettysburg on July 3, at North Anna on May 24, 1864, and at Petersburg on June 16, 1864. Wright mustered out on October 6, 1864.[1]

Captain Abraham Wright, Company A, 2nd U.S. Sharpshooters. Courtesy the Brian T. White Collection.

---

1. Peteler, "Narrative of the First Company of Sharpshooters," 511; civilwardata.com (accessed January 8, 2023); U.S. War Department, *Regimental and Company Books of the 2nd U.S. Sharpshooters Regiment.*

Company B: Captain Adolphus A. Guest

Adolphus A. Guest, a clerk before the war, entered service on October 29, 1861, as a private in Company H, 8th New York State Militia for three months of service. Guest attained the rank of first sergeant on November 6, 1861, when he joined Company B. He was promoted to second lieutenant on April 2, 1862, then to first lieutenant on April 2, 1862. Guest received wounds at Antietam on September 17, 1862, but returned to the regiment after 20 days of leave. He attained the rank of captain on October 14, 1862, and mustered out on October 10, 1864. At the time of his enlistment, Guest was 22 years old, five feet eight inches tall with a light complexion, hazel eyes, and brown hair.[2]

Captain Adolphus A. Guest, Company B, 2nd U.S. Sharpshooters. Courtesy the Brian T. White Collection.

Company C: Captain Ira J. Northrop

Ira J. Northrop, a laborer living in Brookville, Jefferson County, Pennsylvania, before the war, enlisted as a sergeant in Company C on October 1, 1861. He was promoted to second lieutenant (date unknown) and then to captain on January 9, 1863. He mustered out on August 21, 1864. Northrop, when he enlisted, was 27 years old, six feet two inches tall with a light complexion, blue eyes, and light brown hair.[3]

---

2. George H. Brown, *Record of Service of Michigan Volunteers in the Civil War, 1861–1865, Volume 44* (Kalamazoo, MI, 1905), 112; civilwardata.com (accessed January 8, 2023); U.S. War Department, *Regimental and Company Books of the 2nd U.S. Sharpshooters Regiment.*

3. civilwardata.com (accessed January 8, 2023); fold3.com (accessed January 8, 2023); U.S. War Department, *Regimental and Company Books of the 2nd U.S. Sharpshooters Regiment.*

Captain Ira J. Northrop, Company C, 2nd U.S. Sharpshooters. Credit: Author's personal collection, scanned from carte de visite portrait photograph. This work is in the public domain and was published in the United States before 1927.

Company D: Captain Jacob McClure

Jacob McClure lived in Rockland, Maine, with his wife Hannah, where he worked as a mechanic. McClure was 29 years old, five feet eleven inches tall, with a light complexion, hazel eyes, and dark brown hair when he enlisted on September 17, 1861. He mustered into service with Company D on November 1, 1861. The Army commissioned McClure as a first sergeant and later promoted him to first lieutenant (date unknown) and then to captain on September 25, 1862. McClure received wounds at Gettysburg, on July 2, 1863, and eventually mustered out on April 11, 1864. An anonymous writer to the *Bangor Daily Whig and Courier* stated that "Major McClure is a gentleman and a soldier—and the best shot in either of Berdan's two regiments. Many a rebel has fallen by his unerring rifle—and he has made the name of our little company of Maine riflemen a terror to the enemy."[4]

Captain Jacob McClure, Company D, 2nd U.S. Sharpshooters. Courtesy the Brian T. White Collection.

---

4. John L. Hodsdon, *Annual Report of the Adjutant General of the State of Maine for the Year Ending December 31, 1863, Appendix D* (Augusta, ME: 1863), 99–101;

Company E: Captain Francis D. Sweetser

Francis "Frank" D. Sweetser was born in Salem, Massachusetts, on June 4, 1833, but had moved to Lynn, Essex County, Massachusetts, during his childhood. Sweetser, a shoemaker before the war, was approximately 26 years old when he enlisted. He mustered into Company E and was commissioned as a second lieutenant on March 15, 1862, being promoted to captain on September 17, 1862. The Army cashiered Sweetser from service on September 14, 1863.[5]

Captain Francis D. Sweetser, Company E, 2nd U.S. Sharpshooters. Courtesy the Brian T. White Collection.

Company F: Captain Edward T. Rowell/ Second Lieutenant Samuel F. Murry

The Army promoted Captain Edward Rowell to major on July 1, 1863, and transferred him to regimental field and staff, leaving Company F under the command of Second Lieutenant Samuel Murry. Wyman White does not mention Rowell during the Gettysburg battle but does indicate Murry was with the men during combat. Therefore, I have included both officers in Company F.

Rowell graduated from Dartmouth College in 1861 and then enlisted as a private in the 5th New Hampshire Infantry. The Army commissioned Rowell as a second lieutenant in Company F on September 21, 1861, to captain on July 13, 1862, and to major on July 1, 1863.

---

civilwardata.com (accessed January 8, 2023); fold3.com (accessed January 8, 2023); Ancestry.com (accessed January 9, 2023); U.S. War Department, *Regimental and Company Books of the 2nd U.S. Sharpshooters Regiment*; Unknown, "Letter to the Editor," *Bangor Daily Whig and Courier*, Bangor, ME, September 18, 1863, page 1.

5. U.S. War Department, *Regimental and Company Books of the 2nd U.S. Sharpshooters Regiment*; Theodore S. Peck, *Revised Roster of Vermont Volunteers* (Montpelier, VT, 1892), 611.

Rowell received a shell fragment wound in his leg at Gettysburg and was wounded again on June 17, 1864, near Petersburg, Virginia. He mustered out on November 27, 1864, and entered the field of journalism with the *Lowell Daily Courier* in Lowell, Massachusetts.

Captain Edward T. Rowell, Company F, 2nd U.S. Sharpshooters. Courtesy the Brian T. White Collection.

Samuel F. Murry was a 20-year-old student in Auburn, New Hampshire, before he enlisted in the Army on November 5, 1861. He mustered in as a sergeant in Company F on November 26, 1861. The Army commissioned Murry as a second lieutenant on July 13, 1862, and promoted him to first lieutenant on August 30, 1863, and to captain on September 10, 1863. Confederate forces captured Murry twice during the war. The first time was on July 13, 1862. His captors held him prisoner for a month before he was exchanged. The second time was on June 21, 1864, when he was imprisoned for almost seven months before he was paroled. Murry mustered out on December 29, 1864. At the time of his enlistment, Murry was five feet 11 inches tall with a florid complexion (which is a red or flushed complexion), blue eyes, and dark hair.[6]

Lieutenant Samuel F. Murry, Company F, 2nd U.S. Sharpshooters. Courtesy the Brian T. White Collection.

---

6. U.S. War Department, *Regimental and Company Books of the 2nd U.S. Sharpshooters Regiment*; Natt Head, *Report of the Adjutant General of the State of New Hampshire, May 20, 1865* (Concord, NH, 1865), 730; Unknown, "Personal Section," *The National Tribune*, Washington, D.C., July 17, 1890, page 4; White, *Civil War Diary*, 165;

Company G: Captain Harvard P. Smith

Before the war, Harvard P. Smith devoted his time and effort to the study of medicine. At the outbreak of hostilities, Smith, at 23 years old, enlisted as a sergeant in Company G. He was commissioned as a second lieutenant on October 10, 1862, and promoted to captain on November 1, 1862. He was wounded and taken prisoner at the Battle of Bull Run but returned to the regiment before the Battle of Fredericksburg. Smith was again wounded on May 6, 1864, during the Battle of the Wilderness. Afterward, considered disabled for active duty, he was detailed for special duty at Washington until mustered out on December 24, 1864. Smith, at the time of his enlistment, was six feet one inch tall and had a dark complexion with hazel eyes and black hair.[7]

Captain Harvard P. Smith, Company G, 2nd U.S. Sharpshooters. Courtesy the Brian T. White Collection.

Company H: Captain Albert Buxton

Albert Buxton was a farmer outside the town limits of South Londonderry, Vermont. He enlisted into Company H on December 24, 1861, and mustered in as a second lieutenant on December 31, 1861. The Army promoted Buxton to captain on December 1, 1862. He received a slight wound in the neck at Gettysburg on July 3, 1863, and received a mortal wound in his leg on May 5, 1864, during the Battle of the Wilderness in

---

Ancestry.com (accessed January 9, 2023); State of New Hampshire, *Journal of the House of the Honorable Senate, of the State of New Hampshire. June Session, 1864* (Concord, NH, 1864), 565–566.

7. U.S. War Department, *Regimental and Company Books of the 2nd U.S. Sharpshooters Regiment*; Natt Head, *Report of the Adjutant General*, 730; State of New Hampshire, *Journal of the House of the Honorable Senate*, 565–566; Kimball Webster, *History of Hudson, N.H.* (Manchester, NH, 1913), 280; George W. Kingsbury, *History of Dakota Territory, Volume V* (Chicago, 1915), 1000–1002.

Virginia. Surgeons amputated his leg, but he died the next day. Buxton, at the time of his enlistment, was five feet 10 inches tall with a light complexion, gray eyes, and dark hair.[8]

Captain Albert Buxton, Company H, 2nd U.S. Sharpshooters. Courtesy the Brian T. White Collection.

---

8. U.S. War Department, *Regimental and Company Books of the 2nd U.S. Sharpshooters Regiment*; civilwardata.com (accessed January 8, 2023); Ancestry.com (accessed January 8, 2023).

Bibliography

Primary Sources

Unpublished Manuscripts

Jackson, James W. *Letter to Montgomery Daily Mail, July 26, 1863*. Library & Research Center, Gettysburg NMP, Gettysburg, PA, 3 pp.

Jackson, James W. *Letter to wife, July 7, 1863*. Library & Research Center, Gettysburg National Military Park (NMP), Gettysburg, PA, 3 pp.

Meade, George. *Letter to Henry J. Hunt, July 22, 1886*. http://www.gdg.org/Research/Hunt/hajuly22_1886.html (accessed May 10, 2022).

Norton, Seymour. *Civil War Papers—Company E Sharpshooters—Memoranda*. Library & Research Center, Gettysburg NMP, Gettysburg, PA, 21 pp.

Oates, William C. *Account of Colonel William C. Oates, 15th Alabama Infantry; Re: Battle of Gettysburg*. Library & Research Center, Gettysburg NMP, Gettysburg, PA, 19 pp.

Oates, William C. *Letter to J.L. Chamberlain, 8 March 1897*. Library & Research Center, Gettysburg NMP, Gettysburg, PA, 4 pp. plus map.

Shreve, William Price. *William Price Shreve Papers*. M29, Historical Manuscripts, Special Collections, The University of Southern Mississippi Libraries.

Online Collections

Brown, Joseph B. "Letter to Matilda Crandall, July 29, 1863." Crandall Family Papers: https://altchive.org/node/13637 (accessed December 1, 2021).

Clark, Nathan S. "Nathan S. Clark Diary, 20th Maine" (2016). *Historical Documents*. Digital Maine Repository. https://digitalmaine.com/hist_docs/2 (accessed December 27, 2021).

Elliott & Co., S.G. *Elliott's map of the battlefield of Gettysburg, Pennsylvania*. [Philadelphia, S.G. Elliott & Co., 1863] Map. Retrieved from the Library of Congress, https://www.loc.gov/item/99447500/ (accessed February 15, 2020).

Graves, Anthony Gardner, Jr. "Letter to John, July 9, 1863." *1862–65: Anthony Gardner Graves, Jr. Letters*. https://sparedshared22.wordpress.com/2021/07/09/1862-65-anthony-graves-letters/ (accessed December 7, 2021).

Pettijohn Chamberlain, E.J., and C.A. Pettijohn. "Something of the Pettijohn (Pettyjohn) Family." Privately printed, 1948. http://www.pettijohn.net/Something_of_the_Pettijohn_Family.pdf (accessed April 18, 2018).

Prince, Howard L. "Capt. Howard L. Prince's Address," *Dedication of the Twentieth Maine Monuments at Gettysburg, October 3, 1889*, http://www.gdg.org/Research/People/Chamberlain/20ded.html (accessed May 27, 2022).

Warren, G.K., *Battlefield of Gettysburg*. [Washington, U.S. Army, Office of the Chief of

Engineers 187-?] Map. Retrieved from the Library of Congress, https://www.loc.gov/item/99448794/ (accessed April 01, 2018).

Books

Alexander, E.P. *Military Memoirs of a Confederate: A Critical Narrative.* New York: Charles Scribner's Sons, 1907.

Beecham, R.K. *Gettysburg: The Pivotal Battle of the Civil War.* Chicago: A.C. McClurg & Co., 1911.

Benedict, G.G. *Vermont in the Civil War: A History of the Part Taken by the Vermont Soldiers and Sailors in the War for the Union, 1861–1865, Volume 2.* Burlington, VT: The Free Press Association, 1888.

Briscoe, J.C. "Capt. J.C. Briscoe's Report of Gettysburg." *Life of David Bell Birney, Major-General United States Volunteers.* Philadelphia: King & Baird, 1867.

Buchanan, Charles J. "Oration by Lieut. Charles J. Buchanan." *New York at Gettysburg: Final Report of the Battlefield of Gettysburg, Volume 3.* Albany, NY: J.B. Lyon Company, Printers, 1902.

Burnham, Janet Hayward, ed. *Notes of Army and Prison Life, 1862–1865.* Bethel, VT: My Little Jesse Press, 2004.

Casey, Silas. *Infantry Tactics, for the Instruction, Exercise, and Manœuvres of the Soldier, a Company, Line of Skirmishers, Battalion, Brigade, or Corps D' Armée, Volume 1.* New York: D. Van Nostrand, 1863.

Chamberlain, Joshua L. *Through Blood & Fire at Gettysburg.* Gettysburg, PA: Stan Clark Military Books, 1994.

Coco, Gregory A. *Killed in Action: Eyewitness Accounts of the Last Moments of 100 Union Soldiers who Died at Gettysburg.* Gettysburg, PA: Thomas Publications, 1992.

Coco, Gregory A., ed. *Recollections of a Texas Colonel at Gettysburg.* Gettysburg, PA: Thomas Publications, 1990.

Craft, David. *History of the One Hundred Forty-First Regiment, Pennsylvania Volunteers, 1862–1865.* Towanda, PA: Reporter-Journal Printing Company, 1885.

Fasnacht, C.H. *Historical Sketch, Dedication of 99th Pennsylvania Monument, Gettysburg, PA., July 2, 1886.* Lancaster, PA: Examiner Steam Book and Job Print, 1886.

Fletcher, William A. *Rebel Private Front and Rear.* Beaumont, TX: Press of the Greer Print, 1908.

Fortin, Maurice S., ed. "Colonel Hilary A. Herbert's 'History of the Eighth Alabama Volunteer Regiment, C.S.A.'" *Alabama Historical Quarterly* 39, no. 1–4. Montgomery: Alabama State Department of Archives and History, 1977.

Frederick the Great. *Instructions for His Generals.* Translated by Thomas R. Phillips. Mineola, NY: Dover Publications, 2005.

Gerrish, Theodore. *Army Life: A Private's Reminiscences of the Civil War.* Portland, ME: Hoyt, Fogg & Donham, 1882.

Goss, Warren L. *Recollections of a Private: A Story of the Army of the Potomac.* New York: Thomas Y. Crowell & Co., 1890.

Hastings, William H. *Letters from a Sharpshooter: The Civil War Letters of Private William B. Greene, Co. G, 2nd United States Sharpshooters (Berdan's), Army of the Potomac, 1861–1865.* Belleville, WI: The Hastings Group, 1993.

Hoisington, Daniel J., ed. "I Never Saw Such Shooting." *Chanhassen: A Centennial History.* Chanhassen, MN: City of Chanhassen, 1996.

Hood, J.B. *Advance and Retreat: Personal Experiences in the United States and Confederate States Armies.* New Orleans, LA: Privately published, 1880.

Houghton, Edwin B. *The Campaigns of the Seventeenth Maine.* Portland, ME: Short & Long, 1866.

Hunt, Henry J. "The Second Day at Gettysburg." *Battles and Leaders of the Civil War: Volume 3, The Tide Shifts.* Secaucus, NJ: Castle Books, 2010.

Johnson, Hannibal A. *The Sword of Honor: A Story of the Civil War.* Worcester, MA: Blanchard Press, 1906.

Jordan, William C. *Some Events and Incidents During the Civil War*. Montgomery, AL: Paragon Press, 1909.
Judson, A.M. *History of the Eighty-Third Regiment Pennsylvania Volunteers*. Erie, PA: B.F.H. Lynn, Publisher, 1865.
Kellogg, Marya (Abbott), and Robert Kellogg, eds. *The Curtis Abbott Papers: Letters and Memoirs from a Civil War Veteran's Long Life*. Scottsdale, AZ: The BookPatch, 2015.
Ladd, David L., and Audrey J. Ladd, eds. *The Batchelder Papers: Gettysburg in Their Own Words, Three Volumes*, Dayton, OH: Morningside House, 1994.
Lasswell, Mary. *Rags and Hope: The Recollections of Val C. Giles, Four Years with Hood's Brigade, Fourth Texas Infantry, 1861–1865*. New York: Coward-McCann, 1961.
Leavitt, Samuel H. "Dedication of Monument. 86th Regiment Infantry Historical Sketch." *Final Report of the Battlefield of Gettysburg, Volume 2*. Albany, NY: J.B. Lyon Company, 1900.
Lee, Fitzhugh. *General Lee*. New York: D. Appleton and Company, 1898.
Longstreet, James. *From Manassas to Appomattox: The Memoirs of the Civil War in America*. Philadelphia: J.B. Lippincott Company, 1896.
Magnin, Albert. "Dedication of Monument, 99th Regiment Infantry." *Pennsylvania at Gettysburg, Ceremonies as the Dedication of the Monuments, Volume 2*, edited by John P. Nicholson. Harrisburg, PA: E.K. Meyers, State Printer, 1893.
Mahan, D.H. *An Elementary Treatise on Advanced-Guard, Out-Post, and Detachment Service of Troops, and the Manner of Posting and Handling Them*. New York: John Wiley, 1861.
Meade, George. *The Life and Letters of George Gordon Meade, Two Volumes*. New York: Charles Scribner's Sons, 1913.
Meier, Heinz K. *Memoirs of a Swiss Officer in the American Civil War (Three Years in the Army of the Potomac or a Swiss Company of Sharpshooters in the North American War)*. Translated by Hedwig D. Rappolt. Bern, Switzerland: Herbert Lang, 1972.
Michigan Gettysburg Battlefield Commission. "Sharpshooters." *Michigan at Gettysburg, July 1st, 2nd and 3rd, 1863*, 113–114. Detroit, MI: Winn & Hammond, 1889.
Miller, R. Howard. "Historical Sketch, Dedication of Monument, 63[D] Regiment Infantry." *Pennsylvania at Gettysburg, Ceremonies as the Dedication of the Monuments, Volume 1*, pp. 359–363. Edited by John P. Nicholson. Harrisburg, PA: E.K. Meyers, State Printer, 1893.
Moore, Joseph A. "Dedication of Monument, 147th Regiment Infantry." *Pennsylvania at Gettysburg, Ceremonies as the Dedication of the Monuments, Volume 2*, edited by John P. Nicholson. Harrisburg, PA: E.K. Meyers, State Printer, 1893.
Murray, R.L., ed. "John Hetherington to his mother, July 6, 1863." *Letters From Berdan's Sharpshooters*. Wolcott, NY: Benedum Books, 2005.
Nash, Eugene A. "Dedication of Monument 44th Regiment Infantry." *Final Report of the Battlefield of Gettysburg, Volume 1*. Albany, NY: J.B. Lyon Company, Printers, 1902.
Nash, Eugene A. *A History of the Forty-Fourth Regiment New York Volunteer Infantry in the Civil War, 1861–1865*. Chicago: R.R. Donnelley & Sons Company, 1911.
Norton, Oliver W. *The Attack and Defense of Little Round Top, Gettysburg, July 2, 1863*. New York: Neale Publishing Company, 1913.
Norton, O.W. "Dedication of Monument 83[D] Regiment Infantry." *Pennsylvania at Gettysburg: Ceremonies at the Dedication of the Monuments, Volume 1*. Harrisburg, PA: E.K. Meyers, State Printer, 1893.
Oates, William C. *The War Between the Union and the Confederacy*. New York and Washington, D.C.: Neale Publishing Company, 1905.
Oates, Wm. C. "Letter to Col. H.R. Stoughton, Nov. 22, 1888." *Berdan's United States Sharpshooters in the Army of the Potomac, 1861–1865*. St. Paul, MN: Price-McGill Company, 1892.
Owen, Joseph L., and Randy S. Drais, eds. "Private John Marquis 'Mark' Smither—Fifth Texas Infantry." *Texans at Gettysburg*. Croydon, England: Fonthill Media Limited, 2016.

Parsons, H.C. "Farnsworth's Charge and Death." *Battles and Leaders of the Civil War: Volume 3, The Tide Shifts*. Secaucus, NJ: Castle Books. 2010.
Peck, Theodore S. *Revised Roster of Vermont Volunteers*. Montpelier, VT: Press of the Watchman Publishing Co., 1892.
Peteler, Francis. "Narrative of the First Company of Sharpshooters." *Minnesota in the Civil and Indian Wars, 1861–1865*, 2nd ed. St. Paul, MN: Pioneer Press Company, 1891.
Phisterer, Frederick. *New York in the War of the Rebellion, 1861–1865*. Albany, NY: J.B. Lyon Company, 1912.
Polk, J.M. *Memories of the Lost Cause: Stories and Adventures of a Confederate Soldier in General R.E. Lee's Army, 1861 to 1865*. Austin, TX: Self-published, 1905.
Polley, J.B. *Hood's Texas Brigade: Its Marches, Its Battles, Its Achievements*. New York and Washington, D.C.: Neale Publishing Company, 1910.
Pullen, John, ed. *Soldiers in Green: Civil War Diaries of James Mero Matthews, 2nd U.S. Sharpshooters*. Sandy Point, ME: Richardson's Civil War Round Table, 2002.
Rafferty, Thomas. "Gettysburg." *Personal Recollections of the War of the Rebellion, An Address delivered at a meeting of the Commandery, State of New York, Loyal Legion, Nov. 7, 1883*, edited by James Grant Wilson and Titus Munson Coan. New York: New York Commandery, 1891.
Ripley, William Y.W. *Vermont Riflemen in the War for the Union, 1861 to 1865: A History of Company F, First United States Sharp Shooters*. Rutland, VT: Tuttle & Co., 1883.
Rittenhouse, Benjamin F. "The Battle of Gettysburg as Seen from Little Round Top." A Paper Read Before the District of Columbia Commandery MOLLUS, May 4, 1887. Washington, D.C.: Judd & Detweiler, 1887.
Rourke, Norman E., ed. *I Saw the Elephant: The Civil War Experiences of Bailey George McClelen, Company D, 10th Alabama Infantry Regiment*. Shippensburg, PA: White Maine Publishing Company, 1995.
Shattuck, A.S. "Address of A.S. Shattuck." *Michigan at Gettysburg, July 1st, 2nd and 3rd, 1863*. Detroit, MI: Winn & Hammond, 1889.
Shuffler, R. Henderson, ed. *The Adventures of a Prisoner of War 1863–1864*. Austin: University of Texas Press, 1964.
Smith, James E. *A Famous Battery and Its Campaigns, 1864–64*. Washington, D.C.: W.H. Lowdermilk & Co., 1892.
Stevens, C.A. *Berdan's United States Sharpshooters in the Army of the Potomac, 1861–1865*. St. Paul, MN: Price-McGill Company, 1892.
Stevens, J.W. *Reminiscences of the Civil War: A Soldier in Hood's Texas Brigade, Army of Northern Virginia*. Hillsboro, TX: Hillsboro Mirror Print, 1902.
Stocker, Jeffrey D., ed. *From Huntsville to Appomattox, R.T. Cole's History of 4th Regiment, Alabama Volunteer Infantry, C.S.A., Army of Northern Virginia*. Knoxville: University of Tennessee Press, 1996.
Stoughton, Homer R. "Companies E and H, Second United States Sharpshooters." *Revised Roster of Vermont Volunteers, 1861–1866*. Compiled by Theodore S. Peck. Montpelier, VT: Press of the Watchman Publishing Company, 1892.
Tolles, C.W. "Army Movements." *The United States Service Magazine, Volume 3*. New York: Charles R. Richardson, 1865.
Toombs, Samuel. *New Jersey Troops in the Gettysburg Campaign from June 5 to July 31, 1863*. Orange, NJ: The Evening Mail Publishing House, 1888.
Tremain, Henry E. *Two Days of War: A Gettysburg Narrative and Other Excursions*. New York: Bonnell, Silver and Bowers, 1905.
Walker, Elijah. "Regimental Dedication of Monument." *Maine at Gettysburg*. Portland, ME: Lakeside Press, 1898.
West, John C. "Incidents at Gettysburg—Recollections of a Soldier Who Fought with Hood in This Battle." *Unveiling and Dedication of Monument to Hood's Texas Brigade*, edited by Frank B. Chilton. Houston, TX: Self-published, 1911.
West, John C. *A Texan in Search of a Fight, Being the Diary and Letters of a Private Soldier in Hood's Texas Brigade*. Waco, TX: Press of J.S. Hill & Co., 1901.

Weygant, Charles H. *History of the One Hundred and Twenty-Fourth Regiment, N.Y.S.V.* Newburgh, NY: Journal Printing House, 1877.
Weygant, Charles H. "What They Did Here." *Final Report of the Battlefield of Gettysburg, Volume 2.* Albany, NY: J.B. Lyon Company, Printers, 1900.
White, Russell C., ed. *The Civil War Diary of Wyman S. White, First Sergeant, Company F, 2nd United States Sharpshooters.* Baltimore, MD: Butternut and Blue, 1993.
Wray, William J. *History of the Twenty Third Pennsylvania Volunteer Infantry; Birney's Zouaves.* Philadelphia: United States Army, 1904.
Wright, A., and F. Peteler. *History of First Company Sharpshooters of Minnesota.* Minneapolis, MN, 1889.

Government Documents

Head, Natt. *Report of the Adjutant General of the State of New Hampshire, May 20, 1865.* Concord, NH: Amos Hadley, State Printer, 1865.
Hodson, John L. *Annual Report of the Adjutant General of the State of Maine for the Year Ending December 31, 1863, Appendix D.* Augusta, ME: Stevens & Sayward, Printers to the State, 1863.
State of New Hampshire. *Journal of the House of the Honorable Senate, of the State of New Hampshire. June Session, 1864.* Concord, NH: Amos Hadley, State Printer, 1864.
United States. *Report of the Joint Committee on the Conduct of the War.* Washington, D.C.: Government Printing Office, 1865.
U.S. War Department. *Regimental and Company Books of the 2nd U.S. Sharpshooters Regiment* (Washington, D.C.: The Adjutant General's Office, 1861–1867), Record Group 94, 4 volumes.
U.S. War Department. *The War of the Rebellion: A Compilation of the Official Records of the Union and Confederate Armies* (Washington, D.C.: Government Printing Office, 1889), Series 1, 27, Part 1, 2, and 3.

Periodical Collections

Anonymous. "Pickett's and Hood's Charges at Gettysburg." *The Southern Bivouac* 3, no. 2 (October 1884), 76–77.
Clark, George. "Wilcox's Alabama Brigade at Gettysburg." *Confederate Veteran* 17, no. 5 (May 1909), 229–230.
Jones, C.A. "Longstreet at Gettysburg." *Confederate Veteran* 23, no. 12 (December 1915), 551–552.
Law, Evander M. "Round Top and the Confederate Right at Gettysburg." *The Century Magazine* 33, no. 2 (December 1886), 296–305.
McLaws, Lafayette. "Gettysburg." *Southern Historical Society Papers* 7, no. 2 (February 1879), 64–90.
Oates, William C. "Gettysburg—The Battle on the Right." *Southern Historical Society Papers* 6 (July–December 1878): 172–182.
Perry, W.F. "The Devil's Den." *Confederate Veteran* 9, no. 4 (April 1901), 161–163.
Purifoy, John. "Longstreet's Attack at Gettysburg, July 2, 1863." *Confederate Veteran* 32, no. 8 (August 1923), 292–294.
Purifoy, John. "The Lost Opportunity at Gettysburg." *Confederate Veteran* 31, no. 6 (June 1923), 214–218.
Ward, W.C. "Incidents and Personal Experiences on the Battlefield at Gettysburg." *Confederate Veteran* 8, no. 8 (August 1900), 345–349.
Youngblood, William. "Unwritten History of the Gettysburg Campaign." *Southern Historical Society Papers* 38 (1910), 312–318.

Newspapers

Allen, L.J. "Berdan Sharpshooters." *The National Tribune.* Washington, D.C.: Thursday, August 12, 1886, page 3.

Bennet, Edward. "Fighting Them Over." *The National Tribune*. Washington, D.C.: May 6, 1886, page 3.
Carr, Ira. "A Sharpshooter at Gettysburg." *The National Tribune*. Washington, D.C.: November 25, 1886, page 3.
Editor. "Berdan's Reconnoissance." *The National Tribune*. Washington, D.C.: July 12, 1888, page 8.
Editor. "The Famous Cavalry Charge." *The Rutland Weekly Herald and Globe*. Rutland, VT: Thursday, April 28, 1887, page 2.
Editor. "Fights of the Sharpshooters." *The Rutland Weekly Herald and Globe*. Rutland, VT: Thursday, April 28, 1887, page 2.
Farley, Porter. "Bloody Round Top." *National Tribune*. Washington, D.C.: Thursday, May 3, 1883, page 1.
Harper's Weekly. Saturday, July 4, 1863, vol. 7, no. 340, page 418.
Parsons, H.C. "A Cavalry Charge." *National Tribune*. Washington, D.C.: Thursday, August 7, 1890, page 1.
Unknown. "Letter to the Editor." *Bangor Daily Whig and Courier*. Bangor, ME: Friday, September 18, 1863, page 1.
Unknown. "Personal Section." *The National Tribune*. Washington, D.C.: July 17, 1890, page 4.
Wilson, William W. "From the Sharpshooters." *The Daily Green Mountain Freeman*. Montpelier, VT: Saturday, July 11, 1863, page 2.
Wright, A. "The 2D U.S. Sharpshooters." *The National Tribune*. Washington, D.C.: February 18, 1909, page 2.

Published Secondary Sources

Books

Balch, William R. *The Battle of Gettysburg: An Historical Account*. Philadelphia: John M. Butler, 1885.
Bates, Samuel P. *History of Pennsylvania Volunteers, 1861–5, Volume II*. Harrisburg, PA: B. Singerly, State Printer, 1869.
Bilby, Joseph G. *Civil War Firearms: Their Historical Background, Tactical Use and Modern Collecting and Shooting*. Conshohocken, PA: Combined Publishing, 1999.
Brown, George H. *Record of Service of Michigan Volunteers in the Civil War, 1861–1865, Volume 44*. Kalamazoo, MI: Ihlilng Bros. & Evrard, 1905.
Busey, John W., and David G. Martin. *Regimental Strengths and Losses at Gettysburg*, 4th ed. Hightstown, NJ: Longstreet House, 2005.
Busey, Travis W., and John W. Busey. *Union Casualties at Gettysburg: A Comprehensive Record*. Jefferson, NC: McFarland, 2011.
Castel, Albert. *Victors in Blue: How Union Generals Fought the Confederates, Battled Each Other, and Won the War*. Lawrence: University Press of Kansas, 2011.
Coddington, Edwin B. *The Gettysburg Campaign: A Study in Command*. New York: Simon & Schuster, 1968.
Collier, Calvin L. *They'll Do to Tie To! The Story of Hood's Arkansas Toothpicks, Third Arkansas Infantry Regiment, C.S.A*. Little Rock, AR: Butler Center Books, 2015.
Commager, Henry Steele, ed. *The Blue and the Gray: The Story of the Civil War as Told by Participants*. New York: The Fairfax Press, 1982.
The Comte De Paris. *History of the Civil War in America, Volume 3*. Philadelphia: Porter & Coates, 1888.
Cowell, A.T. *Tactics at Gettysburg as Described by Participants in the Battle*. Gettysburg, PA: Gettysburg Compiler Print, 1910.
Crawford, Kim. *The 16th Michigan Infantry in the Civil War*. East Lansing: Michigan State University Press, 2019.

Desmond, Jerry R. *Turning the Tide at Gettysburg: How Maine Saved the Union.* Camden, ME: Down East Books, 2014.
Dunn, Craig L. *Harvestfields of Death: The Twentieth Indiana Volunteers of Gettysburg.* Carmel, IN: Guild Press of Indiana, 1999.
Earley, Gerald L. *The Second United States Sharpshooters in the Civil War: A History and Roster.* Jefferson, NC: McFarland, 2009.
Foard, Glenn. "English Battlefield 991–1685: A Review of Problems and Potentials." *Fields of Conflict,* edited by Douglas Scott, Lawrence Babits, and Charles Haecker. Washington, D.C.: Potomac Books, 2009.
Fox, William F. "New York at Gettysburg." *Final Report of the Battlefield of Gettysburg, Volume 1.* Albany, NY: J.B. Lyon Company, Printers, 1902.
Fox, William F. *Regimental Losses in the American Civil War 1861–1865.* Albany, NY: Albany Publishing Company, 1889.
Freeman, Douglas Southall, ed. *Lee's Dispatches.* New York: Knickerbocker Press, 1915.
Gilbert, J. Warren. *The Blue and Gray: A History of the Conflicts During Lee's Invasion and Battle of Gettysburg.* Harrisburg, PA: Evangelical Press, 1922.
Guelzo, Allen. *Gettysburg: The Last Invasion.* New York: Vintage Books, 2014.
Hall, Hillman A., W.B. Besley, and Gilbert G. Wood. *History of the Sixth New York Cavalry, Second Ira Harris Guard, Second Brigade, First Division, Cavalry Corps, Army of the Potomac 1861–1865.* Worcester, MA: Blanchard Press, 1908.
Hamlin, Charles. "The Battle of Gettysburg." *Maine at Gettysburg.* Portland, ME: Lakeside Press, 1898.
Hamlin, Charles, C.T. Stevens, S.W. Thaxter, G.W. Verrill, and C.E. Nash. "Company D, Second U.S. Sharpshooters." *Maine at Gettysburg,* 349–353. Portland, ME: Lakeside Press, 1898.
Hamlin, Charles, C.T. Stevens, S.W. Thaxter, G.W. Verrill, and C.E. Nash. "Fourth Maine Regiment." *Maine at Gettysburg.* Portland, ME: Lakeside Press, 1898.
Hays, Gilbert Adams. *Under the Red Patch: Story of the Sixty Third Regiment Pennsylvania Volunteers 1861–1864.* Pittsburgh, PA: Sixty-Third Pennsylvania Volunteers Regimental Association, 1908.
Hess, Earl. *The Union Soldier in Battle: Enduring the Ordeal of Combat.* Lawrence: University Press of Kansas, 1997.
Hessler, James A. *Sickles at Gettysburg.* New York: Savas Beatie LLC, 2010.
Hewett, Janet B., Noah Andre Trudeau, and Bryce A. Suderow, eds. *Supplement to the Official Records of the Union and Confederate Armies,* 51 vols. Wilmington, NC: Broadfoot Publishing Co., 1994–97.
Ingersoll, Ralph. *The Battle Is the Pay-Off.* New York: Harcourt, Brace and Company, 1943.
Kingsbury, George W. *History of Dakota Territory, Volume V.* Chicago: S.J. Clarke Publishing Company, 1915.
Maine at Gettysburg. Portland, ME: Lakeside Press, 1898.
Marcot, Roy M. *Civil War Chief of Sharpshooters Hiram Berdan, Military Commander and Firearms Inventor.* Irvine, CA: Northwood Heritage Press, 1989.
Marcot, Roy M. *U.S. Sharpshooters: Berdan's Civil War Elite.* Mechanicsburg, PA: Stackpole Books, 2007.
Marshall, George C. *Infantry in Battle,* 3rd edition. Richmond, VA: Garrett & Massie, 1986.
McWhiney, Grady, and Perry D. Jamieson. *Attack and Die: Civil War Military Tactics and the Southern Heritage.* Tuscaloosa: University of Alabama Press, 1982.
Minnigh, Luther W. *Gettysburg: What They Did Here.* Baltimore, MD: W.K. Boyle & Son, 1892.
Norton, John Foote. *The History of Fitzwilliam, New Hampshire, From 1752 to 1887.* New York: Burr Printing House, 1888.
Nosworthy, Brent. *The Bloody Crucible of Courage, Fighting Methods and Combat Experience of the Civil War.* New York: Carroll & Graf, 2003.
The 155th Regimental Association. *Under the Maltese Cross, Antietam to Appomattox,*

Campaigns 155th Pennsylvania Regiment. Pittsburg, PA: The 155th Regimental Association, 1910.
Orr, Timothy J. "On Such Slender Threads does the Fate of Nations Depend: The Second United States Sharpshooters Defend the Union Left." *The Most Shocking Battle I Have Ever Witnessed: The Second Day at Gettysburg.* Edited by Chris Little. Gettysburg, PA: National Park Service, 2008.
Pegler, Martin. *Sharpshooting Rifles of the American Civil War.* New York: Osprey Publishing, 2017.
Pullen, John J. "Introduction." *Soldiers in Green: Civil War Diaries of James Mero Matthews, 2nd U.S. Sharpshooters.* Edited by John Pullen. Sandy Point, ME: Richardson's Civil War Round Table, 2002.
Rose, Alexander. *Men of War: The American Soldier in Combat at Bunker Hill, Gettysburg, and Iwo Jima.* New York: Random House, 2015.
Sauers, Richard A. *Gettysburg: The Meade-Sickles Controversy.* Lincoln, NE: Potomac Books, 2003.
Scott, Kate M. *History of the One Hundred and Fifth Regiment of Pennsylvania Volunteers.* Philadelphia: New-World Publishing Company, 1877.
Spruill, Matt. *Decisions at Gettysburg: The Nineteen Critical Decisions that Defined the Campaign.* Knoxville: University of Tennessee Press, 2011.
Spruill, Matt. *Summer Thunder: A Battlefield Guide to the Artillery at Gettysburg.* Knoxville: University of Tennessee Press, 2010.
Sword, Wiley. *Sharpshooter, Hiram Berdan: His Famous Sharpshooters and Their Sharps Rifles.* Woonsocket, RI: Andrew Mowbray, 1988.
Tucker, Phillip Thomas. *Storming Little Round Top, the 15th Alabama and Their Fight for the High Ground, July 2, 1863.* Cambridge, MA: Da Capo Press, 2002.
Tzu, Sun. *The Art of War.* Translated by Samuel B. Griffith. Oxford: Oxford University Press, 1971.
Unknown. *Lectures on Land Warfare: A Tactical Manual for the Use of Infantry Officers.* London: William Clowes and Sons, Ltd., 1922.
Vanderslice, John M. *Gettysburg Then and Now.* New York: G.W. Dillingham Co., 1897.
Von Clausewitz, Carl. *On War.* Edited and translated by Michael Howard and Peter Paret. New York: Alfred A. Knopf, 1993.
Webster, Kimball. *History of Hudson, N.H.* Manchester, NH: Granite State Publishing Co., 1913.
Willson, Arabella M. *Disaster, Struggle, Triumph. The Adventures of 1000 Boys in Blue.* Albany, NY: The Argus Company, 1870.
Wise, Jennings C. *The Long Arm of Lee or the History of the Artillery of the Army of Northern Virginia, Volume II.* Lynchburg, VA: J.P. Bell Company, 1915.
Woods, James A. *Gettysburg, July 2, The Ebb and Flow of Battle.* Gillette, NJ: Canister Publishing, 2012.
Yee, Gary. *Sharpshooters 1750–1900. The Men, Their Guns, Their Story.* Broadmoor, CA: Sharpshooter Press, 2009.
Young, Jesse B. *The Battle of Gettysburg, A Comprehensive Narrative.* New York and London: Harper & Brothers Publishers, 1913.

Articles

Bruner, Gary P. "Up Over Big Round Top: The Forgotten 47th Alabama." *Gettysburg Magazine,* issue 22 (July 2000), 6–22.
Erdmann, Charles E. "Application of Geology to the Principles of War." *Bulletin of the Geological Society of America,* vol. 54 (August 1943), 1169–1194.
LaFantasie, Glenn W. "William C. Oates Remembers Little Round Top." *Gettysburg Magazine,* issue 21 (July 1999), 57–63.
Henley, Lana J. "Lt. Col. Benjamin F. Carter." *UDC Magazine,* vol. 73 (December 2010), 16–18.

Bibliography

Online Sites

Astronomy Scope. *Dawn vs. Sunrise.* https://www.astronomyscope.com/dawn-vs-sunrise/ (accessed May 1, 2022).

Bateman, Robert. "Understanding Military Strategy and the Four Levels of War." *Esquire*, 25 November 2015. http://https://www.esquire.com/news-politics/politics/news/a39985/four-levels-of-war/ (accessed May 10, 2018).

Cissel, Anne. "From Mechanicstown to Thurmont." https://www.emmitsburg.net/history_t/archives/places/mechanicstown_to_thurmont.htm. (accessed May 28, 2022).

Elder, S.G. *Berdan's Sharpshooters; Air Yankee Doodle.* New York: H. De Marsan, 1. https://www.loc.gov/resource/amss.sb10033b (accessed May 4, 2018).

Ledoux, Tom. "Roster for 1st Sharpshooters, Company F." https://www.vermontcivilwar.org/units/ss/rostersf.php (accessed December 13, 2021).

MacArthur, Douglas. https://www.brainyquote.com/authors/douglas-macarthur-quotes (accessed May 24, 2022).

Military Factory. https://www.militaryfactory.com/dictionary/military-terms-alphabet-list.php?letter_group=D (accessed April 20, 2022)

Peale, Norman Vincent. https://www.brainyquote.com/quotes/norman_vincent_peale_159732 (accessed May 27, 2020).

Shreve (William Price) Papers, The University of Southern Mississippi—McCain Library and Archives, https://lib.usm.edu/spcol/collections/manuscripts/finding_aids/m029.html (accessed May 4, 2022).

Tactical Withdrawal. https://tvtropes.org/pmwiki/pmwiki.php/Main/TacticalWithdrawal (accessed February 8, 2019).

Maps

Kissel, Tim. *Gettysburg National Military Park.* Battlefield America: A Civil War Map Series, Map #104. Aurora, CO. Trailhead Graphics, Inc. 1 sheet.

Personal Communications

Cameron, James. Personal communication, November 12, 2021.

Heiser, John. Former park ranger, Gettysburg National Military Park. Personal communication, February 11, 2019.

Phillips, Gar. Licensed battlefield guide, Gettysburg National Military Park. Personal communication, March 27, 2022.

Index

Numbers in ***bold italics*** indicate pages with illustrations

Abbott, Corp. Curtis 63, ***63***, 81, 84, 84*n*3, 88*n*2, 100, 102, 104, 113, 120, 120*n*3, 124, 126, 129, 149, 152*n*6
Alabama Infantry: (4th) 96, ***97***, 107, 111, ***112***, 113, ***118***, 122, 123, ***124***, 125, 127–128, 149, ***150***, 152, ***153***, 182, 184; (8th) 58–59, ***62***, ***66***, 67, ***69***, 70, ***72***, 182; (9th) ***69***, 182; (10th) 37, 58–59, 61, ***62***, 64, ***66***, 67, 68, ***69***, 70–71, ***72***, 182; (11th) 37, 58, 59, 60–61, ***62***, 65, ***66***, 67, 68, ***69***, 182; (15th) 17*n*1, 83, 96, ***97***, ***98***, ***99***, ***103***, 104, ***105***, 110, ***112***, ***114***, ***118***, 120, 122, 123, ***124***, ***126***, 129, 130, ***131***, 132, ***132***, 133, ***134***, 136, ***137***, ***138***, ***141***, ***146***, ***148***, ***151***, ***153***, 154, ***156***, ***160***, ***161***, 163, ***163***, 164, 173, 182, 184; (44th) 96, ***97***, ***98***, ***103***, ***112***, ***114***, ***118***, 122, 122*n*2, ***124***, 125, ***126***, ***131***, ***132***, ***134***, 137, ***137***, 138, ***138***, 139, 140, ***141***, ***146***, ***153***, ***156***, ***160***, ***161***, ***163***, 182, 184; (47th) 96, ***97***, ***98***, ***103***, 104, ***112***, ***114***, ***118***, 122, ***124***, ***126***, 128, 129, 131, ***131***, ***132***, 133, ***134***, 135, 136, ***137***, ***138***, ***141***, ***146***, ***148***, 150, ***151***, ***153***, ***156***, ***160***, ***161***, ***163***, 175, 182, 184; (48th) 96, ***97***, ***98***, ***103***, 104, 110, ***112***, ***114***, ***118***, 119, 122, 122*n*2, 123, ***124***, 125, ***126***, ***131***, ***132***, ***134***, 136, ***137***, ***138***, 139, ***141***, 142, 145, ***146***, ***148***, ***151***, ***153***, 155, ***156***, ***160***, ***161***, ***163***, 173, 182, 184
Aldritt, Pvt. Edwin 14, 87, 88–89, 90–91, 113
Alexander, Col. E. Porter 75, ***76***
Allard, Pvt. Wilman D. 90
Allen, Sgt. Lewis J. 60, ***61***, 64–65, 68–70, 71, ***72***, ***73***
Anderson, Brig. Gen. George T. 96
Anderson, Maj. Gen. Richard H. 37, 182

Arkansas Infantry (3rd) 96, ***97***, ***98***, ***99***, ***103***, 106, 107, 108, ***109***, 110, 112, 140, ***141***, 157, 182, 184
Aschmann, Capt. Rudolph 7, ***8***, 13, 41, 43*n*1

Bachman, Capt. William K. 96
Baker, Capt. James H. ***72***, ***73***
Baltimore Road/Turnpike 24, 96
Bane, Maj. John P. 110, 124
Barziza, Capt. Decimus 125
Bennet, Edward 15
Benning, Brig. Gen. Henry L. 96
Berdan, Col. Hiram 1, 5, 6, ***6***, 7, 8, 11, 12, 13, 34, 35, ***35***, 36, 38, 40–41, 47, 54–56, 59, 59*n*1, 63, 65, 67–68, 70–71, 74, 75, 76, 143, 178
Berlin, Pennsylvania 49
Big Round Top 15, 15*n*3, ***16***, 17, 20, 24–25, 32, 75, 77, 80, ***81***, ***82***, ***85***, 92, 94, 94*n*2, 95, 102, 103, 104, 106, 107, 108, ***112***, ***114***, 115, 116, 117, 118, ***118***, 119, 120, 121, 122, 123, ***124***, 125, ***126***, 127, 128, 130, ***131***, ***132***, 133, 134, ***134***, 135, 136, ***137***, 138, ***138***, 142, 143, 144, 145, ***146***, 147, 149, 150, ***151***, ***153***, ***156***, 158, 159, ***160***, ***161***, ***163***, 164, 165, 168, 172, 175, 176, 178
Birney, Maj. Gen. David B. 5, 30, ***31***, 32–33, 34, 39, 44, 47, 50, 51, 52, 54–55, 56, 59, 68, 74, 75, 76, 78, 80, 90, 92, 158, 179
Bonnafon, 2Lt. Sylvester 33
Boynton, Corp. Richard C. 89
Briscoe, Capt. J.C. 54–55, 56, 59, 67–68, 75, 76
Brown, Lt. A.J. 28, 37
Brunson, Capt. Ervin B. 27

Bryan, Lt. Col. King 117, 128, 155
Buchanan, Corp. Charles 64, 70, 71, 74
Buford, Brig. Gen. John 43, 44, *47*, 48–49
Bulger, Lt. Col. Michael J. 123
Bushman Farm/farm road *16*, 20, *85*, 86, *88*, *89*, 90, 91, *97*, *98*, *99*, 103, *103*, *112*, *114*
Butterfield, Maj. Gen. Daniel 48–49, *49*, 63, 71, 74, 76, 77, 79
Buxton, Capt. Albert 84, 84n3, 102, 116, 126–127, 180, 194–195, *195*

Calef, Lt. John H. 43, *44*
Camp of Instruction 8, 10, 12–13
Campbell, Maj. James 104
Candy, Col. Charles 25, *26*, 181
Carr, Pvt. Ira 87, 89–90
Carter, Lt. Col. Benjamin F. 106–107
Cashtown Road 54
Cemetery Hill/Ridge 24, 26n1, 36–37, 45, 75, 79
Chamberlain, Col. Joshua L. 144, *145*, 147, *148*, 154, 160, 162–163, *163*, 164, 175, 176, 180
Chambersburg Turnpike 37, 79
Chancellorsville, Battle of 5
Clark, Lt. George 58, 61
Clark, Capt. Judson A. 43
Clark, Corp. Nathan S. 147
Codori, Nicholas house 167
Cole, R.T. 127
Confederate scouts 77–78, 83, 92–93
Congdon, Corp. Henry C. 84, 88n2, 89, 90
Cooney, Adjutant John M. 86, 90, 104, 142
Culp's Hill 26n1, 28, 45, 79, 168
Cummins, Lt. Col. Francis M. 142

D-shaped field *16*, 20, *85*, *103*, *114*, 118, *118*, 119, 120, 121, *124*, *126*, 127, 128–129, *131*, *132*, *134*, *137*, 178
Danks, Maj. John A. 21, 23, 179
Dearborn, Dr. F.A.: letter to William C. Oates 121, 160
delaying action 1, 15, 16, 17, 142, 175, 176, 178; *see also* tactical withdrawal
De Trobriand, Col. Régis 80, 96, 180
Devil's Den 1, *16*, 26, 26n1, 39, *40*, *82*, 100, 107, 110, 115, *124*, 129, 139, 157, 158, *160*, 176, *187*
Devin, Col. Thomas C. 43, *43*
Diamond, Corp. George W. 89
Dolson, Pvt. John O. 89, 91–92
Doubleday, Maj. Gen. Abner 167

Early, Gen. Jubal A. 44–45
Egan, Col. Thomas W. 139, 142, 180
Ellis, Col. Van Horne 77, *77*, 179
Emmitsburg, Maryland 20–21, 22, 23, 29 35, 41, 49, 50–51, 52
Emmitsburg Road 6, 20, 21, 22, 23, 24, 26, 29, 30, 33, 34, 35, *35*, 36, 39, *40*, 41, *42*, 43, 44, 46, 49, 51, 52, 53, 54, 56, 58, 59, 60, *61*, 63, 65, *72*, 73, 75, 76, 78, 79, 80, *81*, 84, *85*, 86, 87, *88*, *89*, 90, 92, 93, 94, 95, 97, *97*, *98*, *99*, 100, 101, 103, *103*, 106, 111, *112*, 120, 123, 129
en echelon 170–171
Ewell, Gen. Richard S. 44–45, 46, 57

Fairbanks, Pvt. Charles 9, 35, 87, 88–89, 90, 93, 94
Fairfield, Pennsylvania 51
Fairfield Road/Turnpike 26, 60, 60n4
1st U.S. Sharpshooters: reconnaissance (1st) 40–43, 54; (2nd) 54–55; (3rd) 55–56, 59
Fletcher, William A. 118–119, 123–124
Forney, Col. William H. 37, 59, 70, 182
Fox, Lt. Col. William F. 158

Gamble, Col. William 43
Garden, Capt. Hugh R. 96
Garnett, Lt. Col. John J. 26, 182
Garrard, Col. Kenner 158, 181
Geary, Brig. Gen. John W. 24, *25*, 28, 29, 30, 31–32, 33, 38, 39, 52, 181
Georgia Infantry: (7th) 104; (23rd) 5
Gerrish, Pvt. Theodore 164
Gettysburg Turnpike 37
Gibbon, Brig. Gen. John 36–37
Giles, Val 123
Gilkyson, Lt. Col. Stephen R. 139, 142, 180
Gordon, Lt. Col. G.T. 27
Graham, Brig. Gen. Charles K. 50–51, *51*, 52, 179
Graves, Jr., Anthony Gardner 166n1
Greene, Pvt. William B. 10, 12
Gregg, Brig. Gen. David M. 48, 49
Guest, Capt. Adolphus A. 179, 190, *190*

Hall, Capt. James S. 77, 79
Hamblet, Corp. Benjamin O. 89, 91–92
Hancock, Maj. Gen. Winfield S. 23, 24, 32
Hanover Road 49
Harrington, Pvt. Elisa 90
Hayman, Col. Samuel B. 5
Hazlett, 1Lt. Charles E. 157, 181
Hazlett's Battery 139, 140, *156*, 157, 158, 159

Index 209

Healey, Pvt. Albert S. 90
Heidlersburg, Pennsylvania 48
Heidlersburg Road 49
Henry's battalion 102
Herbert, Col. Hilary A. 58–59, 67, 70, 182
Herr's tavern 79
Hetherington, Lt. John 65, 70
Higgins, Lt. Col. Benjamin 141, 179
Hill, Lt. Gen. Ambrose P. 26, 182
Hood, Maj. Gen. John Bell 1, 14, 15, 45, 46, *46*, 57, 58, 77–78, 80, 81, 83, 90, 92, 93, 94, 94*n*3, 95, 96, *97*, 100, 101, 102, 104, 105, 113, 115, 116, 128, 142, 149, 170, 172, 174, 175, 176, 181, 182, 184
Houck's Ridge 1, *16*, 20, 26, 34, 39, *40*, 76, 77, 78, 80, *81*, *82*, 84, 98*n*2, 103, 106, 108, 109, *109*, 110, 111, 119, 122, 122*n*2, 136, 137, 140, *141*, 142, *146*, *160*, *163*, 168
Humphreys, Brig. Gen. Andrew A. 2, 51, *51*, 180
Hunt, Brig. Gen. Henry 31, *32*, 37, 52–53, 53*n*1, 54

Indiana Infantry (20th) 80, *81*, *82*, *85*, 97, 98, 98*n*2, *99*, *103*, 108, *109*, 110–113, 142, 179
Infantry Tactics by Brig. Gen. Silas Casey 117

Jackson, Col. James W. 96, 133, 135, 182
Jerome, 1Lt. Aaron B. 63, 71, 74
Johnson, Sgt. Hannibal A. *35*, 59, *60*, 64, 70, 72
Jordan, William 132

Key, Col. John C.G. 96, 182.

Ladd, Pvt. Francis W. 89
Lakeman, Col. Moses B. 33, *34*, 56, 68, 70, 72
Lane, Maj. John 26
Latham, Capt. Alexander C. 96
Law, Brig. Gen. Evander M. 1, 15, 24, 56, *57*, 57*n*1, 58, 78, 92, 93, 94, 94*n*2, 95–96, 100, 101, 103, 104, 105, 106, 107, 108, 110, 111, *112*, 119, 122, 122*n*2, 123, 129, 130, 133, 137, 142, 149, 155, 158, 159, 170, 172, 173, 174, 175, 178, 181, 184
Lee, Gen. Robert E. 44, 45, *45*, 46, 56–57, 58, 77, 83, 92, 94, 95, 100, 165, 168, 169, 170, 171, 172–173, 174, 176, 181
Leister, Lydia 36
Little Round Top 1, 3, 6, *16*, 17, 20, 21, 25, 26, 29, 31, 32, 34, 40, *40*, 52, 57, 63, 75, 77, 78, 79, 80, *81*, *82*, 83*n*1, 92, 102, 104, 105, 109, 117, 120, 120*n*3, 121, 127, 128, 128*n*1, 133, 136, 137, *138*, 139, 140, *141*, 142, 143, 144–145, *146*, *148*, 150, *151*, *153*, 154, 155, *156*, 157, 158, 159, *160*, *161*, *163*, 165, 166*n*1, 168, 173, 174–175, 176, 178; *see also* Sugar Loaf Mountain
Longstreet, Lt. Gen. James 1, 6, 17, 45, *45*, 46, 56, 57, 58, 59, 75, *76*, 77, 78, 79, 83, 90, 94–95, 100, 110, 115, 119, 121, 171, 172, 173, 174, 181
Lowrance, Col. William L.J. 27–28, 183

Maine Infantry: (3rd) 33, *34*, *35*, 55–56, 59, *60*, *61*, *62*, 64, *66*, 68, *69*, 70–71, *72*, 73, 74, 179; (4th) 21, 22, *23*, *24*, 29, 30, 55, 77, 80, *81*, *82*, 84, *85*, *109*, 115, 117, 121, *126*, *131*, *132*, 133, *134*, 136, *137–138*, 139, 140, *141*, 142, 143, 145, 176, 179; (17th) *109*, 110, 112–113, 180; (20th) 17, 144, *145*, *146*, 147, *148*, 149, 150, *151*, 152, *153*, 154, *156*, 159, *160–161*, *163*, 164–165, 175, 176, 180
Manning, Col. Van H. 96, 182
Marble, Capt. Frank E. 41
Marshall, Billy 125
Massachusetts Infantry (1st) 30
Matthews, Sgt. James 21*n*1, 35, 39, 107, *108*, 152*n*6
McClelen, Pvt. Baily 58, 64, 68, 71
McClure, Capt. Jacob 180, 191, *191*
Mcintosh, Maj. David G. 26, 182
McLaws, Gen. Lafayette 57, 77, 78, 100
Meade, Maj. Gen. George G. 28, *29*, 31, 32, 33, 36, 37, 38–39, 40, 46, 48–49, 50, 52–53, 53*n*1, 55, 76, 79, 168, 170, 171, 174, 179
Meade, Capt. George, Jr. 37–39, 52
Mechanicsville, Maryland 168, 168*n*2
Merrill, Col. Charles B. 109, 180
Michigan Infantry: (3rd) 96–97, 98, *99*, 180; (5th) 44, 180; (16th) 145, *146*, 147, *148*, 149, 150, *151*, 155, *156*, *160*, *161*, *163*, 180
Millerstown Road *16*, 20, 51, 54, 56, 59, 60, 60*n*1, *61*, 63, 64, 68
Moore, Maj. John W. 22, 23, 30–31, 33, 97, 142, 179
Morrill, Capt. Walter G. *147*, *148*, 149–150, *151*, *153*, *156*, 159, *160–161*, 162, *163*, 164
Morse, Corp. Argyl D. 89
Murry, Lt. Samuel F. 192–193, *193*

Nash, Eugene 17
Nash, Capt. William H. 167

Nesbitt, Capt. Robert A. 22, 26
New Jersey Infantry: (6th) *138*, 139, *141*, 180; (13th) 100
New York Battery (4th) 75, 80, 94
New York Cavalry (6th) 48
New York Infantry: (40th) *138*, 139, *141*, 142, 180; (44th) 15, 17, *141*, 145, *146*, 147, *148*, 150, *151*, *153*, *156*, *160*, *161*, *163*, 166n1, 180; (86th) 80, *81*, 109, *109*, 110, 141, *141*, 179; (107th) 158; (124th) 77, *77*, *81*, *82*, *85*, *99*, *103*, 109, *109*, 110, 113, 141, *141*, 142, 179; (140th) 155, *156*, 174, 181; (146th) 158, 181
North Carolina Infantry: (34th) 27, 183; (38th) 28, 183
Northrop, Capt. Ira J. 179, 190, *191*
Norton, Oliver 3, 121
Norton, Adj. Seymour F. 84, 84n2, 84n3, 86–87, *87*, *88*, 90, 116, 117, 120, 121, 128, 133–135, 145, 149, 149n5, 150, 162, 164, 167, 185

Oates, Col. William C. 17, 17n1, 96, 104–105, *105*, 110, 120–121, 122n2, 122–123, *126*, 129–130, 131, *132*, 133, 135, 136, 142–143, 145, *146*, 152, 152n6, 154, *156*, 159, 160, *161*, 162, 164, 165, 173–175, 176, 178, 182
Ohio Infantry (5th) 25, *27*, 29, 181
O'Rorke, Col. Patrick 155

Parsons, H.C. 128
Patrick, Col. John H. 25, 26, *27*, 181
Peach Orchard *16*, 20, 22, 26, 29, 33, 34, *35*, 36, *40*, *42*, 43, 44, 52, 53, 53n1, 54, 56, 57, 59–60, *61*, 64, 71, *72*, 73, 75, 76, 79, 80, 83, 84n1, 96, 100, 168, 172, 174, 176
Pegram, Maj. William J. 26, 182
Pegram's Artillery Battalion 27, 28, 43, 182
Pender, Maj. Gen. William D. 26, 27, 28, 182
Pennsylvania Infantry: (63rd) 21, 26 29, 179; (83rd) 3, 121, 144–145, *146*, 147, *148*, 150, *151*, 152, *153*, *156*, 158–159, *160*, *161*, *163*, 176, 180; (99th) 21, 22, 23, 30, 33, 80, *81*, 97, 98n2, *99*, *103*, *109*, 110, 111, 112, 142, 179; (147th) 25, 26, 29, 181; (155th) 157, 181
Pennsylvania Reserve/Bucktails 157, 158
Perry, Col. William F. 96, 122, 137, 138–139, 140, 182
Petersburg Campaign 177
Pettijohn, 1st Sgt. Dyer B. 87, 87n4, 89, 91

Pierce, Col. Byron R. 96, 180
Pitzer Run 67
Pitzer Woods 1, 6, 55, 56, 59, *61*, *62*, *69*, *72*
Pleasonton, Maj. Gen. Alfred 46, *47*, 48–49
Plum Run *16*, 20, 25, *40*, 80, *81*, *82*, *85*, 103, *109*, *112*, *114*, 116, 117, 118, *118*, 119, 119n3, 120, 123, 124, *124*, 125, *126*, 130, *131*, *132*, 133, *134*, 135, 136, *137*, 145, 176
Plum Run Valley 1, 25, 26, 39, *40*, 46, 77, 80, *82*, 84, 98, 102, 109, *114*, 115, 117, *118*, 120, 121, 122, 128, 136, *138*, 139, *146*, 157, 159, 176
Polk, James M. 106, 108
Polley, J.B. 125
Potomac River 167
Powell, Col. Robert M. 15, 96, 120, 182
Prince, Capt. Howard L. 162
Pulford, Col. John 44, 180

Randolph, Capt. George E. 38, 76, 180
Reilly, Capt. James 96, 102, 108
Richardson, Maj. William J. 26
Robertson, Brig. Gen. Jerome B. 1, 15, 95–96, 101, 103, 106–107, 110, 111, 112–113, 119, 122, 122n2, *124*, 182, 184
Rogers, Peter house 41, *42*, 54, *72*, 73
Rollins, Pvt. Ledrue M. 89
Rose (George) farm 60, 97
Rose Woods 1, 26, 80, *81*, 82, *82*, 98, 98n2, 107, 109, *109*, 110, 111
Rounds, Corp. John H. 89
Rowan Artillery 102
Rowell, Capt. Edward T. 180, 192–193, *193*

Sanders, Col. John C.C. 37, 59, 65n5, 67, 67n2
Sawyer, Lt. Charles F. 23, *24*, 30, 136
Scales, Brig. Gen. A.M. 27, 183
Scribner, Sgt. Grove 84, 84n3, 85, 86, *86*, 87, 87n2, *88*, *89*, *97*, *98*, *99*, 102, *103*, *112*, *114*, 116, 117, *118*, 119, 120–121, 122, 123, *124*, 125, 125n4, *126*, 127, 128, 129, *131*, *132*, 133, 134, 134n2, *134*, 135, *137*, *138*, *141*, 143, 144, 145, *146*, *148*, 149, 149n5, 150, *151*, *153*, *156*, 159, *160*, *161*, 162, 163, *163*, 164, 176
Scruggs, Col. Lawrence H. 96, 118, 123, 182
Seddon, James A. 169
Seminary Ridge 67
Sharps breech-loading rifle 7, 12–13, 14

Index

Sheffield, Col. James L. 96, 122, 139, 182
Sherfy, Joseph house 29, 33, **35**, 41, **42**, **61**, 72, **72**, 73
Shreve, William Price 34, **36**, 41, 73
Sickles, Maj. Gen. Daniel E. 21, **22**, 23, 29, 30, 32–33, 35, 37, 38–39, 40, 44, 46, 47, 48, 49, 50–51, 52–53, 53n1, 54, 55, 56, 67, 68, 74–75, 76, 79, 80, 81, 139, 172, 173–174, 176, 179
Slocum, Maj. Gen. Henry W. 24, 53n1, 181
Slyder, John 14, 78
Slyder Farm/house 1, 15, **16**, 20, 84, 85, **85**, 85n2, 86, **88**, **89**, 96, **97**, **98**, **99**, 101, 102, 103, **103**, 111, **112**, 118, **118**, 119, 120, 121, 122, 123, **124**, **126**, 128, **131**, **132**, 143, 159, 174, 175, 178
Slyder farm road **16**, 20, 80, **82**, 84, **85**, 86, 87, **88**, **89**, 90, 93, 96, **97**, **98**, 99, **99**, 100, 101, 102, **103**, **112**, 120, 128, 129
Smith, Capt. Harvard P. 180, 194, **194**
Smith, Capt. James E. 76, 94, 140, 180
Smither, Mark 123
sniper 178
Snyder, Phillip (house) **61**, 64
Spangler Woods 37, 58, 59, 63, 68
Stannard, Brig. Gen. George J. 167
Stevens, 1Lt. Charles A. 1, 12, 47, 67, 119, 129, 178
Stevens, J.W. 129, 155
Stoughton, Maj. Homer R. 9, **9**, 34, 35, 36, 39, 40, 49, 63, 75, 78, 80, 82, **82**, 83, 84, 85, **85**, 86, 87, 87n2, 87n3, **88**, 93, 96–97, 98, 98n2, **98**, **99**, 101, 102, 104, 109, 111, 113, 114, 115, 116, 117, 119–121, 127, 128, 129, 130, 132, 133, 136, **137**, 139, 142, 143, 145, 159–160, **161**, 162, 164, 167, 174–175, 176, 179
Sugar Loaf Mountain 33, 36, 39, 39n2, 129; *see also* Little Round Top
Sweetser, Capt. Frank D. 180, 192, **192**

tactical withdrawal 114, 115, 117, 119, 120; *see also* delaying action
Taneytown, Maryland 20, 22, 31, 43, 44, 48
Taneytown Road **16**, 20, 24, 36, 38, 96, 165
Taylor, Lt. Col. William C.L. 97, 142
Terrell, Capt. Leigh R. 142
Texas Infantry: (1st) 96, **97**, **98**, **99**, **103**, 106, 107, **109**, 110, 112, 122n2, **138**, **141**, 182, 184; (4th) 96, **97**, **98**, 99, **103**, 106–107, 107n3, 108, **109**, 110, **112**, **114**, **118**, 119, 122, 123, 124, **124**, 125, 126, **126**, 127, **131**, **132**, **134**, **137**, **138**, 140, **141**,

146, **148**, 150, **151**, **153**, 155, **156**, **160**, **161**, **163**, 182, 184; (5th) 15, 96, **97**, **98**, **99**, **103**, 106–107, 110, 111, **112**, 113, **114**, 117, **118**, 119, 122, 123, **124**, 125, **126**, 127, 128, 129, **131**, **132**, **134**, **137**, **138**, **141**, **146**, 148, **148**, 150, **151**, **153**, 155, **156**, **160**, **161**, **163**, 182, 184
Thurmont, Maryland 168n2
Tolles, Chief Quartermaster C.W. 2, 86
Toombs, Pvt. Samuel 100
Tremain, Maj. Henry E. 49–50, **50**, 51, 52–53, 54
Trepp, Lt. Col. Caspar **7**, 8, 34, 35–36, 40–41, 54, 56, 59–60, 63–64, 71, 73–74, 179

U.S. Sharpshooters: characteristics 8–14; eligibility 9–10; regiments comprised of 8; skirmishing 11–12; uniforms 12; weapons 12–14

Vermont Cavalry (1st) 128
Vincent, Col. Strong 139, **140**, 144, 174, 178, 180

Wadsworth, Brig. Gen. James S. 28
Walker, Col. Elijah 22–23, **23**, 26, 29, 30, 55, 77, 136, 138, 179
Walker, Col. R. Lindsay 26, 182
Ward, Brig. Gen. J.H. Hobart 30, 31, **31**, 33, 39, 56, 75, 78, 80, 93, 94, 96, 98, 98n2, 100, 101, 102, 104, 108–109, 110, 111, 112, 124, 136, 139–140, 142, 174, 179
Ward, W.C. 124, 127
Warfield, James (house) **61**, 64
Warfield Ridge **16**, 83, 96, **97**, 103, **103**, 111
Warren, Gen. Gouverneur K. 2, 52, 139, **140**
Warren map 2, **16**, 64, 85n2, 128
Weed, Brig. Gen. Stephen H. 157–158, 181
Welch, Col. Norval E. 145, 180
West, John C. 106, 108
Westminster, Maryland 43, 46, 48, 49
Wheatfield **16**, 20, 33, **35**, **40**, 53, 71, 80, 109
Wheatfield Road **16**, 20, 26, **35**, 39, **40**, **42**, **61**, **81**, **82**, 84n1, 109
White, Pvt. Wyman 9, 10, **10**, 10n2, 21, 35, 82, 83, 99, 111, 113, 116, 117, 119, 129, 135, 144, 150, 152, 154, 158–159, 165, 167, 176, 192
Wilcox, Brig. Gen. Cadmus M. 37, **38**, 58–59, 60–61, 75, 182

Wilson, Capt. John 41, *72*, *74*
Wilson, Pvt. William W. 65, 65*n*3, 67
Winslow, Capt. George 93
Work, Col. Phillip A. 96, 107, 182
World War I 177, 178

Wright, Capt. Abraham 113, 166–167, 179, 189, *189*

Youngblood, Pvt. William 83, 128

www.ingramcontent.com/pod-product-compliance
Ingram Content Group UK Ltd.
Pitfield, Milton Keynes, MK11 3LW, UK
UKHW041958140426
5217IPUK00015B/870